Peatlands

About the Author

Alys Fowler is a queer gardener and writer. She has contributed to the *Financial Times*, *Gardens Illustrated*, *Observer Food Monthly*, *National Geographic* and *Country Living* and wrote a weekly column on gardening for the *Guardian Weekend* magazine for many years. Alys trained at RHS Garden Wisley, The New York Botanical Garden, and the Royal Botanic Gardens, Kew and has a master's degree from University College London in Science, Society and the Environment. She has presented on BBC's *Gardeners' World*, *Great British Garden Revival* and *Our Food*, as well as her own six-part series *The Edible Garden*. She regularly contributes to radio and podcasts.

Her previous book, *Hidden Nature*, was shortlisted for the Wainwright Prize.

ALYS FOWLER

Peatlands

A journey between land and water

hodder
press

First published in Great Britain in 2025 by Hodder Press
An imprint of Hodder & Stoughton Limited
An Hachette UK company

The authorised representative in the EEA is Hachette Ireland, 8 Castlecourt Centre,
Dublin 15, D15 XTP3, Ireland (email: info@hbgi.ie)

1

Chapter illustrations by Alys Fowler

A CIP catalogue record for this title is available from the British Library

Hardback ISBN 9781399727563
ebook ISBN 9781399727587

Typeset in Sabon MT by Palimpsest Book Production Limited, Falkirk, Stirlingshire

Printed and bound in Great Britain by Clays Ltd, Elcograf S.p.A.

Hodder & Stoughton policy is to use papers that are natural, renewable
and recyclable products and made from wood grown in sustainable forests.
The logging and manufacturing processes are expected to conform to the
environmental regulations of the country of origin.

Hodder & Stoughton Limited
Carmelite House
50 Victoria Embankment
London EC4Y 0DZ

www.hodderpress.co.uk

To Justin Lyons, and all those who care for bogs

Contents

Part Three

Prologue

I have always loved bog landscapes, wide, low places in plums and browns and greens, the sense of expansiveness that comes with them. But why bogs? Why not fens, brackish marshes or swamps? Fens have more flowers – there's certainly more chance of seeing orchids – brackish marshes conjure adventures of the sea beyond, and swamps have more interesting trees. Aren't bogs the flattest, most wearisome wetland? You can float across the others in a boat, but not a bog.

I feel at home in such places. Despite their sogginess, it isn't hard to learn how to move in ways sympathetic to their pull and suck. It might have something to do with my queerness and their queer nature. You can't easily walk, run or ride over bogs; you can't build a house on them or grow crops. Their stagnant water invites fear: mosquitoes favour bogs; you could sink, drown, disappear, but nothing rots completely away here. From a distance a bog reveals little of itself: its earthy tones flatten the landscape it rolls over.

These are places of neither this nor that. As landscapes, bogs embrace ambiguity and edges, the sensibilities that come with changing perspectives. They hold their multitudes within them, at a distance to anyone who affords them a glance.

It's easy to mistake them. It's easy to mistake us. Queer people, peatlands, we have complicated histories. At times people have tried to erase us, retold our stories, feared and ignored us. Neither of us is easy to categorise. We shift our edges, our definitions, our demands. Yet we are here, persisting.

bell hooks once said, 'I often identify myself as queer-past-gay . . . queer as not belonging . . . queer as not being about who you're having sex with (that's a dimension of it); but queer as being about the self that is at odds with everything around it and that has to invent and create and find a place to speak and to thrive and to live.'

It made me think about us, but also about mosses.

A lot of peat is made up mostly of mosses that are seemingly at odds with everything around them and are creating a place where they (and others) can thrive. Peat is formed from layers of its former selves. There's a little gay kid in me and then there was a straight conforming one: there are bits of me, like bits of the peat, that are dead but not gone, and that's what we have to build on. This speaks to me of queerness.

Perhaps most of us can relate to that a little: we are all many selves – lovers, parents, friends, siblings, sometimes good, sometimes bad. I think about this a lot and nowhere more than when I am standing on peat. Then I have time to think such things, because I am away from clock-time environments. I am in the air, on water and land all at once. If you found some peat to stand on, you wouldn't necessarily think about being queer or selfhood, but I'm sure you'd find time to think. This is one of peat's gifts: vast, slow space.

Part One

1

Wet Places

When I started this journey, I thought I knew quite a bit about bogs. My feeling for wet places grew when I was young. I was in love with our local stream, which I thought of as a friend, like my dog or the few other kids that peppered my childhood. It was endlessly available for play, with hidden spots that adults couldn't or wouldn't go to. I spent summers walking up and down the woodlands that bordered it, through the warm softness of its waterweeds, peering into its sandy spots, and swinging into muddy banks. I take such pleasure in wet soil; I love the suck, slurp and smear of earth with water. When I was training as a gardener, I found I wasn't alone: a huge swathe of plants liked the strange conditions of waterlogged soil and sculpted themselves into alien shapes to make the most of it.

Waterlogged conditions are naturally low in nutrients, particularly nitrogen, and no more so than in a bog, where the slow rate of decomposition, plus the water and the acidity mean that whatever is available is severely limited. Carnivorous plants have evolved to eat in order to survive. They eat the animals around them, mostly insects, occasionally amphibians and even, in extreme examples, small mammals. Carnivorous bog plants tend to go for small prey. Sundews and butterworts have sticky leaves rich in enzymatic residues that trap small flying insects and dissolve them slowly. Some use mechanised traps to suck in their prey, such as the bladderworts. They grow in peatland pools and have underwater or underground vacuum traps: when their tiny prey touch the trigger hair, the trapdoor flies open and the prey is sucked into the bladder to be digested. At the same time, the leftover watery remains of the previous victim are ejected and the trap resets itself. In North and South America, pitcher plants grow a long vase to lure insects down slippery sides to drown in a soup of enzymes. In Borneo, pitcher-plant vases grow large enough to hold at least three litres of deadly digestive fluids and small mammals have been found in them.

One of my jobs as a student at Kew Gardens was looking after the unheated side room at the Princess of Wales Conservatory, where the temperate carnivorous plants, the tiny sundews and butterworts, were kept in small fish tanks filled with sphagnum moss. It was here that I first fell truly in love with bogs. It was not a glamorous room. It didn't have the spectacular species of North America or South East Asia. It was a tiny cold damp room off a tropical conservatory paradise and nearly every visitor opened the door to shut it promptly. I was often alone with the mosses and the sundews. I remember layers of condensation, grey and wet, from their glass tanks to the windows of the conservatory and the greys of the sandstone rock garden beyond – the quiet, wet heaviness of it all.

I thought knowing the plants was to know their places. It's certainly a handy indicator as to where you can step and where you will sink on a bog – the grasses are your friends as they tend not to sink too much – but the more I looked into bogs, the more I realised how little I knew.

I mean I knew a lot about peat physically, you cannot train in horticulture and not know the stuff, it has for years been used as the main growing media for the industry, the majority of pot plants are grown in varying amounts of peat, be that bedding or house plants, trees for new development, herbs from the supermarket, those tomato grow bags, shrubs, perennials, cactus and succulents. Once removed from the bog, dried and milled it becomes a bland, pleasing, porous substance to grow every plant imaginable. It is a blank canvas to create an industry on. For years, I have been campaigning, along with many, many others, that we need to get rid of this habit. I have written and pleaded, I have shouted and implored and yet, here we are still extracting peat from the earth, still tearing apart a precious and unique habitat and with it releasing tonnes of greenhouses gases into the air. I decided I'd try another tack. I, perhaps rashly, quit my job. I put away my gardening tools and left the garden to tend to itself and I walked into the heart of the matter, onto the bog to ask for its story. And with the help of many bog lovers, I learnt how to peel back the layers and hear the bog's song. I hope I have rendered it prettily enough that when you hear it, you will be moved to understand the space and why we cannot plunder our peatlands any more. I also hope you might venture to these spaces, each one has their own song, each one their own ways that they murmur and guggle and trill for you to hear. Bogs are strange, funny beings. Like anyone who has had to play the ogre or the beast in too many stories they are shy; their beauty, their compassion even, is often hidden, so you have to tread gently, carefully, as you ask to get to know it. But I cannot of think of another landscape, once you've become acquainted, that will teach you how much of being it really is. Before you go, there's a few things to know.

When I wasn't knee deep in getting to know living peat, I was buried in books. Recently, I'd been awarded a fellowship with the Royal Literary Fund, which gave me a room in one of the modernist buildings at Aberystwyth University, many confused students to tutor, and unlimited access to the library. As a quasi-staff member, I could take out books and keep them until someone wanted them back. When I wasn't with students, I haunted the library, learning where the peat was hidden. I found it in the geography, botany, ecology, restoration, agriculture, history, Welsh studies, medicine, archaeology, industrial history, pollution and environmental economic sections. The mires oozed over the library just as they do over our landscape, touching almost every part of the Dewey system.

I started with the doorstopper *Mires and Peatlands of Europe* by Joosten, Tanneberger and Meon, a thick book, half of which was dedicated to categorisation and language, including a dictionary of all the peatland and wetland terms, their roots and related words. 'Bog' comes from the Irish Gaelic *bogach*, meaning soft and flexible, but also perhaps from German *bogen*, an arch or weapon for shooting arrows: an intact bog, particularly a raised bog, is often a bow- or arch-shaped raised dome. 'Mire' has its roots in the Proto-Indo-European mother tongue, which gives rise to *mere* in early English, *mare* in Latin, *mope* in Russian, and is believed to come from *mori* or *meri*, meaning sea or stagnant water or *meu-r*, wet or dirty. So, if you have a landscape covered with moss (derived from an Indo-European root meaning 'damp and wet'), there are many ways in which that the bog enters your language. From our mires we get 'miry', an antiquated version of 'bogged down' – 'I'm in a miry about how all these roots of language work' – mired, meaning stuck in mud or in a complicated situation that might end up in a quagmire, which is a shaking, quivery bog that gives way underfoot, or an awkward, complex or hazardous situation. The pattern is quite clear: if you can't walk across a landscape, it quickly becomes synonymous with difficult to deal with.

I can't say the first half of *Mires and Peatlands* illuminated much on the sticky problem of classification, but it gave me a list of words to build on. I learnt about poor, rich and transitional fens, raised, blanket and quaking bogs, open mires, wooded mires and shrub-covered mires, mire margins and expanses, hummock-hollows and hummock-mud bottoms, aapa mires, palsa mires, sloping bogs, mound blankets, flarks, eccentric raised bogs and concentric ones. I was dizzy by the end and had resorted to flipping through the pages to look at the pictures of far-flung bogs in Siberia, the Faroe Islands and Azerbaijan.

I got in touch with Dr Peter Jones, who oversees much of Wales's peatland restoration and is a self-confessed nerd when it comes to classification, and admitted how confused I was by the many categories and subcategories that merged, parted and skirted each other over the landscape. He suggested that I start somewhere a little less ambitious than *Mires and Peatlands* and recommended I start with *Peatlands* by P. D. Moore and D. J. Bellamy (yes, *that* David Bellamy, for those old enough to remember wildlife TV of the 1970s and 80s). I bought a 1970s copy online – it has a lurid green cover photograph of a ghostly swamp with dead trees growing out of it. Several weeks later I was starting to master a little more of plaudification, or how bogs are formed, expanded, and how peat grows.

Armed with the basics, I threw myself into the current academic literature, and stacks of paper built up beside my desk, on the kitchen table, the sofa, beside the loo and my bed. Peter Jones introduced to me to 'grey papers', which are as white as any other printed material but are not peer-reviewed or published, and I threw myself into the subterranean world of the unpublished peatland hydrology classification. It's a much better read than it sounds.

Slowly but surely, the peat layers began to filter into order and I found I could read the landscape in a new way. At first, I thought studying the minutiae of this world – pollen grains and cation exchanges in moss cells, nutrient supplies of rainfall and microtopography – was just another way of burrowing into a subject so that I didn't have to engage in the increasing panic I felt about the state of the world, the damage we're doing to our environment, the horror of our politics. (A cation is an ion – a charged atom or group of atoms – with a positive charge.) But as my understanding grew and the words in the papers and books started to read clearly, I found the opposite. Those origin words 'quagmire' and 'morass' have one thing right: mires are complicated, but they're the opposite of bogged down or stuck in their ways. Their roles in the wider system gave me something I'd forgotten. I thought I needed hope in the light of climate change, but instead I needed wonder.

Peatlands offer complexity: the further you wade into their intricacies the more complex they become, down to the cellular level, where a whole new world races by. What they give me, when I can put aside the desire for hope, is something much more. I revere their complexity. In other words, I've found a kind of faith in them. And in my attempts to understand these places, I found something on the other side of knowledge: the vastness is such that all you can do is leap into it with astonishment and amazement.

Ecosystems are alive. A wood is more than just a group of trees; a desert is not just sand; a river runs because everything in it decides to do so; and a bog is a beast with a body as complicated as any other. There's a heartbeat under the mosses, driven not by blood but by water, and this bog sighs: it breathes with all the life that is in it. This landscape has crystallised my thoughts on animism. It is alive with body, soul and ancestor.

I found myself lifting my head from the stacks of books, from the microscope work, the papers, and walking slowly with the old dog up the greenways behind my house and into the hills. When she was weary we'd sit, just high enough to see the mountains begin to roll up and away and in the other direction the flat line of the shimmering sea. I was high enough in elevation and in spirits to imagine the roll of the waves over the sea's kelp beds, which would seed the atmosphere with iodine to form wisps of cloud that would race along until they met the hills, then the mountains, and release their waters to the bogs that blanket them. In turn those mossy places would slow and filter the waters down through hills till they hit the source of the river and washed back into the sea to feed the seaweeds. I find myself in this loop between algae, water and moss, able to travel back and forth between the deep blue of the horizon, the browns and greens blanketing the hill behind me.

This is an old story then, of finding faith in the seemingly miraculous life that swirls around us.

It was during this time of intensive study that I met Richard Lindsay, often affectionately referred to as *the* godfather of peat by the peatland community (there are many godmothers too). For decades he has been working tirelessly for peatlands to be recognised as important habitats for biodiversity and for their role in climate mitigation. He was one of those instrumental in saving the Flow Country, the largest peatland in Britain, found in the north-east corner of Scotland, from becoming entirely afforested in the 1980s. Afforestation is simply to make a forest, to plant trees in a landscape where there hasn't been tree cover in recent history.

Standing among the rushes, in a pair of snow shoes (to lessen his impact, because this is a man who loves mosses), a giant mustard waterproof, a thick waxed wide-brimmed hat, bushy eyebrows and, dare I say it, twinkling eyes, he sounds like a parody of the kindly scientist, listening intently and, at times, with some amusement as I tried to get all my questions out at once.

Me: Could you explain cation exchange in mosses?

Richard: Like fly papers. Everything sticks to them.

Me: What do you think about a genetic pool of micropropped mosses?

Also me: What's with all the weird mire classifications? Are AI and digital mapping a good way of finding unknown peatlands? What about wind turbines' footprint on the bog? What's that huge hairy caterpillar by your foot called? (An eggar moth, very common on bogs.) Can we save the bogs in time?

To the latter he sagely replied, 'On whose timescale?' and looked quizzically at me.

I realised he wanted a reply. 'I don't know. Two hundred years?'

I said, plucking out a number based on my understanding of woodland ecology.

'Two hundred?' he said, raising those great eyebrows. 'There are peatlands that have formed over two hundred thousand years of climate change. We are standing on peat at least two thousand years old.' He pointed at his feet. The bogs left alone, he said, would look after themselves. We aren't restoring the bogs to save them, but to save ourselves.

Many things stayed with me after our meeting, but the one I come back to again and again is his comment about honouring and respecting peatlands as an entirety, as a body in their own right. 'The last time we revered bogs as a society was the Iron Age,' he said. 'The bog bodies as boundary markers, the buried hoards of butter and gold,' were, he said, 'a mark of respect, of veneration.'

Once upon a time we knew a lot about bogs. We knew them intimately as places of wonder, but also of prosperity. We've forgotten an awful lot, but many people know of the bog bodies, our ancient ancestors, found buried deep in the peat. Whenever I told anyone I was writing a book about bogs, the first thing they would ask, once I'd clarified it wasn't a joke book about toilets, was 'Are you writing about those buried souls?'

Fascination with the bog bodies is so often tied up in the violence of their deaths that we've perhaps missed the point of why the bodies were buried there. This landscape was so important to our ancestors that they sacrificed their own people in the knowledge that they wouldn't rot: they were not trying to hide the bodies, they were preserving them. They interred their dead in the bog as a votive or ritual offering that marked an edge, be that a territory of the living or the dead. When an actual body is suspended between this world and the next, the notion of the bog as a portal to another realm becomes visceral.

Today those bodies are buried deep, but there's a good chance that they weren't hidden. They would have been near-the-surface watery graves where people might have gone to peer down at them, offerings at the edge of their world. We will never know to whom the offerings were made: gods, other forces, warnings to enemies or other tribes. They certainly couldn't have imagined they would be dug up and preserved in museums. Those bodies were supposed to stay in their bogs. Perhaps we have unleashed something in removing them. Their re-emergence is possibly better seen not as a grim tale of mutilation and torture, but as an offering to us from our distant ancestors: take heed of these places and their importance in our lives, our climates, or prepare for their reckoning.

*   *   *

The more I learnt of peat, the more it presented itself to me. Some was obvious: I was getting much better at pattern recognition for its distant colours and found I could map my way home to mid-Wales through peat, up there to the right, again on the left, perhaps some degraded blanket bog, a little marsh, learning to look for signs of mineral soils or peat. It was easiest done looking for haggs, which are not witches hiding in the hills but the bare face of peat, eroded by water, wind and livestock. They're like miniature cliff faces. If the haggs are black, the soil is peat, but if they're light-coloured or glint with sandstone, siltstone or mudstone, then it is not peatland but dry heathland. A damaged, dried-out peatland often looks remarkably like a heathland, blanketed in heather and purple moor grass.

I sought out stories about peat, devouring Sarah Moss's *Ghostwall*, a must-read in conjunction with *Bog Bodies* by Melanie Giles, and *The Fell*, a cautionary tale of walking on mires at night. Peat appeared when I wasn't looking, too: I found bogs in my father-in-law's calendar of photographic scenes of Australia (Tasmanian bog); I realised the picture that hangs above my dear friends' Pip and Kath's sofa shows a bog and remarked as much to Pip, who disputed it. 'But that's deer grass,' I said, pointing to the distinct orange glow of the grass in autumn.

I realised my obsession with crime dramas was as much about backdrop as it was about intricate and convoluted plot lines. I'd shout 'Peat!' every thirty seconds as I binge-watched the BBC's *Shetland*. And that obsession flitted to every Nordic crime drama, not solving the crime, spotting the peat. I found peatlands in my local cinema: *Emily* (set on the Brontës' Yorkshire moors), *The Wonder* (set in the nineteenth-century Irish midlands), the tropical swamp peatlands in *A Crack in the Mountain* (a film about the world's largest cave, Vietnam's Son Doong). I'd wander into an art gallery and find myself drawn to a piece only to realise it was created using bog pigments or had bog wood in it.

I started to keep a running list of all the places other than bogs where I found peat or, at least, where I found it haunting my imagination. Often it represented the obvious: the remote, distant uneasy terrain, but it also suggested freedom away from the steady and ordinary. These hauntings hinted at tumultuous places that provided a great source of inspiration whether through their reputation for preserving the dead, with transformative properties of erasing the boundary between present and past, or because peat comes with a kind of autonomy or self-determination, a place that decides where you can go and the sort of people who want to go there.

2

Misrepresented Places

Peatlands have a desultory history that says they, particularly bogs, are just a filthy pit of mud and not much more. It has a lot to answer for. I want to go back to the bogs' beginning and let them tell their story.

These strange places offer something far closer to euphoria than desolation. Many people are politely baffled as to why I might write a book about bogs, but others understand. They talk of the dizzying excitement of so many wonderful little green things; they instantly catch on to the freedom inherent in a place that can't be controlled. They come maybe for the birds or the moths or the dragonflies; they love the pseudoscorpion and are fans of the giant horseflies, with their beguiling green eyes, and all the other strange things that make their home in these places. Maybe it's the water or the peat itself. Many of these people make up the peatland community, and are doing everything they can to restore these places to their glory. They are scientists of every order, biologists, chemists, system-modellers, computer scientists, engineers, hydrologists, and practitioners of everything from sculpting and keying peat back into itself, to blocking cracks and drains, pulling up errant conifer seedlings, probing the depth to measure the peat, and they are planters of tiny mosses.

If you are still thinking, I've been up on the moors and stood on those places and they are windswept and not full of much, let me take you first to the few that have not been ruined. When you say 'bog' or 'moor', most people think of very damaged habitats. Damage has been inflicted for centuries. The peatland might have been dug, certainly burnt, often polluted and eroded into a thin few species and some black haggs. They have a certain wild beauty in what's clinging on, but they shouldn't be judged in the state to which we brought them. The few that have by chance or luck been able to hold on to part and sometimes all of their glory show that peatlands can have all the complexity and intricacy of ancient forests, just at a scale that sits mostly beneath your feet rather than towering overhead.

*   *   *

I know people who have lived their whole life in my area of mid-Wales and never been to my local bog, Cors Fochno, in Borth. They know and love the estuary that lies nearby. They have run up and down Ynylas's shaggy dunes covered with marram grass; they know its wide, sweeping beaches and the petrified forest that appears at low tide; they are aware that it is famous for its meeting of many edges; they will talk of salt marshes and perhaps the brackish waters, of the osprey, the plovers; they have got up early to see the dolphins and porpoises; they know of strange, local lore about toads and witches that live in its backwaters, but have never been to those backwaters, the bog, never stepped on it. I know people who have driven past it time and time again and couldn't even point out where on that flat plain it sits. But if you said, 'Borth Bog,' they'd all nod in recognition, so you might think they'd go out of curiosity. But this is the fate of many a bog: to exist as an endless space that, to many people, cannot be entered.

Of course, there are others who know its great mysteries, of how it can move time and sound, how you can hear clearly the dog barking miles away, and the rustle of the beetle walking through the lichens, how the weather is different on the bog, covered in occult mists at one minute, blazing in brilliant sun at the next. How it hides the homes of so many, but if you sit quietly what seems like an inanimate landscape will, in just a little time, start to dance with life. Life that hasn't changed much in thousands of years.

You don't have to venture far for it to give up some of its best jewels. Late into the summer night you can wander to the edge and hear nightjars whirl and shudder in their strange songs, and if you stay up late or rise before dawn you will hear a willow warbler. The adders are sweet enough beings that will slip away before you can fear them and hide themselves so well you never spot them again. You will find that the bog smells sweetest in autumn when the oils of myrtles are concentrated in the opening buds and in late spring when the waters are clear and cool. And, oh, the summer, when the skylarks are in full swing and their song fills the whole space with such energy, and the smells of the high sun on your skin, and the humidity that rises from the bog is somehow akin to a sweaty night dancing in a club with too many hot, beautiful bodies. I know that sounds fantastical, but when I hear the skylarks run their song at tempo, I come away yearning for a dark basement nightclub.

And I do love that bog, more perhaps than any other bog. It is a rare bog. There aren't many like it, where you can sit in the middle of a plain of peat and smell the sea and hear the wind rush down from the mountains. Its location may be rare, but the peat itself is not. There are peatlands all over this island: they make up around 13 per cent of the UK's land mass, from the famous fens to the east, the many moors south and north, the upland hills of Wales, the meres and kettles and strange quaking bogs of the Midlands, to our many wet edges and the carr woodlands that grow by rivers and streams. You are never very far from peat. History has kept peatlands hidden, called them wastelands and wet deserts, has seen them as flooded as in drowned, rather than flooded as in abundance. Not just here but around the world.

The bogs, the swamps, the fens, the marshes and the wet woodlands – all that sit on peat – have had the wrong stories told about them. Stories about dangerous, barren spaces that are full of loss, shame and deception, as if their liminality means they aren't to be trusted. There are centuries of these tales and if you follow them back to their beginnings you'll find they all spring from some men's desire to own. You cannot own such a liminal space, that is as much wet as it is land, unless you drain it of its lifeblood, its waters.

Then you can lord over it, you can dig it up, burn it, extract from it. And when you do these things to peat, you'll claim you have conquered it: 'Look, we took something worthless and made use of it.' And, yes, peat when dry does burn and, yes, when dry, it can be turned into growing fields and potting compost and, yes, when it's dry, it can flavour whisky barrels, but when it's wet, it holds the balance of life in its body because the peatlands are one of the ways in which this earth stays cool enough to be inhabited.

I felt that to retell bogs' stories I needed to get to know one in particular, to come back again and again until the bog felt familiar and friendly. It made sense that it would be Cors Fochno, just over the hill, a distance short enough for me to go regularly, even if it was just to swing by and look over it from the top of the hill. I thought of these visits as popping in to say, 'Hi.'

*   *   *

I left home in a blaze of sunshine, but in the seven miles and two hills between me and Cors Fochno, the wind had whipped the clouds together. By the time I was approaching the middle of the bog the distant mountains had disappeared behind the clouds and the near hills washed in and out of vision. A sea mist had rolled in and crept down into my thin layers. I hunted through my pockets to find waterproof gloves and zipped my coat hood right the way up, cursing that I had made the rookie error of not putting on waterproof trousers. I walked on down the monitoring boardwalk passing the lone rowan, hunched over like an old person from years of battling winds and poor conditions.

The rowan is one of a number of obvious visual peaks in that seemingly endless flat space. It is only growing there because it managed to make its life on one of the ditches of years past, when people cut the bog for fuel. The slope of the ditch means the peat has dried out enough for the acid-tolerant rowan to get a foothold. Not that life is rich, for this tree is short and twisted from lack of nutrients, but still it stands above most of the rest of the bog.

When I knew that no one was around, one of my favourite things was to go down to one of the more solid sections of the boardwalk and lie on my back and watch the world from the bog's perspective: the trill and rat-a-tat-tat of the skylarks, the drumming of the snipes, the drone and buzz of insects, the gurgle and glug as my weight settled on the bog.

Half of the boardwalk had recently been replaced with bright yellow slats of new wood and half of it awaited repairs. Inevitably, over the pools of water the walkway rotted quickly and thus the most treacherous bits are missing. I tiptoed over these, going further into the middle, so I could get to the 'lawns'. Acid mires or bog complexes are covered with sphagnum mosses, the key species of this habitat. If you are walking over a landscape of wet mosses and seemingly nothing else, you are, without doubt, walking on highly acidic peat. But it is not a landscape of a single moss: it's a carpet of sometimes a few and, in the best cases, many different species. Like the 'Land of Counterpane', it rolls up and down so that you find flat lawns of certain species, hummocks of species that can tolerate drying out more, and roll down into pools for species that must remain submerged.

I'd come to better my sphagnum identification, which stood at about three of forty species. I had a lot of work ahead. Sphagna are a tricky lot, many often only truly identifiable under a microscope, where the thinnest, gossamer fragment allows you to peer between the cell walls and make sense of which one you are looking at. Their ability not only to adapt but maintain in such difficult conditions of acid peatlands means they are shapeshifters: loose and lanky in pools but, if need be and conditions dry up, tightening into neat columns, so that the easy identification of wet-loving submerged types and dry-tolerating hummocks can flip on its head in just a few metres.

On that day I noticed something I would feel over and over again with every new peatland I visited, that a landscape dominated by many varieties, the varying hues of greens, browns, reds, whites, coupled with the patterns of tight-knit hummock dwellers and loosey-goosey submerged types, does something quite extraordinary to the brain. Once you relax into your near rather than distant view, your brain gets very excited and your senses highly stimulated by varying repetitions, by the depth and brilliance of the jewel-like colours. It is a heady magic carpet for the eyes to ride upon, and that you can't launch yourself onto it – well, not without potentially sinking rather deep – somehow adds to its mysterious nature. It's begging you to trip into the unknown so you have to steady yourself and hold both of you accountable. I found myself shouting to the bog through the wind, 'I'm not doing that! I'm not coming in.' I startled a jacksnipe that rose low from its hiding spot and, like a fighter pilot, took off at speed, rattling in alarm.

Two Canada geese circled me so low that I could hear the taut rip of their wings against the wind. They honk periodically and did this over and over again. I moved on, they moved away, they returned, low and wide, and all I could do was pivot on the boardwalk to watch them, certain they knew they had the upper hand.

I guessed they were new parents and my presence was troubling.

I am not used to Canada geese being so put out. Their urban counterparts are mostly indifferent to humans, but so few people come to visit this bog that all the inhabitants, from the tiny brown moths to the fieldfares that dance across the sky, notice me. I can't say they are as bothered as the geese, but they all know I'm there.

In such a wide space where the sky is often more of a presence than the land, clouds can race across the pools with dizzying effect and it's easy to become disoriented: far seems near and near seems infinite. When you peer past the clouds, the pools are portals to a whole other world. It's a landscape where you transcend distance and often time. There's something about the flatness of lowland bogs that loosens how you manage time. It's all a little relative out here if you relax into it.

When I first met Justin Lyons, the land manager of the Dyfi National Nature Reserve and keeper of the bog magic, he asked straight away if I'd found the scientific boardwalk that leads to the middle of the bog. Had I gone down the non-public board-walk, the one with the sign saying it isn't a public right of way? It's there, as its name suggests, to let scientists onto the bog to do research. Sections are marked with a white line and corresponding number. Dotted along it at either side are various scientific experiments, glass boxes to measure gas exchanges and older side paths, their timber struts sinking back into the bog, and various dipwells for measuring the waters below.

I admitted sheepishly that I might have used it once or twice. I couldn't work out if he was bothered by that, but I realised he was making me a formal invitation. This was the first of many walks together where he would point and teach me about mosses and birds, pondering my questions seriously. I was left with so much from these visits – more to read: often he'd bring papers he thought I'd find interesting, more people to meet, but mostly he'd offer new ways of seeing. I've looked at the world much more carefully since I met Justin.

We were with Jake White, the New LIFE for Welsh Raised

Bogs project officer, who is based at Cors Caron, Tregaron Bog. Initially, I'd ask Jake to take me to Cors Caron, but once he knew the nature of the book, he insisted that 'no one knows a bog more intimately' than Justin, and he'd be happy to introduce us. So, between sphagnum identification and peatland engineering chat, the three of us walked out to the middle of the bog. Pointedly, Justin marked out the terrain around us – I guess he could tell a wanderer when he met one. 'Over there are hidden ditches from turf cutting. I almost lost the all-terrain vehicle in one. Use this rowan if you get lost on this side to find your way back. That island over there, the Jenkins family call it coed wirion. It means "the crazy wood".' I asked if he'd ever been there and he looked at me so incredulously that I shut up. He explained that the edges were the easiest places to cut turf, and a hundred years on they might have looked just like the centre, but the deep cuts remain and are now soupy pools of peat hidden by mosses. It is into the cuts, where the magic carpet of moss hides the perils below, that people fall.

Justin told me that only last summer a man had to be air-lifted out: he was trying to capture the sunset on camera and was so enamoured of the distant view that he had taken one step too far. He'd pulled his false hip out of its socket trying to struggle free. Thankfully, his phone was in his shirt pocket and not water-logged so he could call for rescue. I liked these stories, not just because they were well told, but because they were peppered with lessons. I moved my phone to my breast pocket.

He also told me more stories of weather, how it rushes in and can catch you unexpectedly. In these unbounded spaces, lightning races to whatever is standing. He told me to be wary of the weather, not to attempt to shelter by the rowan or anything else that stuck out of the bog, but to find a solid bit of sphagnum turf and lie flat till it passed. This was not a joke: he knew of a scientist who had lost two research students to lightning on a bog.

It took many more visits to different bogs for me to learn that you have to temper, as much as your wanderlust, your ability to sit with your mood. There is nothing to run to or, for that matter, to run from. It's just you, the weather and all that knowledge buried deep beneath your feet. It is not like walking on mountains or up a hill: there's no better view to prize; you can't hide in the nook of a rock or the might of a tree if the wind comes looking. If you don't pay attention you will probably get wet and most likely stuck. If you take your worries to the bog, they will race around its vastness or wobble on its uneven terrain. But if you can sit with these uncertainties and sigh with the breath of the bog, if you can slow your clock-time thoughts until they seem as distant as the edges, the magic of the Lilliputian world will take over, the sparkle of the sundew, the pop of spores in mosses, the creak of the crow's wing, the song of the toad, the dart of the damsel fly . . . Before you know it, you can sink into the pace of the place. And there is something here in this ancient world that is not easy to find elsewhere, something about distance and depth and slowness, and how it may not reveal itself on your first, second or even third visit. You have to wait till it's ready, till you're ready, but when it comes, my God, it comes.

*   *   *

The track to Cors Fochno is fringed with young birch on one side. Their coppery stems smoulder against the smoke signals of fireweed seed heads. On the other side there's a ditch. Here, huge, luxuriant royal ferns sway, with their orange seed heads, as bog pondweed, *Potamogeton polygonifolius*, covers the dark water below. As I reach the start of the bog, a little stream gushes as it drains into the ditch, and recent rain means it pools over the little bridge pathway. I peer over the edge and the water glows blood red with tannins.

The bog in autumn is the colour of sweetness. It is toffee before it cracks, browning butter and caramel just as it swirls into shape. The bog myrtles are orange, the heathers brown, the sphagnum mosses cream, yellow-green, pink-red and brown. There are forests of bog asphodel seed heads in caramel and coffee, and cotton grass in hues of orange and yellow. There are fiery red deer grass and, among the bog rosemary, dotted here and there, the last pink flowers of cross-leaved heath all born from the sweet, fudgy soil of the peat below.

A small common darter flits over the silvered surface of one of the pools, and the milky orb of the late-autumn sun burnishes the wider landscape. I shudder: I feel high on all of this. I turn around and around trying to take it all in, too excited to know where to start. Try to identify all of the mosses? Meet the various sedges, find the sundews and bladderworts, stay low and hope for a bird of prey?

A while back, someone sensibly understood that if you wanted us to view bogs as important, valuable and worthy of being turned into a nature reserve, you should probably allow us onto them. That's not an easy thing to do in a world where you can't be sure-footed, where sinking is more likely than propelling forth. So, conservation organisations and public bodies started to build public boardwalks to allow the public to get a little closer to the magic.

In the end, I lie on my belly and peer between the slats of Fochno's boardwalk, which is a strange thing to do in six hundred or so hectares of wild open space but it calms down the nature rush until I breathe in tune with the belly of the beast, its long, slow rise and fall. I turn over to lie on my back and allow the landscape to enfold me.

I know a deep contentment here. For a good while, lying on my back on the boardwalk, with a fringe of oranges and pinks to the world, I try to think of something that would make me happier and I cannot. By which I mean I try to think of other things but I can only dwell on this landscape, the mountains behind and the sea beyond. It absorbs me wholly and, I realise, physically too as my feet are hanging over the edge of the board-walk, soaking up water. I sit up and determine to be less smug about my luck, but it doesn't last.

I have always loved this kind of landscape. I can trace this back to my earliest memories of sitting on moors as a very young child in Lancashire, the purple of the heather outside and a room full of sombre people in dark clothes and thick accents inside. Though sometimes I imagine I might have had other bog lives: a pile dweller, a forager, a farmer, a peat cutter, a witch, perhaps.

You are a lover of bogs. You may not know it, but deep in your gene pool there it sits. We all carry wet people inside us. Among our earliest ancestors, *Homo habilis* lived on wetlands. Some were nomadic, while others remained permanently on bogs, burying their dead, their butter and their stories in these places.

Wetlands are good places for those who go looking: there are plenty of wildfowl, ducks and geese, herons and cranes, beavers and otters, fish, too, and molluscs. And plenty of material that's seemingly impervious to wet decay: reeds, grasses and sedges are easy to weave into nets. The wet woodlands would have been rich in nettles, with fibres for clothing, leaves for eating and medicine, and seed full of protein. When one of the most famous bog bodies, the Tollund Man from Denmark, was found, his stomach was full of nettle seeds. For millennia people lived by and on wetlands, and did very well. Life was damp, but rich.

This is not a governable richness: foraging breeds a certain freedom and nonconformity. It is hard to round up people who can sink away. There is a long history of wetland people who evaded conforming to other powers. Eventually, though, some of our ancestors bowed to the grain and the domestication of cereals, which required drier lands and less nomadic ways.

Grain requires that you stay with it, to tend it, to protect its precious harvest. The semi-nomadic pastoralists who went with the ebb and flow of wet places found themselves in contested spaces, as contested peoples. Slowly, but surely, humans started to drain wet places, to cut away at the peatland, to hold the places and their people in submission to tame them.

Dramatic things have always befallen these landscapes: before we drained them the seas rose over them, and in their turn, the wetlands rose over lakes and forests. Even now the drama continues as we alter our climate: they are drying out and releasing a vast history of carbon stored deep in their veins. Now we are racing to save them. We need to re-wet the dry places rapidly and restore the damp cycles to allow them to grow once more.

Part of this race belongs to us, to you and me, for it is time to be a good citizen, to come back into community with our wet past. We need to talk these places back into our language, with stories, folklore and fantasy. This is best done by visiting them, getting to know them. The places are as much our ancestors as the buried people sometimes found in them; we need to befriend the bogs, to make kin with the mires and the fens and all who inhabit them. These places are good company, playful spaces of uncertainties: what looks solid shakes; what looks like sky is ground; what looks like water is soil. To honour these places we must delve back into their beginnings and learn to read their stories.

The bog makes this possible because it has been keeping a diary of its existence since it was born, layer upon layer, of all that has happened to it and all the secrets it promised to keep. It is possible to read whole histories of places, people and lost-to-time beasts. Eventually we will rise out of these dark soils to find ourselves in the wide space of above-ground treasures, of insects and insect-eating plants, of mosses and more, but also of futures.

3

Lost Places

One simple way of telling whether you are standing on peat is to jump up and down. Peat always vibrates: it wobbles, quakes. It resembles soil and is made up of semi-decomposed dead things; organic matter in suspended animation, dead but not completely decayed. It started to rot, but it couldn't fully break down because the conditions were too wet and therefore too low in oxygen for all the microbes that take on the final act.

The leaf litter, plant material, dead animals and insects, their bones, poo, petals and pollen started to decompose where they lay, but a new layer of material fell upon them and buried what had come before in a place where rotting just couldn't happen. A place lacking in air, thick with water and often very acidic.

Wales is full of it. So are the uplands of the north of England, and there are even greater swathes across Scotland. Down south, there are the Somerset Levels and Dartmoor, and to the east, the Norfolk fens. But peat isn't only British: it is found across the world in at least 180 countries, and spans all of the continents, from forested peatlands in Central and Northern Europe, tropical peat swamps in South East Asia (Asia has the most peat world-wide, mostly in Russia), to vast permafrost peatlands in Arctic Russia and Canada, and the high mountain peatlands of the Andes and Himalayas.

These are surprisingly different places. Peatland depends on peat's two mothers: the rock beneath it, which shapes its birth, and the sky above, which forms its future. If the peat is wet enough, it keeps on growing. A peat that is growing is known scientifically as a mire. That is a broad term and encompasses the many different ways in which the geology and hydrology of a place come together to form peat. At its simplest there are two categories: fens, which are alkali to neutral, and bogs, which are acidic. Fens are fed by the landform and the sky, by rivers, streams and underground water courses. Bogs get their water only from the sky: they are cloud dependent. Because of this, they lack the flush of minerals from their parent rock or accumulated surface waters, so they are thin places of poor nutrients, which means that only a handful of plants can make a bog their home. Driven by these stark conditions, the main plants that grow here, mosses, are fiercely protective of their home and maintain these wet-acid conditions to keep down competition. That they are some of the smallest, oldest plants in the world should come as no surprise: these small plants are quite the chemists. They build the bog, and store a third of the world's carbon in their millimetre-long leaves – just another of the many marvels of life here.

Rain-fed bogs are ombrogenous, meaning they are born of clouds. The word is taken from the Latin, *ombro* meaning cloud, and from the Greek, *genous* meaning born. There are also ombro-trophic, again, from *ombro* but this time with the Greek, *trophos* meaning nutrition, meaning that their minerals come from the clouds too. meaning that their minerals come from the clouds too. Lucky for bogs: etymology is poetic and romantic.

Fens don't fare so well with their language: they are minero-trophic, rich in minerals that the surface water has collected. They are also soligenous, meaning created by water born of the land, the inflow of surface water, as well as what falls from the sky. They are fed by these waters too, making those that live in them rheotophilous, nourished by that flow. In short, fens have more riches as the minerals mean there is a greater diversity of plant life, insects and birds. But that doesn't make bogs the poor cousin: instead it makes for a rich marriage because there is no such thing as a bog or a fen sitting alone in the landscape.

At some point, fens may become bogs as they lay down their layers of peat, which impedes their water flow. Many bogs find themselves with fen flushes, moments at which the underlying geology ripples or rises and will flush minerals through the acidity. In fact, the best way to talk about this landscape is not as bogs, fens, swamps, marshes or moors, but as mire landscape complexes.

Fens are among the largest wetlands in the world – part of the Florida mangroves and much of the Indonesian forests are also fen peatlands. In the UK, the fens of Norfolk are low, plashy areas that are frequently flooded. Here, where the peat meets the rich nutrient soup of the underlying ground watertables bio-diversity flourishes. The peat-muds are full of flat worms, insect larvae and other things that squirm. Under a microscope a jam jar of black peaty water seethes; above ground, where enough light is let in, there is a carpet of lichen and liverworts between towering reeds, rushes and grasses and a meadow's worth of flowers, ragged robin, kingcups and marsh thistles.

Fens are a particular landscape with a particular people. I don't know them well, but I understand their beauty, as do many others. Much has been written about them and I will not retread those boards. I am biased for bogs. There's something about the acid and the paucity of nutrients that come with it that makes the things that cling to these spaces so tenacious. I'm laying my cards out flat: I'm here for the mosses and the world they build. This is shamelessly a book of bogs.

I have come to the conclusion that part of the magic of the peat bog is to understand how it is born, how it dies and resurrects itself. Partly because it is another example of how wondrous our world is and the system it creates, but also because in exploring peatlands, I found new ways of thinking about being, found light in one of the darkest places, saw action between us and the peat that is working, creating community, building possibilities. In those layers of half-rotted material there is a metaphor about the huge, unending complexity that is our world and how we might start to dance differently with it.

When Ele and I told people that we were moving to Wales inevitably someone would say, 'Oh, all that rain!' or, 'You'll get depressed with all that rain.' And we wondered privately if that might be true. It does rain a lot, but I might have stopped noticing it or at least I don't find the idea of it depressing any more: this landscape is rich because of the rain and nowhere more so than all those bogs. When it rains, sometimes endlessly, I now think of how happy Cors Fochno must be, how fat Cor Caron must be swelling, how rich the blanket bogs must feel. Being on bogs in the rain has changed the way I look at grey. It's an oppressive dull colour if viewed from inside a house, but in the open it is made of so many hues. I have stood on the bog marvelling at the many tones a clouded sky can bring. Learning about the bogs has changed so much of my thinking, perhaps especially about water, of its immense power over the landscape. It can move, build and destroy at its own whim.

Peatlands occur only in wet conditions; they are married to water. Their wetness slows the rate of decomposition, which in turn allows the peat to accumulate. It is essential for peat growth, but also plant growth, and peatland plants have found many ingenious ways to adapt to being constantly wet.

Water is essential for the growth of all parts of the peatland, so it must be present, but it must also act in certain ways. It must move slowly; it must be impeded. Slow water, less agitated water, becomes oxygen poor, particularly as partially decomposed matter accumulates. The more it accumulates, the more nutrient and oxygen poor the water becomes, creating a better place for peat to build. There must be rain or high humidity throughout the year, but particularly during the growing season. The largest peatlands in the UK are oceanic blanket bogs, which can occur only in areas with regular precipitation, be that rain, hill fog, dew, morning mists, clouds at ground level or overall cloud cover. In the UK, that generally means areas with at least 160 days of rain annually.

Healthy peatlands can survive periods of drought and drying out: they do so because the lower levels of peat jealously guard their water by binding it in the intra- and intercellular spaces in the peat. Once the lower level is wet it stays wet as long as it is allowed to remain intact. The top parts, the active layer of peat, which is growing plants, loves and needs the rain because the plants have adapted to living with wet feet, and although they aren't without some surprising methods to survive drying out, they can only thrive when wet.

In northern climates, all those tiny mosses and short shrubby plants may not look much, but they are growing. They may lack stature, but they are impressive builders of peat. In tropical conditions, where the peatlands are mainly under swamps and forests, plant growth is faster because it's so warm. Importantly the atmosphere is very humid, and there is more rainfall than evaporation. Hot, wet, sunny conditions mean a lot of fast growth, but because the swampy soils are waterlogged these areas build peat rapidly: fast growth + wet soils = a lot of peat formation, all year round; on the other hand, temperate peatlands slow down in winter.

Peatlands are essentially a lot of dead material, breaking down very, very, very slowly once you go deep into the peat. The peat we dig up is old, often thousands of years old. In the northern hemisphere, it takes a year to grow a millimetre of peat, ten years to grow a centimetre and somewhere around a thousand years to grow a metre. A lot of our peat is very old, but it isn't stuck in the past. If it's healthy, it can continue to grow. A healthy peat bog is doing just that, slowly but surely increasing year on year, swelling with the wash of its water, thickening and spreading as it lays down peat.

The peat we see in our soils is pretty modern in geological terms. An even more ancient version is millions of years old, under layers of geology and rock, compressed by time and weight: coal. If peat is allowed to age for its entire geological lifetime in its natural environment, it would turn first to lignite, then charcoal, anthracite (a high-rank type of coal) and eventually graphite. But if you dig up any of this, whether it is peat to be used as compost or fuel, or you drain it for agriculture or you extract it as coal, it goes back into the atmosphere as carbon dioxide.

That some of the fossil fuels we are burning, hurtling us into an uncertain future, were once bogs and peatlands is not irony but a lesson. The earth was burying all this dead organic material for a reason: to reduce atmospheric carbon and make life habitable here. Peatlands weren't born by accident: they were formed by the earth's complex systems to keep the living world cool.

4

Dark Places

To understand bogs, you have to delve deep into their belly, into the thick, fudge-like substance that makes up the meat of them. You have to push to their edges to learn how things change here, how they compress and shift their acidic ways to adjust to the outer world around them. Finally, when you have taken notice of this dense, muffled underbelly, you must drive upwards to the living layer that blankets and protects, that builds and renews all that is dark below.

The living layer is easy enough: if you place each foot carefully, you can walk on to it and take in its surface at least, the best part, but the stuff below, the only way to know that is to go uninvited. The bog never wanted you in its belly, never asked to be prised open and taken from but, as with so much of our knowledge, we have learnt through extraction, from digging up and draining, from milling away what lies below.

I want you to know how the heart beats inside the beast, of the waters that pump through the system like blood, of the hidden soul. Then, every time you find yourself on peat, you'll start to think of all the marvellous, sometimes mysterious things that happen below. You look for the edges, peer into the pools of water as portals into the underworld, glimpses to the other side.

*   *   *

Peat is half land and half water, and held in the land is a great, ancient store of carbon, about 600 gigatonnes of carbon dioxide worldwide. That's double the carbon stored in all the world's forests and about 44 per cent of all soil carbon. So that you can visualise this a little better a single gigatonne is the equivalent of 200 million elephants or 5.5 million blue whales. We talk a lot about carbon and carbon dioxide these days, and we know it is bad, but why does it occur so abundantly and why does the earth have to lock it away?

When I started to look into this, I knew little more about carbon than what I'd held on to from school science lessons, which was not much. I best understood carbon through my compost pile and my garden's soils. Plants growing in organic soils full of carbon are resilient and steady compared to the rank growth in soils dominated by nitrogen.

But carbon cycles, stores, sequestrations, carbon rings and chains, carbon oxidisation? I had to clamp my jaw shut to concentrate. And this became a problem. When I was at the bog, I was happy and relaxed; when I was reading about bogs and carbon cycles, I was gritting my teeth so hard that I was starting to crack them. When I let go of all this concentration, I could hear my jaw muscles snap back.

My friend Naomi told me about her brilliant acupuncturist – 'She used to be an archaeologist, likes bog bodies. You should go and see her.' It instantly seemed to make sense to see an acupuncturist. I like the symmetry of probing around peat and the needling of the treatment, that both require hunting into hidden layers to extract the truth.

After some weeks, Jody relaxed my jaw just enough that I

could keeping the snapping quiet, but she taught me something. She said on my first visit that I was stuck on decision-making and this rankled because I like to think of myself as decisive, not afraid to make big leaps, but my jaw was saying otherwise. I argued it was not a decision-making issue but about concentration. She smiled knowingly. We'd talked about bogs, and wind farms, about Neolithic people, about academia and ancient arts as she placed her needles week after week, and I began to see she was right: it was all about decision-making, about what word to use next.

It turns out that all of our carbon originally came from outer space, which has oodles of the stuff, locked up in the stars and hanging between them. Long before the earth was as we know it, when it was a lump with an iron-rich core hurtling madly about, it ran into another lump, a baby planet with a carbon-rich crust. It consumed the planetary embryo, with all of its carbon.

This run-in changed a lot for the earth: once there was a source of carbon, life could (eventually) get going. From one strand of DNA, a world is built, and when the first green things crept across the land, the earth had a dilemma about what to do with all this energy. As the earth's climate changed because more DNA was replicating and more plants grew, there was suddenly an abundance of material, and some of it was carbon, more than could be recycled, so the systems needed to find a way to store it. And one of those ways was peat.

These days, we dance with carbon in many different ways, but let's start with the basics. Plants capture sunlight and convert light energy into chemical energy through photosynthesis. Think of it like this: plant leaves are solar panels. What's left over from converting light energy into chemical energy is carbon, which is stored as carbohydrates, sugars and starches, and the rest is released as carbon dioxide.

Let's look at this through the lens of peat. Plants store carbon throughout their tissues, in their leaves, stems and roots, but just as much is given to the soil. They release around half of their energy to feed the soil food web around their roots. So here we have two forms of stored carbon: in the growing plants and in the community in the soil. When the plant dies, in a stable perennial system, a wood or a forest, a grassland, a hedgerow, it rots back to where it came from, and this carbon is recycled into the soil or the atmosphere to create new energy for the next generation. In nearly all terrestrial ecosystems this rate of production, plants-grow-plants-die-plants-rot, is equally balanced, meaning that the soil depth remains pretty much constant. However much compost you put on your garden, it doesn't rise in height. We are not drowning in rotting organic matter because it is recycled by the system, or the soil food web. The great fallen tree in the wood eventually crumbles to soil. This constant makes most ecosystems store carbon as long as they are in equilibrium, but most do not result in a reduction in atmospheric carbon.[*]

Most, that is, but not all ecosystems.

Peat-forming ecosystems, because of their watery ways, create a situation in which plants grow faster than they can decompose; over time the dead plant material builds up. Peatlands rise, and this slowly increasing build-up of dead plant material leads to a reduction in atmospheric carbon. So a peat bog is a carbon store and a carbon sink. It takes in carbon as it grows, but it keeps hold of all its past carbon, thousands of years of it, or, in the case of fossil fuels, millions of years, as the peat bog is slowly compressed and incorporated into rock, then converted to coal.

The build-up is not necessarily noticeable when you look across the landscape, though some raised peat bogs do appear to mound. Most actually flatten the landscape; they blanket dips and hollows. But probe, and there can be metres of peat. Even though peat forms only a tiny proportion of the land mass, just 3 per cent, it is currently thought that nearly half of the world's carbon

---

[*] The exception is early stage succession in, say, a forest, where the rapid growth of trees does result in a reduction in atmospheric carbon, but this is balanced out when the forest matures and older trees grow more slowly.

stored in soil is held in peat. That's more than half of the current atmospheric stock of carbon dioxide – a lot banked.

Right now, 80 per cent of peatlands in the UK no longer hold onto their carbon. They are broken. This damage is repeated more or less around the globe. The living layer has been either lost or is deeply degraded: the waters that keep the peat safe are draining away. And with this, the deep layers of stored carbon are rapidly oxidising, returning their stores to the atmosphere, no longer acting as a sink or a store.

There are many reasons for this: they are dug up, milled for compost and fuel or they have been drained for agriculture. The East Anglian Fens are a 'successful' example of this; the drains across most of our upland blanket bogs a disastrous version (both fens and uplands are dedraded and releasing greenhouse gases, we just profit more from fens). I came to this story in part because my relationship to peat might have started as some distant memory of childhood, but quickly turned into my use of peat in gardening. My industry is fuelled not by burning peat but by growing stuff in it. Peat-based compost is still the most widely used potting compost for the amateur market, for growing culinary pot herbs, for plants used in landscaping schemes, municipal bedding displays, houseplants for offices, trees for conservation schemes – the list is endless. There's a deep irony: we horticulturalists like to think of our industry as green – growing plants means supping up carbon, which is a good thing, right? Not if they are grown in ancient peat that releases carbon at its source, its home, but also while it is degrading in the pot. Peat only stores carbon if it is wet.

I learnt about the destruction of peat bogs for compost when I was seventeen, doing work experience in the orchid unit at Kew Gardens in my summer holidays. I remember it clearly. I was with an older Kew student: he was French and I thought he was impossibly cool. My job was to mix the potting compost for the rare and wildly beautiful orchids. It was mostly bark compost used because many orchids are epiphytes, growing high on tropical trees, so their roots need lots of oxygen to survive, mimicked by bark in pots. The Frenchman explained that Kew was peat-free: all its plants grew without it. Peat was precious habitat and it made, he said, no sense to destroy one home to make another. I hung on every word he said and followed him round like a lamb. At the end of the summer, he sat me down and told me how to apply to do the Kew Diploma in Horticulture, so I could become just like him. I did everything he said. I became a student, a passionate advocate of being peat-free. It was the motivation for my entire journey, but I thought my industry and the fuel industry were to blame for peat extraction. I knew very little of the damage of draining, of afforesting peatlands, of overgrazing, of the effect of atmospheric pollution and intensive agriculture. Of the land-grabbing for railways, motorways, wind turbines in the UK and far, far away. For instance, a huge percentage of the world's palm oil is grown on drained peatlands.

Which is not to let gardening off just yet: in 2019 we extracted somewhere between 600,000 and 800,000 cubic metres of peat (a quick reminder that it grows at just a millimetre a year) in England, Scotland and Northern Ireland (Wales has banned peat extraction). That doesn't cover all of the peat we import from Estonia, Poland, Romania, Canada and China, to say little of what other countries are doing. Germany, Holland and France are all major producers of plants and there's only a nascent peat-free movement in those places. China is a huge growth market for gardening, and from a cursory glance at the internet you'll find there's a growing interest in extracting peat for this market as well as for export. So peat extraction still needs a lot of shouting about it. If someone says, 'Oh, but we planted some trees to offset that,' ask where those trees are – afforestation is still a colonial tool – and what they were grown in.

All of these examples, whether extraction or drainage, result in the peat drying off: what's left is exposed to the air and starts to break down. This releases stored carbon, but also destroys the mechanics, the architecture of how peatlands work, which in turn means the peatlands start to erode. Lost to winds, washing away in floods or winter rains or, increasingly, in our long, hot summers, peatlands are catching fire and burning away. Fires can creep down into the layers; the surface may appear free of flames, even cool to the touch, but below fire burns deep in the belly for months, even years. Not only is this the loss of a physical landscape, it may increase flooding, affect drinking water, agriculture, increase atmospheric pollution through smoke, destroy habitats and more.

In the UK only 22 per cent of the total peatland area remains in a near-natural state, that's undrained bogs and fens, meaning that the vast majority of peat is not sequestering carbon. It's either tenuously holding onto or rapidly losing it. The picture worldwide is not dissimilar, though in some places, such as the palm-oil plantations in Indonesia, it is far, far worse.

This is sobering, but peatlands have an inherent resilience to draw on if given a chance. Restored peatlands call back the mosses and cotton grasses to clothe them and grow again as their top layer starts to knit back together. And if the top layer is intact, the magic below can start to happen again.

5

My Place

I live in a small cottage on a very busy road that runs down a valley to the sea. If I walk behind my home, the land at either side quickly rises and rises again, and soft, rounded foothills spread as far as the eye can see. To the north there is Eryri (Snowdonia) National Park, and to the west, the Cambrian mountains, and where my hill rises eventually into Pumlumon, a patchwork of blanket bog complexes cover the mountains in mosses, rushes and reed grasses. Sheep graze there. So, the landscape above my head is one type of peatland, blanket bog, but just to the north and the south there is another type.

I live between two important raised bogs, Cors Fochno and Cors Caron, known in English as Borth Bog and Tregaron Bog, after the towns they lie adjacent to. If I could have persuaded my wife to live next door to either, I would have. To me, they are places of unequivocal beauty. When I first proposed we should move to Wales and live by a bog, Ele named all the bad bog words: damp, depressing, desolate and bleak. I know when to pick my battles and we found a neat little house in Aberystwyth.

Cors Fochno is near, just a few hills away, so I can see the bog whenever I wish.

Every time, without fail, when I turn the final corner and see Fochno my heart skips, and I have lost count of how many times I have veered my car across the road to view the bog. All the eager anticipation of seeing a loved one. I know I don't have any right to claim that – I'm too new here, I don't speak the language, I haven't seen out seasons or generations – but still I feel it. Sure, the hills surrounding it are pretty darn beautiful, while the back-drop of sands, the dunes on the shore and Aberdyfi in the near distance are all very good, but it's the flat brown middle that has my heart.

My home is in a triangulation of bog classification because Cors Fochno is a single raised bog, Cors Caron is a raised bog complex (three raised bogs are nestled together), and the moun-tains behind are covered with blanket bog complexes. There is one other type, the quaking or Schwingmoor bog, and there's a good one about an hour away, just outside Builth Wells. I'm nestled into a landscape of soft, wet places.

All bogs have interesting origins. Like all peatlands, they are born of a relationship between the ground they sit on, the water that runs with them and, of course, the plants that make them alive. But in a bog's case the relationship is as much about sky and the water it holds, as it is the landscape. Where and how this falls and pools determines what kind of bog you get.

*   *   *

All raised bogs were once depressions in the landscape: a shallow glacial lake or a wet hollow. They filled with water that ran down from surrounding hills and mountains. The water was rich enough in nutrients that the margins of the depressions became colonised by wetland vegetation. From the reeds and rushes, fens developed, and trees grew at the drier margins of the lake. As the wetland vegetation lived out its lifecycle, debris started to accumulate in the

41

basin of the depressions and in these dark, anaerobic conditions the first peat started to form. The depressions began to change: where there was once an open body of water now there was only a clear middle. The depression slowly filled up with organic matter until it was eventually no more. Now it was becoming a marshy fenland, and the plants and trees that once inhabited the edge started to take over. In the place of open water, in the middle, there was a floating turf of plants with uncompacted dead material below.

Very few things like to live at the centre of a covered lake, the waters of which are becoming increasingly acidic and anaerobic. The only plants that can successfully colonise this sort of space are the sphagnum mosses, which thrive in wet, cold, acidic conditions. Despite the sphagnum's slight nature, its continual and rapid growth weighs heavy over the water table.

Peat starts to form initially from submerged rushes, then from the trees that took over and failed because the conditions became too acidic. Eventually, as the sphagnums dominate, the peat is formed almost entirely of those. The peat rises and swells, the depression in the landscape is lost and, in its place, the raised dome of a bog appears. All that is left of the wet depression is a thin line that circles the dome, known as the lagg fen.

The rivers and streams that fed the depression still feed the lagg, but the raised dome has created its own water table perched above the mineral soils and is wedded to its acid state. The only things that will grow on it now are the mosses, the cotton grasses, and on its sloping edges, known as the rand, a few short shrubby types, bog myrtles, bog rosemary, cranberries and such. The centre of the bog is now several metres higher than the surrounding landscape and made up of a series of hummocks and hollows covered with lawns of brilliant green, golden yellow, red and brown mosses, so thick as to suggest that you might be able to run across them. If you did, the hummocks would mostly sink and rebound behind you, the hollows would wobble, wave and threaten to sink you, and the way you came would never be the way you left.

Cors Fochno began as just such a shallow depression, left behind by the last Ice Age, when the many rivers of the surrounding hills, the Leri, Clewtr, the Ddu, Einon, the Melidwr and, most famously, the Dyfi, fed a large wide estuary with steep slopes dotted with rocky outcrops that are still visible in the hillsides. The sea created a long shingle spit to the south-west, which forms the base of Borth town. Behind it, a salt marsh built up. Over time the sea rose and the salt marsh turned into a large brackish estuary that sat on top of clay mud. If you take the train from Machynlleth to Borth and sit on the right-hand side, you'll see the characteristic mudflats, islands of salt-tolerant grasses, and the flush of fen landscape of the many *Juncus* rushes and *Phragmites* reed grass, with marsh birds and the sheep that graze there. It's a stunning landscape.

Around six thousand years ago, the shingle spit was moved eastward by the sea, and sand dunes started to develop, which prevented the sea from flooding the fens, and the vegetation built to above the flood zone. Slowly the reeds and grasses turned into wet woodlands of alder carr. As the soils continued to rise and the sea retreated, the natural succession of alder, oak and pine grew from a wood to a forest. The shallow lake depression lay in the heart of the forest. To imagine what that mighty forest might have looked like, go down to Borth beach at low tide and you will see, rising from the sand, the petrified stumps of oaks and pines, even occasionally the footprints of our ancestors as they walked among them.

At some point the River Leri broke its banks and found a more direct route through the shingle spit to the sea. Today it is canalised: a rod-straight line that runs parallel to the beach until it hits the estuary. You cross it on the train that goes from Dovey Bridge to Borth: it has to be one of the prettier sections of line in the UK. But you can see the ghostly ancient Leri footprint in the landscape: it snakes off around the golf course and its shadow runs down the sea; it's full of common reed, *Phragmites australis*, that dances in the wind reminding us that the ghost of the river is still alive. There's a good chance you might also see Justin's wild ponies, which keep the fringes of the bog grazed.

Back when the Leri first escaped to find the sea, it formed a second, smaller estuary, which played no small part in the fortunes of Borth. But right now, at four thousand years before the present day, the Leri's new route creates a way for the sea to creep back through the wetlands to lap at the forest edge.

The sea will slowly creep and rise over the next millennia. Again and again the land is flooded, killing off the pines and returning the area to wet woodland of alder carr and oak. The shallow lake begins to fill in and the peat builds. It does so uninterrupted for the next five thousand years. And that is how a raised bog is born. It rises out of the landscape.

A raised bog can sit alone, like Cors Fochno, or make up a complex, like Cors Caron. You can find raised bogs across North America, northern Europe, western Siberia (which has the largest raised bog landscape in the world), on the southernmost tip of South America at Tierra del Fuego, in South East Asia and in the Amazon basin.

Most of the European examples are coastal or Atlantic bogs that tend to form close to the sea, like Cors Fochno, but there are also plateau bogs, found in the warmer climates of north-west Europe, in particular Germany and Holland, the largest of which was Bourtange Moor, which once covered 2,700 kilometres but now only a tiny fraction of that as the Bargerveen Nature Reserve, one of the world's first bogs to be restored. Finally, there are Kermi bogs, which make up huge complexes of the low raised bogs that run through northern Russia, western Siberia and Finland and make up some of the world's largest bog complexes. Many raised bogs in Europe were born around eleven thousand years ago at the end of the most recent Ice Age, though some are younger and a few, particularly in other parts of the world, are much older.

There is, of course, a very different kind of bog. Blanket bog is generally a much thinner layer of peat that makes a continuous blanket across the landscape, and it is found almost exclusively in cold, wet climate regions. It can have deep spots, fen flushes and edges where streams run through; they can have a wooded section in the clough, the narrow ravines the streams often run down, but as their name suggests they cover the landscape in a layer of moss. They tend to be younger than raised bogs and many started life between five and six thousand years ago, though, again, a few examples are much older.

These bogs generally cover upland areas, hills and mountains, draping over the hollows and up and down gentle slopes, like a bedspread. If the landscape gets too steep and the water drains too quickly, the blanket bog will abruptly stop but expand again where it can. Anyone who's climbed high in the north of the UK will have come across these soft blankets of moss that carpet and swathe rocky landscapes. They tend not to build the great depths of peat you find under raised bogs or tropical peatlands, but they can spread vast distances, such as the Flow Country in Scotland, which covers 1,500 square miles and is thought to be the largest continuous expanse of relatively intact blanket bog anywhere in the world. Blanket bogs exist because of high rainfall and constant high humidity. In the UK that means the Pennines, the Yorkshire Dales, the Peak District moors, the Southern Uplands of Scotland, the Scottish Highlands, Clyde Forth and south Solway, the mountains of Wales, the rolling hills of Exmoor and across the vast upland expanse of granite in Dartmoor. In the far north and west of Britain, as well as in Western Ireland, they occur at much lower altitudes, though, in coastal regions of Sutherland, Caithness, Shetland and the Hebrides, County Clare, Donegal and Mayo, where the Atlantic Ocean provides a continual mist to keep them moist.

Many blanket bogs are complex landscapes shaped by time, geology, plants and, lately, humans. The top of a blanket bog complex can be made up of quite distinct individual mire units (or 'macrotopes'), but deep below the peat mantle these can all still be connected by their stored water, like a large undulating lake, and thus, hydrologically, they are all linked.

One final type of bog is worth distinguishing. They are dotted all over the place, the Highlands and islands of Scotland, in an impressive gathering in Cumbria, west and east Wales, the Midlands, Cornwall, the Isles of Scilly, and there's even one in the New Forest. They are often described as transition mires because they sit somewhere between the acid bog and the more mineral-rich fen. They are unstable underfoot, which makes them the most fun bog but also the most terrifying. A quaking bog quakes. All wet peat wobbles when you walk or jump on it, but you can make the whole surface of a quaking bog ripple – the trees and shrubs will shake, not just immediately but across the bog. This bog is a mat floating on water.

A quaking or Schwingmoor bog's formation is not too dissimilar to that of a raised bog, but the lake that bore it was much deeper. A quaking bog has not filled in the lake basin: it is sitting on top of the lake. If you could peel back the bog, you would find the ancient lake still very much intact. These underground lakes tend not to have inflow or outflow streams.

As these depressions in the landscape filled with water, the edges were slowly colonised by plants that grew, died, fell into the water, sank to the oxygen-poor bottom and started to form peat. This changed the pH of the water and gave a competitive edge to pioneering peatland plants, such as the mosses, particularly the hollow-loving types. As they colonised, they allowed the establishment of more mosses and eventually quaking mats of vegetation over the water. Slowly the lake disappeared under a moss mat. In some quaking bogs, the mat is thick enough to support trees, mostly pine, but birch too. There are numerous examples, particularly in the US, of quaking bogs detaching themselves from the edge of lakes and creating floating islands Whatever the vegetation composition in a quaking mire (whether bog or fen), the vegetation surface follows the water fluctuations.

That's why when you walk on it you create a wave formation and the whole thing trembles.

Just down the road from me in Wales is Cors y Llyn (which means 'bog on the lake') just outside Builth Wells. To me, it's the perfect little bog and my favourite pit stop on my way to my parents'. The wet meadows around it are filled with marsh orchids in late spring, and its fen flush edges are spectacular, with marsh cinquefoil, common hemp nettles, ferns and a thick band of birches. Then you pass through to this strange, otherworldly quaking bog, a low landscape of mosses and cranberry and, perhaps most surprising of all, a perfect tiny forest of stunted Scots pine, no more than two metres tall yet at least a hundred years old. The trees are escapees from a plantation that sits to the south of the bog. Their land-based siblings tower at forty metres, but on the bog the pines have bonsai'd. I like to think the trees know they are sitting on a moss mat and would sink through it if they grew larger, but the more prosaic reason is that as their weight increases and they sink into the floating mat, their roots become waterlogged and inhibit growth. I also read somewhere that the trees were ring-barked in the 1970s. Still, they make for a strange sight.

Chartley Moss, in Staffordshire, is one of the UK's largest quaking bogs. It sits over a six-thousand-year-old lake that is more than ten metres deep. It's said that the underground lake is littered with whole pine trees suspended in the water. David Bellamy, the peatland scientist and BBC wildlife presenter, jumped into one of the open holes (there's nearly always a breathing spot somewhere in the mat) and popped up out of the bog as a TV stunt.

6

Growing Places

Occasionally the earth reveals a slice of the past and, for a few seconds, while you marvel at it, time changes. The enormity of the scale of time is suddenly made clear. One of the joys of Cors Fochno and the wider Borth landscape is that the scale swirls around it as the salt waters of the sea meet those of the mountain. It's a double-page spread of a landscape, torn from some 1950s picture book, on how water moves through the world.

The submerged six-thousand-year-old forest that can be seen on the Borth beach at low tide now appears only as ghostly stumps; this ancient former margin of the great bog is washing away. The theory is that the new flood-defence work, the great mounds of rock that sit mid-shore to protect the town from winter storms, has altered the currents. Once upon a time the forest appeared only after a storm shifted great volumes of sand. Now it's there to see every afternoon. Exposed to the air, it is oxidising and falling apart, just like peat. Little bits flake off, and whenever I am walking that way, I cannot help but pocket these ancient relics. They tend to dissolve into mush, and when Ele borrows my jacket I notice how gingerly she puts her hands into the pockets, disgusted by the combination of seeds, soil and degrading plant matter I've collected. But if I were to pull out the fragment, you'd swear it must be a twig from last autumn, or if it was a large piece and you peeled it apart, you'd be looking inside something that last saw light millennia ago. There's a thrill to it: it's a kind of exploration.

A healthy bog is good at keeping its historic – and prehistoric – secrets. You can tease it and poke it, but it won't budge. Whatever fell on or into it as the peat grew rests peacefully. That is its promise to life. But a degraded bog cannot afford such luxuries, which gives us a window into a hidden world. The haggs, the gullies, the milled bottom layer: among them lie fragments of a long-lost past seeing sunlight once again. Some of these things are so small you'd need a microscope, but there are often much larger objects, such as bog wood, trees that fell into the bog when it was forming and, through the process of peat building, were preserved whole. In Ireland I saw a metre-long pine trunk, blackened by the tannin of the peat and moss, like a giant stick of charcoal. Wolf, dog, deer and other animal carcasses have been found and many smaller objects: roots, scales, seeds, buds, leaves, insect bodies, eggs, foraminifera sands (very simple, single-celled organisms with a test, or shell, that is preserved and appears to the naked eye to look like sand), bryozoas (sessile animals that form colonies that look a little like seaweed), tiny molluscs and bivalves from a period when coastal bogs were flooded with sea and brackish waters.

It is hard to look at degraded bogs when you understand what is happening. Like many other hill walkers, I'd assumed that exposed peat was just part of the landscape. I have marched past countless peat haggs, sloshed and slipped through peaty paths imagining that this was like any other bare soil, that it would quickly be recolonised once the pressure was off. But that isn't so. It is partly due to the layering of peat: the bottom layer isn't suitable for the stuff growing on top.

Seeing any amount of exposed peat means it's degrading and releasing greenhouse gases, so bare peat is never good . . . but it's hard not to be fascinated by it. You are seeing the past, being invited to peer into a timeline of life. On many a peat adventure, while some kindly peat expert is describing a restoration project, I've been lost in looking at the peat, trying to distinguish the layers. Once you know this, you can start to pick apart the peat's timeline. It's only through these exposed scars that we get to peer into the archive.

Peat is formed in very thin layers like rings on a tree; they are sequential. In a tree the central rings are the oldest; in peat it's the bottom layer. But the layers are not the same, and there is a distinct shift as you move through the peat. There are two realms to these layers: the living layer, the acrotelm, which sits on top and goes down 40 centimetres or so, and then the lower, denser, fudge-like layer, the catotelm, which can be metres deep and reaches down until you hit the mineral layer, the rocks on which the bog is built.

You can quickly spot the difference between the two because the acrotelm is a pale straw colour and contains visible plant material, is spongy and a little airy, while the catotelm may be much darker, often appearing black when dry. Catotelm is generally denser than the acrotelm by some 50% or more; nearly all the plant fibres may have disappeared, leaving just a mass of leaves and stem fragments obvious only under a microscope. If you find this layer when hill-walking, it often means that the top layer has been eroded and you are looking at a damaged section of bog.

A healthy acrotelm is alive, with an almost continuous layer of sphagnum mosses, cotton grass, rushes, dwarf bog shrubs known as heaths and the various berries (bilberry, cowberry and bearberry), with sundews sitting on top. Common heather is not a true plant of a bog: that space belongs to the cross-leaved heather. Heathers can be dense, particularly on degraded bog, and there may be mosses between the stems of heath and the bog myrtles. A healthy bog has very little common heather, but if it is there it has more soft growth on the heather and fewer silvered woody stems. Between and just below this vegetative layer there is a land rich in much smaller things. The giants of this group are the fruiting bodies of fungi, but there are also diminutive microbes of all feasible shapes and sizes, assemblies of photosynthesising bacteria and diatoms, tiny organisms invisible to the naked eye that whirr and whizz about, things that chase and suck and consume all organic matter that is living and dying in the world above. This layer accounts for a surprising amount of energy and carbon storage.

If the acrotelm is healthy, it is wet. The water table should be near or on the surface. Sometimes you can see this. At others you have to feel for it: sink your hand into the mosses and below them you will find cool wetness, sopping even: across the micro-topography of this layer, there are hollows and pools of hidden waters. Some of the mosses are suspended deep within them. Others float on top. Although both layers are governed by it, this layer visually, and physically if you try to move over it, gives a sense that it is a place of water as much as land. When heavy with rain, the water table is so high it glints, sparkles and mirrors. Just after a summer downpour, when the sun comes out again, I've seen bogs on which every inch of the surface is bejewelled with droplets and sparkles – gold and silver over emeralds, topaz, peridots and citrines from mosses growing below and rubies that are sundews. Yes, on a dull, cloudy day it's a landscape of dun and brown, but stay out long enough and the climate of most bogs means that at some point it will glisten.

In physical terms, the living layer sits above the permanent water table and fluctuates seasonally. A healthy acrotelm can go through periods of drought, the mosses seemingly withering and bleaching white as the landscape sucks back into itself, slumps even, but with the first rains of autumn it swells. Sometimes I think of the acrotelm as a magic carpet or a jewelled and intricate tapestry, a cloak hiding the magic below, a layer of skin freckled, dimpled and marked, the icing on the cake to the dark, dense peat below. The acrotelm is variable and at times mercurial, in part because it embraces oxygen in a way that can't happen in the catotelm.

The ability to be wet and dry creates the potential for an oxygen-rich zone, which is essential for many of the plants growing on it. The underground stems, the roots, their tips and the fine root hairs, as well as the many microbes and fungi that live on and around them, need oxygen to thrive. There's a lot of energy in this section. Thus, the acrotelm can be seen a little like the leaves on a tree: this is the growing section of any peat.

The acrotelm is a strange place, though, because if you peeled back the top layer of living plants a casual glance would suggest it's mostly dead, but in all this darkness it's very much alive. The first 40 centimetres or so is the one place in peat where rot is fully accepted: the dead and dying from above ground are breaking down. Not exactly rapidly, but rotting nevertheless. Decomposition releases just enough nutrients to keep the plants above going while feeding the fungi and bacteria doing the break-down work.

Despite the oxygen present, it is still a world dictated by water. When the water table is high the work of the microbes and bacteria is considerably slowed down. A healthy bog should have pockets of surface water, pools dotted across it and the rest, the mosses, should be saturated with water too. But there are often periods, particularly over the summer, when much or just parts of the acrotelm dry out. When this happens, the microbial community gets back rapidly to the work of breaking things down. This is essential because the dead parts of the living layer need to break down so they can be compressed into becoming peat. There need to be periods when the acrotelm dries and drains a little to let this happen. But what a fine balance it is: too long a period of drying out and more rot takes place, with a release of more carbon dioxide.

The system, of course, has buffers in the form of species composition. The intricate detail in the tapestry layer isn't just beautiful, it stops too much drying and draining. The lower part of the acrotelm consists of broken bits of sphagnum stems and branches, roots of cotton grasses, which knit together to form a tangled scaffolding that provides a significant proportion of tensile strength to the system. It serves as a protective 'geotextile' matting of fibres and sits over the more amorphous peat below. The sponge-like qualities of sphagnum ensure that the living layer is incapable of completely drying out on top, but their resistant, fibrous nature makes sure it can drain just enough to let in the first stages of rot. Together the mosses and other bog plants create the structure necessary so that the beast beneath is protected.

To meet that beast we must delve deeper. It will be dark, cold and a little claustrophobic. We are now too far from the surface for light to penetrate and everything here is compressing a bit more. The material is still partly rotted, the roots, the leaves, the pollen grains, insect bodies, their eggs, cases are nestled into layers, compressed but not compacted. Things are slumping a little more; the odd microbe hardy enough to work in this acidic, anaerobic environment, does so very slowly. But in a healthy catotelm, the organic matter is rising in denser and denser layers, suspended in the bog water. Only when the bog is drained, do we see significant compression.

Eventually the lack of oxygen means nothing can survive and we enter the world of the dead. When our ancestors thought of the bog as a portal to another side, they were, wittingly or not, evoking the catotelm because it is here that the world as we know it becomes turned on its head. And the rules that govern the surface disappear into a world floating in its dark waters. In this airless, claustrophobic realm the final stage of life fades away and all that is caught here is held in limbo.

The catotelm is permanently saturated as it sits below the water table. This also makes it anaerobic. The little oxygen present is soon used by the few microbes that live on the border between the two zones and any further decomposition quickly comes to a halt. In the catotelm, time stops. In this constantly waterlogged world, this layer also ceases to compact.

In its natural state, water is incompressible. Try as hard as you might, you cannot make it take up less space. Hydrogen loves oxygen; the bond is strong, so there's little space left between molecules. Plus it is naturally fluid in nature: the tetrahedral alignment of the molecules' endless roll over each other creates a cohesive structure that cannot be squeezed down or compressed. This means that from here on down, everything is actually going up.

Time may have stopped here, but space hasn't. When you can't squeeze something down there is only one other way to go: the bog grows, as the peat rises from its landscape. In every other soil in any other ecosystem the organic matter slowly but surely rots away: the soil doesn't rise in height; in the bog the opposite happens.

The way this gentle beast engineers the waters and the land to make its world is a marvel. In doing so, it creates a kind of air-conditioning unit for the earth, holding on to carbon so it doesn't overheat. But this is also its downfall: the catotelm produces peat that is worth extracting. We all know this layer much better than we do the living one: that potted basil from the supermarket is growing in catotelm peat, as are nearly all of the mushrooms you eat; that black 'soil' you find on bagged new potatoes, that's sterilised peat added to make you feel you are buying something earthy; plus much that is for sale at the garden centre and outside the supermarket, and all of the peat that has been milled for fuel, for power stations and home fires. Swiftly or slowly, thousands of years of stored carbon has been let back into the atmosphere.

*　　*　　*

There are a lot of folks beneath our feet. The bog, and peatlands in general with their stark pH, might once have been thought a limited environment for microbes and soil fauna, but this idea is slowly being exploded. That was why Justin invited me to tag along on a visit to Cors Fochno with some European scientists, who were on a cross-European fieldwork tour in part to look at exactly that. Dr Janna Barel and her team were from Radboud University in the Netherlands and they were buoyant with energy for their upcoming adventure.

Many of the near-natural bogs, like Cors Fochno, are studied a lot and appear across countless papers. It's strange sometimes to think about such obscure places attracting such notoriety, but the bogs are legendary for more than just myth, and there was a strong sense of lineage about Jana's work. Plus, she and her team had spent a week in Sweden on the crème de la crème of moss identification courses, which I'd heard whispers about, and they were keen to show off their skills. It turned out that Justin was just as keen to show off his best hummocks and hollows.

It was hot, the bog looked a touch dry, and the extensive restoration work of the winter still looked a little raw, but the blue sky, the faint smell of the sea beyond, the mountains behind and all this energy for knowledge made the heat bearable. For all my love of bogs, once the sun comes out, though, I'm really not suited to such exposed conditions: I turn pink, mottled with heat rash, and I long for woodland.

As they set up their equipment for the next few days, I quizzed them about their work on peatlands, why they were here and not there, what they were looking for. At one point, as they toyed with the best way to get onto the bog and how to minimise their impact, Janna blew open a hole in my understanding of the living layer. I peered into a whole new world.

Acidic bogs are famous for not having earthworms. One of their defining factors is that earthworms can live in nearly every soil but bogs. Earthworms are supreme ecosystem engineers: great recyclers of organic matter, architects of aeration with their finely built tunnels. It makes sense, then, that they might hate wet, airless soils. If you find earthworms on peat it is a sign that the system has been hugely altered and is drying out. I had carried this as a fact: bog don't have worms.

'But,' Janna said, 'they do.' She explained that peatlands soil ecology and food webs are not so massively different from other organic soils. It's just that their worms are very much smaller. Peatlands can be rich in enchytraeid worms, or pot worms.[*] They look just like earthworms except they contain no pigment so are ghostly white and a fraction of the size, less than 30 millimetres at adult stage. You might have seen them in your compost, those thin white strands. Just like earthworms they eat bacteria, fungi and protist, and decompose organic matter. They, in turn, are eaten by other soil organisms. They, too, influence the soil structure: they burrow, they eat, they defecate, and their faecal pellets mix the mineral and organic matter. There are many different species, though they all have a preference for wet, cold, organic soils with a low pH. So, there are earthworms and then there are bog, or pot, worms.

I marvelled at this fact, as I did each nugget a scientist fed me about the bog. I kept feeling that maybe I'd made the wrong choice with gardening: that perhaps I was supposed to be out there. It was a growing, creeping notion that I had left the careful, ordered world of cultivation and wandered into the wilderness. Everything out there was more expansive, not just the long views, but the ways of being. All my life I've been taught that these soils are unproductive, but to whose ideal of productivity? Not to the pot worm or the methanogens or cyanobacteria living inside moss cells. I was beginning to realise that much of the way I garden, we all garden, was ignorant and arrogant with it.

At some point Justin had told me there was a record, a nineteenth-century engraving, of one of the far pools, which contained white waterlilies, *Nymphae alba*, but no one in living memory had seen them growing there, though they did occur on the other side of the site. I asked Justin in all innocence why he didn't take a bit from the other side and introduce it back into the pool. He said, with a hint of incredulity, 'You mean do some gardening?'

* Andersen, R., Chapman, S. J., & Artz, R. R. E. (2013). 'Microbial communities in natural and disturbed peatlands: A review'. *Soil Biology and Biochemistry*, 57, 979–994.

If I didn't audibly snort at his remark, I did so internally. But as the weeks, then months passed out on bogs, I started to understand what he meant about scale and time and notions. When I found myself at a particularly good lawn of moss, kneeling to peer at a hummock covered with different species of moss, when I saw my first dwarf birch in Scotland and dwarf willow hugging the mountains at home, or wild cranberries creeping over mosses with their autumn colours or the summer blond seed heads of bog asphodel stretching out as far as the eye could see, I started to wonder why we garden when our very best attempts were such obvious imitations. And the kick, the actual thrill of such visions having absolutely nothing to do with you, I started to get it. Not, I must admit, so much that I gave up gardening: I still think mostly with my stomach and the soft green of vegetable seedlings is a habit I can't put down, but I saw another side, which I didn't try to curate or extract from, but studied instead.

I often think about Justin's comment when someone asked him what he'd do with all the government money to fix the bog. He said he'd just look at the bog for a good few years to understand the impact of the recent intensive restoration works, so he really knew what was going on. At the time, I'd thought we didn't have a couple of years for just observing things, that the work was necessary right now, this minute. But Justin's ways of looking were rubbing off on me, and the more time I spent with the bog, the more I realised how little I knew, how little we all knew. We have had four hundred years or so of Newtonian science and Cartesian logic, which said that to understand anything we had to strip it back to the raw material, then build blocks, brick by brick, until we'd made a wall. Nature, though, is very clear that a wall of knowledge does not build an ecosystem: a web of relations does.

Anyway, after Janna exploded my tiny gardening brain, I decided I had to look at pot worms. I didn't steal any peat from the bog, though I admit I thought about it. Then I remembered another cold, wet, acidic bit of my life: my compost heap. I dug around until I found some worms and stuck them, with a little compost so they didn't feel too exposed, under the microscope to peer hard at their ways.

They really do look like ghostly versions of their larger cousins, the earthworm. They have the earthworm's gentle pointy nose-mouth and distinct segments, the muscles they use to move their food along their bodies, and because they are pigment-less and therefore appear white, you can see everything inside them, their lunch, their pellets in production, their veins. I learnt that soil that has passed through a worm, is cast out, is known as the drilosphere and this thin region, a couple of millimetres at best, is some of the nutrient-rich layer in the soil. The drilosphere contains a whole world of other microbes and bacteria, fixing nitrogen and mobilising nutrients. It has implications as pot worms like to hang out in certain layers in the peat, nearer the surface. Their layer is cool and this hampers how efficient they are – it's a limiting factor. But warm up that cold, wet soil and you get more pot worms eating, and that 'alteration in the feeding preferences of key decomposers [. . .] could result in the mobilization of previously unavailable carbon pools'.[*] But that's another worm hole. In short, the worms are necessary but if they eat too fast they might start releasing old carbon back into the atmosphere.

* Andersen, R., Chapman, S. J., & Artz, R. R. E. (2013). 'Microbial communities in natural and disturbed peatlands: A review.' *Soil Biology and Biochemistry*, 57, 979–994.

7

Tiny Places

My mother-in-law, Gill, arrived from Devon with a trunk packed full of frozen dinners, cakes, various bread experiments, pickles and jams and settled into a weekend in Wales. We took her out to the Spanish wine bar, the nicest beach, the highest views, but by Sunday morning she was impatient. She was up early, and as I stumbled into the kitchen to make tea, she was sitting by the microscope and asked, 'When are we going to look at something?' It was posed as more of a declaration than a question: drink tea and get ready.

She had instigated my purchase of a neat little microscope. Initially I'd thought I'd collect a few samples of mosses and take them to Devon to use her fancy model. She's a retired professor of cardiovascular and cell science and has spent a lifetime looking down a microscope. But I realised that the four-hour drive to Devon, from us to her, was too long and, on a whim, I bought my own.

I'd sent her a text message saying I'd like to buy a simple second-hand microscope mainly to look at rotifers, amoebae and other small things that live in sphagnum moss. She advised that I should go to Brunel Microscopes in Wiltshire: 'At the moment they have a field microscope from 1910 which will give you approximately x 100 mag. It's £245 plus VAT, so a bargain and comes with a case, nice.'

Then there was a flurry of messages. She recommended a more modern brand that 'comes with a range of good objective lenses'.

Hope that's of some help, but if you are going for an antique microscope buy from a company that can provide spare bulbs, etc, or you'll find you're stuck with an interesting artefact rather than a thing of use. Xxx

She knows me well. I've a penchant for old, impractical things. I wrote back:

Is it silly to go for an antique one because it looks better? Are you getting more from a modern one?

The optics are probably better, but it's the fact you can replace parts. With an antique microscope you are paying for brass patina and history, which is lovely, but if Leeuwenhoek were alive today he'd go for an SP21/22 and love it.

Sold. The SP22 arrived the following day, which is the swiftest delivery of whim I think I've ever had. In the meantime, I looked up Leeuwenhoek. He was a self-taught Dutch scientist, known fondly as the father of microbiology and the executor of Vermeer's will.

As with nearly every other compulsive purchase in my life, I neglected to read the instructions. In this case, I didn't even buy the *Introduction to Microscopy* book. I figured I'd done enough biology in school and that it must be like riding a bike: you can't forget how to focus.

Focusing, it turned out, is not that easy. I crashed into the slide and then, reversing, crashed into my eye socket. I couldn't for the life of me think where the oil for the oil lens would go. Did you move the stage up or down? When did you turn the lights up? I eventually got a blurry vision of a tip of moss leaf and then I remembered you had to prepare your slides. It's easy to forget when you're looking down the microscope and that tip of moss leaf is monster magnified and you're after a sliver of cells, not the whole shebang. I felt defeated.

I video-called Gill to ask for advice. Stephen, her husband, pointed out that the oil for the oil lens doesn't go on the specimen, thus suffocating whatever you're looking at, but between the lens and the cover slide to create further magnification. Between them they rattled off a dozen other bits of advice. Clearly, my confusion was evident enough. I don't want to suggest that the prospect of seeing her daughter in her new home wasn't enough, but Gill arrived surprisingly swiftly after the microscope appeared in the house.

I took the tea to Ele in bed and dressed hurriedly. 'I've got a microscope lesson with your mum,' I explained.

'Now?' Ele said.

*　　*　　*

'Where are your specimens?' Gill took the microscope in hand, swung round the eye piece – a revelation to me: I'd been using it backwards.

'Not backwards, it's a preference, but I think it makes the stage easier to handle this way,' she said. 'Such a nice little stage,' she added, patting the microscope, like a pet.

I told her I'd watched a YouTube video on how to prepare a slide, and described it.

'Don't be silly,' she said. 'You'll ruin your slides that way. Go and get the chopping board.' Then, with a scalpel I'd procured from Ele, she proceeded to mash up the moss leaf, by which I mean she chopped madly in every which way. 'You're looking for cells, Alys. They are tiny! You need to turn your material into mush and then go hunting.'

She took a tiny tip's worth of material on the scalpel, put it onto one of the urine-sample jars I'd also stolen from Ele and added a little water, then told me to shake it 'as vigorously as you can for a minute or so'. She went back to setting up the microscope, saying she would send me pipettes in the post once she got back to Devon.

She took a few drops of the shaken material on the scalpel and prepared the slide, showing me how to tip the cover slide over the water so you don't get too many bubbles. Then under the lens it went and she oohed and aahed for a while. 'There,' she said. 'Have a look.' Tiny fragments of green moss were floating around but at greater magnification. Between these cells were all sorts of other things that darted between the material, others floating as if on air, a whole world. 'Miraculous, animal-cules!' as someone in Leeuwenhoek's day might have cried, a whole world of tiny, unicellular organisms and bigger things, and even bigger cells of the moss.

She taught me how to go hunting, to start on the lowest lens, find a flicker of interest, then turn to the next higher lens. If you lose your interest, switch back, find it again, then move forward. When you'd had a good look, go on to the oil lens, where the minute became masters of their world, where you can see not just the distinct pattern of large hollow cells and smaller pigmented cells of the moss, but a world inside those cells. The moss doesn't just provide a forest for tiny things to live around, there's a whole zoo living inside its bloated cells, a world within a world within a world.

It's a revelation to see inside those tiny leaves in which a whole life force is going about its ways. If you peer closely at anything it will reveal another world, a puddle, your eyebrows, your gut, the dog's claws – the microbial world is vast, an unseen landscape of others. The moss world is a place of great interest to scientists because many of the tiny-celled organisms that are in and around the moss are also capturing carbon. They play an important role in the functioning of peatlands.

In the weeks after Gill went home, I would spend hours, whole days and into the evening when I would barely lift my head away from the microscope. That was despite Gill's warning that I should take regular breaks or I'd do my eyes in. She said it as she rubbed her eyes and put on her glasses after looking up from the eye piece – a habit from a lifetime of peering.

Other than slide preparation, the correct way to flip the eye piece and the right direction to move from one lens to the next, the most important thing Gill taught me was to draw what I was seeing. The minute she found something she liked the look of she asked for pencil and paper. Then, keeping one eye looking down the lens, she used the other to start sketching what she could see. She told me it was imperative to draw everything, to label with the date, the lens strength, the material used. This would be how I started to see patterns and make sense of what I was seeing.

This strange split way of seeing, of using one eye to draw, the other to search, quickly became second nature and I covered pages of a notebook (stopping to read 'Microscopic Life' in *Sphagnum*, by Marjorie Hingley) with what I was seeing. First the hyaline cells, then the small photosynthetic ones, amoebae, rotifers, nematodes, mites and then, one day, when I thought my material had become too old and I'd quite given up, the prize of all the zoo: a tardigrade, albeit a dead and slightly squished one, but it was there.

I sent Gill a picture of my squashed tardigrade. She sent back a cute cartoon version with the message: 'I think you've got yourself a water piglet. How big was it?'

Tardigrades, often known as water bears or moss piglets, are tiny, eight-legged micro animals, up to a millimetre in length, but mostly much, much smaller, that live in thin films of water. They have an extraordinary ability to dry out and spring back to life. In their dried-out state, known as the 'tun' stage, they can also withstand temperature extremes, down to a degree above absolute zero, that's −272°C, the temperature at which molecular motion stops. This property has seen them live through five mass extinctions, which means they've been around for roughly 600 million years. They live short lives, though, a few weeks at most, but many spend great periods, years even, of their lifespan, in tun, reduced to a third of their size, waiting for the next drop of water. In this way they are perfectly adapted to live in mosses with their wet-dry cycles.

In fact, water piglets rather relish the dry periods and there are far more species in woodland mosses or your roof moss than in sphagnum mosses because peatland mosses have evolved to dry out only rarely. I'd been looking for days and rather given up, so I was thrilled when I finally spotted one.

Still, not as thrilled as when I saw my first rotifer on a successful hunt. I'd got so enraptured by life down the lens that hours had passed as I hunched over the microscope and I quite forgot I was looking down something. I'd passed into the microscopic world and was drifting among the slow float of amoebae, fragments of moss cells, moth wings and pollen grain. When a rotifer rushed across my vision and darted back, hunting for food that it proceeded to locate, opened its mouth and sucked in, I jolted back in surprise and thumped my eye socket back onto the ocular – such a diminutive, dramatic world whirling round, in and between those tiny moss leaflets.

What wilderness is held there, what magic and marvel in those strange-shaped animals, the single-cell organisms that look like hot-air balloons or complex clubbed balls, moth-wing fragments like stained-glass windows, mites that resemble giant monsters with their strange alien eyes and weird mouthpieces, to say little of the rotifers, with their comical wheel organs for moving about, and their penchant for letting you know what they've eaten, with their see-through bellies, many algae and, if lucky, desmids – which happen to be the prettiest of the algae world.

Desmids love the acid pools of boggy land, and many live in

association with sphagnum moss. They are in a state of constant movement: they glide very slowly, no one quite knows how, but they do it almost poetically. They are single-cell biomass algae, floating cells that are photosynthesising, fixing energy from the sun, passing it on to animals like rotifers. In this way the moss is photosynthesising, capturing energy, storing carbon, but so is the world that floats on, in and around it.

The world has many of these tiny beings doing vast work. Along with the desmids there are diatoms, also microalgae and an even larger group of cyanobacteria, blue-green algae, microscopic photosynthetic organisms that represent some of the most important primary producers in nature. They are found in many different wet habitats from oceans to stream sides to moss worlds. They are the beginning of everything because they are the start of the food chain. They evolved billions of years ago, learning to capture light into energy and turning our planet into an oxygen-rich atmosphere. You and I breathe easily because of these tiny organisms. They are also a favourite food of rotifers – someone has to eat someone else to keep this show on the road.

Rotifers get their name from the Latin, *rota*, meaning wheel, and *–fer*, meaning bearing, and are truly tiny animals, large enough to have a brain, but mostly around 0.1 to 0.5 millimetres thick. Leeuwenhoek was fond of them and described many. Recently, scientists brought back to life a 24-thousand-year-old specimen found in Siberian permafrost: the last time that guy was awake woolly mammoths were still roaming the world. They mostly eat waste, dead bacteria, algae and protozoans; they are nutrient recyclers, grazing continually on bits and bobs, and are a favoured meal of tardigrades.

The menagerie that lives on the sphagnum is like no other fauna of any other habitat. Nearly everyone who lives there is small enough to live in the film of water in the cavities of the moss leaves, which can be as little as 300 micrometres or 0.3 millimetres. I'm not talking about the whole moss plant, but one of the tiny tear-shaped leaves: all of this life is to be found in the cupola of one. If each moss leaflet is an asteroid, each strand a star, a hummock or hollow of mosses a galaxy, then a bog is a universe.

No one knows the extent of life hiding inside the bog. There's a good idea of what we can expect to find, but scientists aren't even sure they've mapped the mosses. The current estimate for species of sphagnum mosses is between three hundred and five hundred. That, and all the strange and wonderful things that live on or because of them are still out to be decided, too. There is a high level of endemism, meaning that many of these tiny algae are found in particular habitats or areas and nowhere else. Which means anyone with a basic microscope and the patience to keep looking, keep drawing, keep learning and recording could very well find their own first. If that's what you're after.

I decided to keep drawing and looking not because I was after naming anything, though I was still thrilled to find something recognisable from the book, but because it was, is, such a marvel, this world down the lens. It was shifting my perspective, the way hours on the moors or bogs did too. There is so much we don't know, which has huge ramifications when we're trying desperately, hurriedly, to restore an ecosystem, but it has some magic, some dance too.

Rather than trying to understand it all, as if the next bit of knowledge will finally shift it all into place, there's a leap of faith again around complexity. We will never be able to see the whole picture, never be able to put all the pieces into place. It is not ours to know but ours to wonder at, not to try to answer but to be in awe of, the tiny organism that moves around with propellers that look like hairy eyebrows and is chased by a water bear no bigger than this full stop.

8

Mossy Places

Sphagnum mosses orchestrate the show. They make the bog: they build the peat; they control who lives on it; they affect its hydrology; they make it acidic and keep it so; they are the bog, so interlinked that it is impossible to unravel one from another. They are the dominant peat-forming plant in the northern hemisphere. In tropical peatland this role is performed by trees; in the Falkland Islands, tall tussac grasses and hair moss dominate. Peat can be formed by any plant, and historically peat was formed in the northern hemisphere by many other plants, but today bogs are dominated by sphagnum mosses.

If you want to know whether or not you are standing on growing peat there's only one thing to look for: a continuous carpet of sphagnum moss. Often growing in all of this are other species, cottontail grasses (bog cotton and hare's tail grass), heathers, not dominating but dotted through the landscape, bog myrtles, various *Vaccinium* berries, insect-eating plants such as sundews and butterworts, but beneath and between, in and around the stems of the shrubs, encircling the base of the grasses and rushes, always sphagnum mosses.

There is a great difference between a smattering of sphagnum and an intact blanket of it. A healthy bog has an almost continuous landscape of hummocks, hollows and lawns of moss. In the moss-dominated peatlands of the northern hemisphere, sphagnum makes up 90 per cent of the volume of the peat. It is possible for trees to grow on bogs, the odd prostrate willow, pines, the occasional birch, though trees are more prevalent in northern and central Europe than in the UK. Trees are spindly on bogs; there aren't enough nutrients for them to grow vast.

A glance-at-it take on whether or not a bog is doing well: from a distance it should look like a sparse grassland of cotton grasses, a scattering of shrubs; up close it should be packed with all sorts of different sphagnum mosses.

It is very easy to miss these details, though. I have taken so many folk to Cors Fochno in a bid to reveal to them that I can predict exactly when the 'Aah' will come from someone new to this world. The first part of the walk is polite – 'What an interesting flat landscape' – and then I take them in a step or two and indicate the mosses, pull out a hand lens, point out that what from a distance looks flat, up close will become a fascinating, undulating terrain of miniature mosses and wait for the penny to drop. Mosses are cute up close. They've yet to fail to entice even the hardened 'just a brown landscape' types. When I point out that the mosses make their own mountains that can reach up to a metre tall, but are usually knee or ankle height, followed by lawns, a flat myriad of different sphagnum species, often in pleasing drifts of acid greens, buttery yellows, brilliant reds and pinks, occasional bleached whites, deep burgundies, then the hollows dominated by species of sphagnum that float in those mysterious pools, well, I've yet to find anyone not taken in by this elfin landscape.

Sphagnum cuspidatum is the easiest moss to recognise. It is present on nearly all bogs, is abundant, often the first to return after restoration, and is nearly always found in the pool. When you pull a bit out it looks just like wet fur or, as Justin once pointed out to me, like a kitten that's fallen into a pond. If you kneel you will get wet (waterproof trousers are a necessity, even in the height of summer), but you will see the wonder and variation of this diminutive world, with its giants, such as grasshoppers and bush crickets, and above your head the whirr of dragonflies or, if you are lucky, our largest moth, the emperor. Then, as your eye begins to rest on the details, the tiny micromoths, the many cobwebs, the spiders that go with them, such as the bog sun jumper, the small butterflies, the dainty damsel flies, the ladybirds, and the many aquatic bugs that live in the pools. You will see many of the smallest of these insects stuck to the sundews and butterworts as they eat their way to better, nitrogen-rich growth. And below all of this above-ground life is all of the wonder that is living on, in and between the mosses. Beneath is the strange world of microbes that live in the acid-rich peat.

On a healthy near-natural or natural bog it is quite possible to walk or, more accurately, hop from one grass tussock to the next. The grasses are your friends; the mosses always sink. On a healthy bog, with just a little knowledge of plant species, it is actually not hard to walk across as long as you don't tread on anything that looks flat, like the lawns or the pools, because you will sink. If there aren't any grasses you can reach easily, aim for hummocks, which may sink as you land. You can't always retrace your steps as those soft stepping stones of moss may disappear, but you can cross the bog. Not that I'm suggesting you go walking across a bog: the nature of this world is easily damaged by trampling. There is a reason that peat conservationists are all seen in snow shoes: they are trying to lessen their impact.

Mosses, with liverworts and hornworts, are part of a group of land plants known as bryophytes. They are ancient beings that arrived on the earth around 450 million years ago when land plants emerged from the green algae group (which includes everything from the green slime on your patio to seaweed). Bryophytes were the first group to appear from the watery world of green algae and quickly made land their home. They are found on every continent and in every ecosystem habitable by plants.

Thanks to their early start on earth, they were the forerunners in creating habitable lands. These earliest colonisers, with their adaptations from watery environments to land, have allowed the rest of the plant kingdom to clothe the earth in green and create the oxygenated world on which we survive.

Bryophytes are still often the first plants to cover bare earth, when glaciers melt or a bit of tarmac is left alone. Mosses stabilise the soil surface and, crucially, slow and retain water, laying the foundation for other plants to grow.

All bryophytes rely on water for reproduction and survival – they have never quite unhooked themselves from their aquatic beginnings – but, unlike other plants, they don't use roots to take up water. Some mosses have root-like structures called rhizoids, but they are used to anchor the plant.

On top of not having roots, they also lack a vascular system: there are no thick-walled xylem tubes structurally holding up the plant, just a continuous sheet of single cells. This means they are destined always to be short; they lack a support system other than water to hold them upright. The largest mosses are always found in wet places, at lake edges, in streams and bog pools where the water can support their weight.

The lack of root and vascular tissues keeps them diminutive as they also lack the internal structures necessary to transport water long distances. Their leaves have to remain tiny, absorbing water directly from where they sit. In vascular plants, the xylem doesn't just add support: it transports water from the roots to the top of the plant in specialised cells that create pipes running up it. The mosses rely on capillary action formed by spaces between the leaves, branches and stems to wick up the water and there's only so far water can be drawn up in this way.

Some mosses are as ancient as can be imagined: they have been around as long as some Cambrian rocks, the limestones and dolomites, as old as the hills that rise around my home. To think of a humble moss born into this world at the same time as limestone rose from under the sea, a time before bony fish existed, which lived through ice ages and several mass extinctions . . . Think of that when you next look down at your feet on the pavement and see moss colonising a crack.

But the mosses that make our peat are evolutionarily very young: they had their growth spurt when the areas that we know as boreal and sub-Arctic were rapidly changing from their former tropical and temperate selves. In short, as the world was rapidly cooling, peatlands were spreading because peat mosses were evolving. The mosses found a new niche to exploit and grew to the challenge as they evolved with the climate, so the peat began to creep up and outwards. It is hard to imagine because our bogs are so degraded, but many once rose ten metres or so above where they stand now, a dizzying height reached by a very small plant.

Sphagnum mosses are quite different from other mosses. First, they don't have rhizoids so they don't anchor themselves to the earth. They also look very different: they have a distinct capitulum, a head made up of a rosette of leaves at the top – this is the only growing part of the moss. This means they grow very slowly but, uniquely to this moss, they decompose even more slowly. They are the zombies of rot: no other plants on the planet take such a long time to decay.

They do this by being alive and dead simultaneously. The tip of the plant grows upwards and everything below it dies back, slowly forming peat. If you think of any other plant, a tree, a rose, then all of the plant is alive, the leaf, the stems, the flowers and the roots; the plant is actively involved with and in relation to the soil around it, but it doesn't build the soil until it dies and rots back to where it came from. In the case of a large tree that might take many decades after it dies. But in the case of the sphagnum moss, it is growing and dying all at once, and in this balance the peat grows.

71

These mosses are forming the living surface of the peat and are also creating the substrate for all the other plants to grow in, the sundews, the grasses and the odd shrub that can tolerate the acidic conditions, to say little of the habitat they are making for the world of microbes and insects.

Different sphagnum species occupy different niches in the bog, and together they curate a rolling terrain for miniature mountains, deep valleys and flat plains. This microtopography is entirely made by the mosses. The miniature mountains are not raised because there's rock beneath them, just pure peat.

There are species that grow into hummocks, or hollows, and some that create lawns. Many are shapeshifters and can grow on the relatively dry hummocks as well as in the saturated hollows. The average hummock is 30 centimetres above the water table, and may sink at some point, but other hummocks are long-lived, akin to the hills of the bog, and may range up to a metre above the bog surface. The hollows, well, anyone who has fallen into one can tell you that they are easily a metre deep and sometimes much more. The deeper hollows appear as pools, dark enough to reflect the sky, though just below the surface the mosses float and the peat is soupy, so not quite the pond they appear to be – neither land nor water but somewhere in between. Where there is neither hummock nor hollow there are lawns or flats and in these places the mosses grow like intricately patterned kilim carpets. The terrain here is often quite stable – you'll sink, but if the bog is healthy, you won't be swallowed.

Sphagnum mosses love a bog, but some species can happily grow on damp heaths, in wet woodlands and beside streams. Anywhere acid, wet enough and not too shaded, they'll give it a go. Below their capitulum, or head. is a stem with two types of branch, those that spread, bearing the main photosynthetic leaves, and pendent ones, which run down the stem and assist in keeping the plant wet. Only the tip and the very top layer of branches are growing, a fraction of the plant, which is why they grow so slowly.

What happens inside those stems and leaves also distinguishes sphagnum from other mosses because, just as the whole plant is at once dead and alive, this pattern is repeated on a cellular level. The main part of the leaf consists of a network of two distinctly different cells: narrow living green cells, known as chlorophyllose, and inflated dead ones, the hyaline cells. The moss is actually more dead than alive: only one in twenty cells is living.

The walls of the hyaline cells contain strands arranged in a hooped or spiral pattern, and each cell is like a balloon. In dry conditions they contain air, giving the plant a colourless appearance and making it brittle. When conditions are wet, they fill with water and usually appear green or tinted with colour. There are numerous pores, like a microscopic sieve, in hyaline cells, to allow for the movement of water but also for microscopic beings to live in them. The movement of water means that a sphagnum moss can hold twenty times its dry weight in water. If you pick up a clump of sphagnum and squeeze it, you'll find it's just like a wet sponge. And it's this ability to hold water that keeps the plant and the surface of the bog humid even in very dry weather.

The difference in humidity between various species is wild: a hummock species may be just a few centimetres above a bog pool, but it offers completely different habitats. The hummock is often very warm, quite dry to touch, though if you wiggle your fingers into its dense mat you will find that it feels moist and cool; dig a little deeper and the temperature can plummet quickly. Moss is a bad conductor of heat so the temperature changes much more slowly in lower layers than it does on the surface. That is why you can use the bog as a fridge or cold store, a fact not lost on our ancestors, who buried butter, cheese, vegetables and meat in bogs for that reason. Meat buried in a bog for two years showed the same pathogen and bacteria count as meat stored in a modern freezer.

The moss is doing more than keeping things cool. It is also modifying its environment chemically, which affects the physical structure of peat formation but also what can grow in it. Damp, soft moss is an inviting bed to explore and many plants would love to get their roots into it, but they would shade out the diminutive mosses with their towering growth. The moss needs to make itself less appealing to remain on top.

The top layer of the moss is where the energy is. The capitulum, that central rosette, is bearing the brunt of photosynthesis, but as you go down through the moss this changes. The lower you go, the wetter and darker it becomes, and there's less and less oxygen. Roots need oxygen, without it they die, but these mosses have no roots. Only the vascular plants have them, the shrubs, the grasses, the berry plants and any trees that grow on the bog. Their roots can't survive past the relatively thin layer of moss growth, which forces anything taller than the moss itself to grow very slowly, thus preventing it from shading it. The mosses drag down anything that wants to grow fast.

As you go further down through the acrotelm, thirty centimetres or so, the roots of shrubs are struggling, and all the sphagnum moss, though present, is now dead. Another chemical change is happening. Any bacteria and fungi that were present at a higher level have used up what little oxygen was left and are now disappearing. In their place are methogens, which do not work fast compared to their aerobic brethren: decomposition is almost, but not quite, halted. Where energy stops, peat builds.

But it's not just because there are fewer and slower rotting workers, the sphagnum is also playing a part. It is actively resisting decay and in this way is bulk-storing the carbon in the peatland. Sphagnum doesn't accumulate peat because it grows fast but because it rots very, very slowly. And it does this by pickling itself and everything around it. Sphagnum mosses have the extraordinary ability to make their world more acidic; they sour the waters. This slows decay but further reinforces that the mosses are staying in charge. The only plants that can grow here have to tolerate being soaked in their acids.

Bogs form in naturally acidic places. A synergy of environmental factors – a lot of rain hitting acidic and nutrient-poor soils, creating a high water table that is low in oxygen – makes for an acidic start, but it wouldn't necessarily stay that way over a lifetime. Other factors would come into play, but a bog remains acid because of the mosses that are actively maintaining the situation.

I can never quite get over this. When I first learnt about the pickling effect, I thought how smart, how acerbic of the mosses, the Dorothy Parkers of the plant world. I saw them as slightly ruthless. The more I learnt and looked, though, the more I realised it was quite the opposite. It seems that the mosses do this to their own advantage, but actually they are levelling the playing field so it works for everyone. There's a lesson in that for sure.

It cannot be stated enough how poor the conditions of the bogs are: there is very little food for growth. The mosses have had to come up with a way not just to survive living on the bog, but to thrive. Sphagnum mosses make acids in their cell walls, which they exchange for cations in the bog water. They are creating a salvage operation in which they swap hydrogen ions for cations that might be helpful to them, like calcium, ammonium, manganese and phosphorus, which are all useful for growing.

The more hydrogen ions you swap, the more acidic the solution becomes. The acids account for up to a quarter of the dry weight of the sphagnum. They aren't just swapping for desirable cations, though: they also bind with nitrogen, which does two things. It means there isn't excessive nitrogen for other plants on the bog, which slows their growth, but the lack of nitrogen also inhibits microbial activity: the mosses are sterilising themselves. The more of these acids a moss has, the more resistant it is to decay. They also prevent anything else that falls into the bog from rotting, such as the bog bodies, butter and shoes. The acids dye everything a reddish colour, which is why the bog bodies are redheads regardless of their original hair colour. The acids also preserve the keratin in horn, nails and hair, keeping them in almost perfect condition, but they decalcify bones, which is why the bog bodies appear shrunken and flattened: their bones are missing, because the mosses dissolved them.

There's evidence to show that our ancestors understood these preservation properties beyond sacrificial burials. Bogs were used as mortuaries: bodies were temporarily buried to preserve the soft tissues, then dug up and reburied elsewhere.

Ancient people might not have known which substance did this, but they understood that the bog was a good refrigerator. As well as bodies and butter, bread and suckling pigs have been found there. They may have been offerings to the gods but perhaps the bog was just a useful storage spot. Norwegians traditionally used bogs to store carrots and turnips over winter well into the nineteenth century. There is good evidence to show that bogs were also used for tanning: half of the complex processes required to turn an animal hide into usable leather are performed by the bog if you bury the pelt and leave it. Historically many communities in Finland got their water straight from bogs. The Vikings were known to take bog water on long journeys, even across seas: it would stay fresher for longer than river water because of the moss acids.

There's an equally long history of sphagnum being used for its healing and antiseptic properties as nappies and period pads. If it can hold twenty times its weight in water, it can do the same with urine and blood. Indigenous peoples in North America used dried sphagnum as bedding, to fill mattresses and pillows, and as insulation in canoes and housing. It was also used to clean fish before smoking, and wet to line cooking pits. In Europe during the First World War, sphagnum was used extensively in bandages: it was harvested en masse, dried, sterilised and packed off to the front line, where it saved countless lives.

Moss creates a varied terrain for the bog surface. Its microtopography, all those miniature hummock mountains and lawn valleys, has created its own little universe of microhabitats, dry mountain tops, wet mountainside and flooded valleys. All sorts live on different aspects: some want vistas and others the richer, more sheltered valley spots.

Once you've got over the marvel of chasing clouds across the surface of a bog pool and peered into it, you'll find that many others visit it, live in its depths, drink its water. The insect life on the bog is rich, and in turn it supports birds, bats, frogs, toads and lizards. This richness is gathered into bog pools: the lifecycles of insects, their eggs, moults, excrements and death, add nutrients. So, the pools are a little richer in nitrogen and other nutrients than the drier hummocks. Hollow sphagnum species grow faster because of this richness, but rot faster too. Hollow species have been found to contain less acids than hummock species. They are often the first mosses to move back into re-wetted bogs that are under restoration. I think of them as the pioneers in getting things back on track, but you can't have a healthy, near-natural bog on hollow species alone.

You need the tiny mountains of hummock species to build the bog. They spend nearly all of the year above the water table. This is a harsh spot, with even fewer nutrients than elsewhere. The hill mosses have to rely on atmospheric dust and the nutrients dissolved in rain. They have to put up with weather too, winds and drying suns, and have had to adapt to make sure they don't dry out. They do this by being smaller in stature than the pool species and they grow cheek by jowl, nestled tightly together, so that they feel like a firm, overstuffed cushion.

To stave off dryness they have had to make other compromises: they have bigger water-holding cells in their leaves, so there is less space for photosynthetic ones. This means they grow much slower than species living in pools. They also contain higher rates of acids, which means they decay much more slowly. Conversely, the pool species, in relatively richer conditions, have smaller water-holding cells. They are sitting in water so they don't need to store it, and more space is dedicated to photosynthetic cells, but because the hollow species rot just as quickly as they grow, they don't build much peat. That task is left to the hummock species with their acid-filled cell walls, which are fighting off microbes and bacteria.

In diversity there is strength. A bog with just one or two species of moss, even if they are doing well, is not as resilient as a bog with many different species. Partly because we don't know what future climates will be like – most likely unpredictable – we need all the players present, but also because the mosses are more community-oriented than their ways suggest. Sure, they act very local, but they think globally. And although many other plants would shrivel in such acid soil, some have found a way to make a good home in the moss.

The top layer of moss, the growing bit, is wet, but it is not anaerobic: there's space for air to breathe, and many of the plants that make up the bog's green surface have found ways to use the moss as a perfectly acceptable place to grow. The insect-eating sundews and butterworts sit gently on top of the moss with their glittering, deadly leaves. The sundews are colonisers of anything they can get their roots into – I've seen them growing on the sheer cliff faces of peat haggs, the exposed sides of a gully brought about either by erosion or peat cutting for fuel. I've been lured by their neon red glimmer and jewel-like glint only to find myself knee deep in a hollow of peat soup.

I'm not the only one tempted by sparkle: sundews get their nutrients by trapping insects on their leaves, which are club-shaped with huge globules, sparkling and sticky with enzymes; small insects are attracted to them and get stuck, as you might if you landed in glue. Once trapped, they are dissolved by the enzymes and absorbed into the plant's systems. Peer closely into the centre of a sundew and you will see a gruesome ending. Butterworts, with their pretty, violet-like flowers, have similar leaves that are lethal to tiny insects that alight on them.

The sundews and the butterworts die back over winter to a bud, which would easily be covered with moss by spring, so the plant in growth has continually to move its growing point (the bud) upwards at the pace of the moss. If you carefully extract a sundew from the moss, you will see the successive shoot generations, ghostly dead versions of past years.

The roots of the bog asphodel, *Narthecium ossifragum*, do

the same thing, constantly moving the growing point of the plant upwards so it isn't swallowed by the moss. Interestingly, it can vary its pattern to the type of moss it's growing in. If it is growing in lawn, which is very wet, it will grow horizontally, like the sphagnum, but if it finds itself on a more stable carpet or slightly more raised area it will grow more vertically. Anything to keep apace with the moss's desire to say on top.

The dwarf shrub species, the heathers, the bog myrtles and prostrate willows and pines must find a different way because of their woody nature. A heather or a bog myrtle might find a dry enough spot to take root, might start to thrive even in the open, sunny position of the bog, but as it grows, its own weight causes it to sink into the mat of sphagnum. As it does so, the surrounding sphagnums creep between its branches and, with their supreme architecture for wicking up water, draw the water column up around the plant. This is like wrapping the lower branches in a wet blanket: it sinks the shrub a little further into the moss. The sphagnum takes advantage of the new light to grow up and around the branches, further weighing down the shrub.

The shrub is now racing with the moss to stay afloat. It must grow rapidly through the moss layer to produce new young shoots or become completely swamped. If it can't, the mosses slowly drown it. As fast as it grows upwards, the sphagnum weighs it down until, eventually, all that is left of it is the cone shape of the hummock. Entombed beneath are the branches and roots of its former self.

The acrotelm, the top layer of the peat, is often littered with ghostly branches, stems and roots of shrubs that have tried and failed to make a living on the bog. If you find exposed peat you can easily pick out the zombie stems. But even in death, these shrubs add structure to the acrotelm, providing this layer with strength so that it doesn't collapse into the catotelm, which adds to the bog's resilience against the vagaries of weather, periods of drought and periods of flooding.

The shrub-moss layers are another way to observe the health of a bog. In a waterlogged, healthy bog the heathers will be made up of mostly young shoots poking out of a moss carpet; in a degraded bog, they will be tall, leggy and old, with a lot of the characteristic grey woody material present.

As with all ecosystems, it is about the balance. Rather than thinking of this as plants in competition with each other (a term surely driven by our capitalist-economic mindset), it is better to understand it as this: a healthy bog has a community of many beings jostling for life; each is needed in its own way.

Sphagnum moss is the skin of peatland: it needs to be intact to keep the beast below healthy. If you keep peeling it off, the nick, the tiny cut, gets a bit bigger and doesn't knit back together. It deepens, gets infected, doesn't heal, is reinfected and eventually the system breaks down. The moss is amazing but, like our skin, it needs to be respected. It is resilient and tough, but not if it is ridden over, trampled, compacted, cut away or frazzled by atmospheric pollutants. Because, like our skin, it holds beneath it the pumping blood of the bog: the water.

9

Historic Places

Cors Fochno might have stayed a perfect raised dome with an intact lagg zone circling if not for the Leri's wild desire to get to the sea quicker. When the river broke its banks and rerouted, it created a little estuary perfect for boats to collect the herrings. A few vessels became a fleet and then an industry. Borth was once one of the herring capitals of the British Isles. So vast were the catches that herrings fed the village, which turned into a town, which turned into a fortune. The herrings also fed the otters, the sea eagles and many others. It was a rich time for Borth.

Then someone had a smart idea. What if the acid peaty soils behind the spit were drained and the herrings were turned into fish meal to feed them too? Those poor soils would become rich, with such a fine source of herring guts. So, the wild, winding Leri, which often let the sea spill over its banks to flood the fast-growing, prosperous town, had to be tamed. And, like so many other histories of peatlands, drainage engineers were brought in to straighten it all out.

If you come to Borth today, you will find the River Leri is a perfectly straight line that runs between the sea and the bog. Around the bog, which is much reduced in size, a series of fields have been drained for agriculture. You can tell they were once part of the bog because deep ditches surround them, and they have lots of molehills made of pure peat.

Of course, the engineers were hardly the first to venture onto the bog. There is evidence of human settlements around the wider area by mid-Palaeolithic (old Stone Age) times, certainly by the Mesolithic (mid Stone Age). The sea level was similar to today's and the bog was beginning to form. No one had settled directly beside it, but we know they were around: they had left behind some tools and traces of fires.

The Mesolithic people used small chipped stones as tools and were largely nomadic. The world's oldest wooden sculpture dates from this time. It was found in a bog, of course – where else could wood have been so perfectly preserved? The Shigir peat bog is in the Middle Urals, Russia. The sculpture is known as the Shigir Idol, and when it was first built it stood as a five-metre-tall totem-like human figure; it has a carved wooden head with a surprised-looking round mouth. On the totem body there are various other figures of humans, with many geometric marks. It is thought it was carved with a beaver jaw. Some say it depicts a creation story, others that the many markings make a map, or perhaps it was a god. Still, it would have stood tall in the hunter-gatherers' landscape.

If Borth Bog holds such a sculpture, it has no intention of telling us.

It's not really until the mid-Neolithic period that we get any sense of how people were using the landscape. Antler and flint tools appear scattered across the beach, suggesting that people were passing through rather than settling, but they were certainly using the area regularly for hunting. The Dyfi river would have been a good place for our ancestors, with the rich pickings of the estuary for mussels and oysters, the river for fish, otters and beavers for meat and fur, and the multitudes of wading and migratory birds. The sea offered bigger fish and eels, and on land there was wood for charcoal, and the peatlands, which would have been fens then, for medicines and dyes, with fibres for nets and traps.

During this period, the fen landscape was waning and the bog was growing strong. Beneath its layers there is undoubtedly more evidence of other lives, but long may they stay buried. Instead, we must look to the wider landscape to understand how the bog was used. By the Bronze Age there were funerary and ritual mounds. The best-known of these is Bedd Taliesin and Ynys Tudor, both of which sit overlooking the bog. During this period we find the first true indication of activity on the wetlands margins. There are burnt mounds, mostly likely used to heat water, and evidence of wooden troughs perhaps used for washing or cooking or as some sort of drainage and water management tool. These things have been found through archaeological investigations.

I was intrigued by the graves that lay high above in the hills behind the bog. I wondered what the view was like. I called my friend Jeremy, who is always good for an ancient-monument hunt, and we met in a local café to consult my maps. Bedd Taliesin is easy enough to find: it is the supposed resting place of the sixth-century bard Taliesin, who might or might not have written *The Book of Taliesin*, a series of praise poems mostly about bloody battles. It's said that if you sleep a night on his burial stone you will either wake up mad or a poet.

It's not hard to find the grave, on a corner of road on a sheep farm. It indeed commands some very good views. But because we found it so easily and because the Ordnance Survey map has so many other intriguing markings we walked a little higher to find other significant stones. Truth is, this landscape is scattered with lots of huge rocks, but every now and then you come across a set of stones, so clearly placed to make a chamber that it's hard not to be impressed. Jeremy made me lie down in several possible grave sites to see if they 'resonated some of that significance'.

It is a beautiful landscape. To one side we could see Cadir

Idris catching the late-afternoon sun. Far below us the sands of the estuary spilt into the milky grey of the cold spring sea and between the orange-brown of the bog still in its winter colours. I'm not sure I can claim the stones said much to me, but the far views gave me a new sense of the bog's position in the landscape, how identifiable it would have been. No one knows if Taliesin is buried there, but whoever it is, they mattered enough to be brought up to rest among such views.

It was the Romans who made the first big mark on the bog landscape. By the time they established themselves in Wales, towards the end of the first century AD, they were prospecting for metal: gold mines in the north and south, and in the central belt, it was lead. There are numerous Roman industrial lead mines.

The A487 that runs above the bog and takes you from Aberystwyth to Machynlleth runs almost on top of an old Roman road, and excavations on the bog show the remains of extensive lead-smelting. The Romans were mad for lead and tin, and across Europe, you find industrial-level smelting going on throughout their empire. We know this because atmospheric lead and tin pollution are found in layers of the peat, particularly that of deep raised bogs. If you have raised bog that is more than two metres deep, you have a record of the atmosphere deposits going back to the Romans and beyond.

Lead was used for all sorts of things, from cauldrons used to boil *sapa,* an intense grape syrup for flavouring and preserving wines, to water pipes for plumbing and aqueducts, and coffins. One can speculate that all of this lead must have been poisoning more than the atmosphere and perhaps many of us are the descendants of deranged men. For whatever reason, in Borth the lead-smelting sites were abandoned, gradually hidden by the encroaching peat bog.

Some of the most substantial archaeological finds of Cors Fochno are typical to many bogs, such as a wooden track that allowed for easier crossing. It was laid after the Romans had given up smelting and the resourceful road-builders used the spent lead-ash to surface the wooden track. It crosses the middle of the bog to the island of Llangynfelyn, a site of early worship for a Welsh saint. We know, too, that the bog was being used for grazing in spring, so whether the track was for cattle or saints, many people put effort into making a safe passage.

By the medieval period the bog covered a large area, much greater than today. There are raised islands of stones within the bog that were settled on during the medieval period. A hoard of medieval coins was found on the island of rocks that is Ynys Fochno during road construction. All of this increased settlement surely affected the bog as it would have been used as common land for grazing, but also for turbary – the right to cut peat – for locals.

By the nineteenth century, pressure for agricultural land meant that large swathes of the bog and the surrounding common wetlands were divided up and given over to more intensive agriculture. There were plans to drain the entire bog. The Somerset Levels and the fens to the east were rapidly being drained of their waters.

In 1815, extensive drains were cut across the bogs, still visible today, a new road, now the B4353, was added in the north, and many new farmsteads ate into the lagg that surrounded the bog. There was much local peat cutting, and in the early twentieth century a steam-powered machine was in use for the purpose. Aerial photographs show thick white scars nibbling all around the edge of the bog, particularly extensive to the south-west where the bog meets Borth. There are several large straight-across scars where, presumably, the cutter munched its way across the bog.

The last period of cutting into the bog occurred after the Second World War, when food scarcity meant that large areas came under the plough as the country aimed to become more self-sufficient. As late as the 1970s, engineers were still being employed to make inroads into the bog, and all failed. By the 1980s, a growing body of people was determined that the bog should be restored to its original state. At least a decade of complicated negotiations followed, to work out who owned which part or had commoners' rights, and to buy land so that Fochno could be designated a nature reserve.

Newly armed with all this history, I would walk out to the middle and become dizzy, trying to locate the various places. The bog's flatness is very good at playing tricks: things that appear to be in a straight line from you, five metres on, are suddenly to your left; car lights in the dusk look as if they are hurtling straight at you when they are miles away; and sound jumps alarmingly from one shoulder to the other. The bog is a trickster to the uninitiated.

10

Night Places

The beings that live on the bog – the birds that migrate to nest or feed over the winter, the badgers, the foxes, the reptiles and the multitudes of insects – have all had to find ways to adapt to the conditions. They need it to be wet, for the hydrology to be intact. Many of the most highly specialised species have evolved for those acidic, nutrient-poor pools. I have watched the first swallows swoop in to feast on the multitudes of bugs that spring forth from the wetness, been spellbound by raft spiders floating on debris, front legs dangling in the water waiting for vibrations to catch tadpoles. I've lost hours peering into eerily crystal-clear waters to see what skulks in them. But the high sun of midday means much of this world goes into hiding. If you really want to know about the bog's inhabitants you have to get up very early or go to bed very late: at night the bog becomes a very different place.

There aren't many people you can regularly ask if they want to go to the bog at night, but my friend Kate Doubleday is one. She loves Borth, wild things and people. That's rare, to be someone who loves a place and everything in it. Many people love wildlife but find people hard, or love the sea but want it tamed so it doesn't batter the town, or love the golden plovers but not the seagulls. Kate loves it all, which makes her fantastically good company. She also knows everyone's story because everyone talks to her. Gradually she was filling me in on the Borth landscape through the people and the people through their place.

Our first night escapade was a spring jaunt, when I had a notion that I would try to follow the Borth toad back to its ancestral breeding ground somewhere on the edge of the bog. The journey started in Rowena's house: every spring she lets toads hop through her house. They squeeze under her back door, leap across her kitchen, occasionally take a detour in her sitting room, and eventually, often in the early hours of the morning, find the front door. They throw themselves at it, until Rowena lets them out at breakfast time. They do this every year. They are not lost, they know the way. It's just that a hundred years or so ago a house was built on their route and they have included its back and front doors in their route.

All toads, given the choice, will go back to breed where they and their ancestors spawned, and their spawn will do the same. Ancestral toad-breeding routes can be very, very old. Rowena's house sits to the south of the bog, so it's not outrageous to imagine that is where they are heading.

Borth has many folk tales attached to it, a huge number of ghost stories, of cities under the sea, changelings, lost ships. And the bog has its own folklore centring on a big old toad and *y hen wrach*, a witch. In the witch tale an old hag didn't like the way she looked. She lived on the bog and had a huge head and serpent-like body. For years she haunted locals on foggy and misty nights by causing them to shake for great periods of time, sometimes killing them, sometimes not. The story goes that on misty and foggy nights if you left your windows open, she would fly in and breathe in your face, causing you to wake shaking. She was, it is said, deeply ashamed of her ugliness and that was why she lived deep in the fog of the bog. It is also said that locals believed the only way to appease her was to cease cutting and burning peat. Which is an interesting detail: to cut peat in Welsh is *mawna*, which directly translates as 'to kill the peat', so there's been a long history of understanding the damage done by using peat as fuel.

The rationale behind the tale is that, until the 1900s, malaria was very much present in the UK, particularly in low-lying marshy and wetland areas. These episodes of shaking relate to the fever associated with the disease. The surprising element is how many deaths there were. It is thought that this was probably due to infections through poor sanitation, and that improved housing had as much to do with ridding the UK of endemic malaria as draining marshes and bogs.

The toad tale is long-winded. It is a localised retelling of part of *The Mabinogion*, the medieval Welsh masterpiece of Celtic mythology, part Arthurian romance and part history, to make sense of British colonisation. It is made up of eleven tales, one of which is about the eagle of Gwernabwy, an ancient bird, who had lost his wife. He needs to find a new bride to live with him. He finds an owl he considers to be of a similar age, but doesn't want to offend her by asking her, so he goes to ask all the other old beings of Wales, a stag, a salmon and an ousel, how old they think she is. Eventually he finds an answer and marries the owl. In the Borth version there is also an old toad to ask.

All the ancient animals have a common motif to their reply: they are so old that they remember a time when the landscape looked very different. The stag can remember before there were forests, the ousel when stones were once mountains, and the toad can recall when the earth was flat. He ate a grain of dust every day and thus carved out the valleys from mountains. In the local version the toad is older than everyone else, not so in *The Mabinogion*, where the salmon has that title. In either case the owl can't believe her luck.

These ancient animal tales appear worldwide in origin stories to remind humans that their world is young and that other beings have roamed the earth for longer than ourselves.

I'm not sure now what I was hoping Rowena's toads would lead me to but I fancied a pool seething with them, a pool that suggested a long-held ancestral breeding migration. Rowena served me tea and sharp humour, but no toads – they were all in hiding the day I went round. Kate knew the previous owner of the house and I texted to see if she, too, had seen the toad procession, but she swore they were frogs.

I went back to Rowena with the frog news, and for the rest of the summer I received deadpan texts with attached photos of a huge toad that lived permanently in her courtyard, too large to get under the gap in her back door.

Kate's next idea was that we all went around the bog listening for toads' mating calls. We tried to drag Rowena along, too, but the night we chose was squally with rain and wind and she politely declined. We didn't find any toads, perhaps because most of the pools on the bog are too acid for toads, but it might also have been because we chose a blustery, cool night and toads are particular about the right mild conditions to mate. We ended up driving around the back lanes behind the bogs with Kate hanging out of the car window straining in vain to hear a single croak.

My next night trip was much more peopled. Justin asked if I wanted to join the yearly rosy moth marsh count that started at 10 p.m. and went on into the early hours. I signed up on the spot.

* * *

Moths and butterflies are part of the warp and weft of the land-scape, woven into it through their metamorphosis from caterpillar to flight. Many species live on peatlands and a number can live nowhere else. Their larvae feed exclusively on acid-loving bog plants, like the large heath butterfly, whose caterpillars dine exclusively on hare's tail cotton grass, *Eriophorum vaginatum*, also known as bog cotton. It is characteristic of the bog landscape in summer. It is one of the first plants to begin growth in spring and was once an important source of early grazing for sheep. Its seed heads are a white mass of cotton fluff, a little bedraggled when wet, but much like that of a hare's tail. They dot the summer landscape, their brilliant white globes of seed heads floating in the summer haze.

The Manchester treble bar (moth or butterfly), the yellow underwing, the wood tiger and the night-flying rosy marsh moth are all species that live for acid. They are as intrinsic to the place as the peat, the sphagnum mosses and the bog asphodels, and they often accompany you: their flight pattern, with its rise and fall, another musical notation in the flat lines of the landscape. If you peer into the low shrubs and grasses, fat caterpillars munch in brilliant greens and bright yellows. Tyrophibionts are restricted to bogs, and tyrophiles live there but feed elsewhere. Although moth and butterfly numbers can seem slight across the landscape, anything that eats has the potential to change a landscape.

Populations can vary widely depending on the caprices of the weather, so yearly numbers are known to explode or decline depending on how specialist their food source is. If you eat only one thing, you either want it to do very well – the hare's tail cotton may only grow on bogs, but it does very well on them – or you want it to be resilient enough to weather a fire or a bad frost. Being rare and niche can mean several things. Perhaps you found a corner to carve out an existence or a way to eat something that no one else could: the length of your tongue or your digestion system adapted. Or you came from another time: many niche species are specialists of a food that was once abundant and now is scarce. Certain central European bog moths hail from a time when forest tundra was more common, but with climate change the bog became the next best thing – a paleorefugium, a fragment habitat close enough to what was once there to offer an island of hope for certain species to cling to.

All niches are good: they are the stuff of rich biodiversity and paleorefugia teach us that what might be common now can easily become rarer with climate change.

Despite this tenuous existence, being niche can also mean that you are particularly hardy to certain things: perhaps you can weather the winter wet or frost because you carry a gene memory of a colder time. This sort of diversity is important because we don't know with any certainty where we are heading: we need to move forwards with the widest pool of genes for everything and everyone.

That slight moth fluttering in the distance is a reminder of how much things can change in a short hop of time, but also how the edges of ecosystems are safety nets to that change. Who might come to live on the bog in the future?

Being niche doesn't mean you can't affect the landscape. If the caterpillars boom, they can easily strip a plant, and their frass (excrement) alone can act as a source of nutrients and nitrogen to a landscape thin in food. Couple that with fluctuating water tables, or hotter summers, or a sudden change in microclimate: you may have more dead organic material that might benefit saprophytic beetles or that slight rise in nutrients means more bog asphodels flowering, which benefit a bee or some pollen-collecting fly. Such are the intricacies of the food web that even a slight tip in numbers can bring about wealth for others.

Keeping track of these entanglements requires steady, meticulous records. Same time, same place, same transact length, details recorded year in year out of the small things most others don't notice. It doesn't have to be the same people every year, but it helps: the person who compiles the information becomes woven into the landscape too. This, I think, is one of the best arguments for the old-school land manager. Justin is as much part of the fabric of Cors Fochno as the mosses. He's been looking after the Dyfi National Nature Reserve since he was in his twenties, working from ranger to manager over many decades, as has his boss and the one before. Sadly, these roles are rare, replaced by project-based management and a more itinerant workforce.

Cors Fochno has its fair share of moths, but none rarer than the rosy marsh moth, *Coenophila subrosea*. It is as pretty as it sounds: it has soft pink markings flecked with iridescence against a chestnut brown background. It's a night flyer, on the wing for the last of the summer. It's found on peatlands as far away as northern Japan, but on just three sites in the UK: Cors Fochno, Cors Caron and a woodland in Cumbria.

Until the 1960s it was thought to have gone, its last sighting was in 1850, but a single moth was found in Gwynedd in the 1960s by a scientist on holiday in Penrhyndeudraeth. A very extensive, but fruitless search was conducted for this rarity. Penrhyndeudraeth literally translates as 'peninsula with two beaches', a far cry from an acid bog.

Two years later and the hunt was still on. There are just two months in which to find the adult, and the search was extended until it reached Borth, which was where it was found. The story goes that it was decided the single Gwynedd moth had hitched a ride on the railway to see a different bit of the coast – Borth and Penrhyndeudraeth are connected by a train, albeit one that splits at Dyfi Junction, so the moth had a layover and a carriage change. The moth remains rare and sits on the Red Data list of endangered beings as the population swings from a handful to several dozen depending on the weather.

The bog is too vast a terrain to go looking for something so small on the wing. Instead, long into the night, you have to hunt for the caterpillars, which, although busy with life, are stationary. Every year, in May, Justin gathers anyone who has even a passing interest in the moth to crawl along the scientific boardwalk, shouting, 'Found one!'

Inch by inch, until three in the morning, across fifteen different points, we knelt, head torches on, seeking them out. Because the boardwalk is only two feet across you have to form a line, so the first person gets the best pickings, 'There's one, there's another,' as the second scribbles down the results. The third and fourth searchers often spend a lot of time calling out caterpillars that the first is already sure they saw.

I turned out to be very competitive about caterpillar counts and weirdly very good at homing in on their distinct stripes of black, white, bright yellow and ochre. A colour scheme I'm sure I've seen as a 1970s shirt or deckchair pattern. Anyway, they can be quite big, seven centimetres or so, and fat, so once you get your eye in, they pop under the glow of the head torch.

You have to note whether the brightly coloured caterpillar is eating, on the move or just hanging out. And if they're eating, what is it? They mostly eat *Myrica gale*, bog myrtle, occasionally bog rosemary and deer grass, though they might just be contemplating things on the deer grass, it being a rather good bouncing route from one place to another. The caterpillars are rarely seen by day. They feed at night, with less predation, though their colours suggest they aren't pleasant to eat.

This night count has been going on since the late 1980s. Some years were disastrous, particularly after a fire ravaged the site, and in others the population fell because of the weather. Last year was dismal and the searchers found only nine. The year I joined we discovered sixty-seven.

I had packed my rucksack full of energy snacks to keep myself going through the night, but other than one quick stop for a refuel, they weren't much needed. The thrill of the hunt, the good company, the vast wonder of the bog at night turned out to be enough.

At one point I overheard Justin saying to one of his colleagues that they could go early if they wanted, as I was clearly staying for the night. I realised I was proving myself as more reliable or more in love with the bog than he might have imagined. After the rosy moth count, I began to understand exactly how precious Cors Fochno is. It may be damaged by fires, its edges missing or cut into and drained, but its beating heart is very near perfect.

When I was walking with rangers over mountains and they

were proudly showing me patches of moss over crisped landscape, I began to see exactly how rare Cors Fochno is, with its rich tapestry of species, from its many sphagnum mosses to its rare moths and butterflies and beyond. How rare, too, someone like Justin is, a true naturalist to his core, always generous with his knowledge and time. I once asked him about some general function of peatland formation and he replied that he wasn't a generalist, that he really only knows about that place. It isn't true: his knowledge is as vast as the bog, but he won't be drawn to theorise about things he hasn't experienced. The more time I spent with him, the more I appreciated his precision: it matches the bog's own ability to keep a careful record in its layers of peat.

*   *   *

The moth night had given me confidence. I understood the wider landscape and its markers so, stars or not, I could pinpoint north and thus a way out. I was also aware that the wind played tricks: that the barking dog could be miles away even if it sounded as if it was mere metres. I was gaining night legs too, surefooted over the boardwalk's wobbly slats.

When we left the bog for the moth count, I'd been deep in conversation with one of Justin's colleagues about old dogs, a subject close to my heart as my Jack Russell was nearly eighteen. It turned out she, too, had a very old Jack. Get two old-dog lovers together and conversation soars with the joys of such love, of the idiosyncrasies and eccentricities of the animals: we missed hearing the first nightjars of the season and the grasshopper warblers.

When we all met back at our cars, Justin quizzed us as to whether we had heard them and we had sheepishly to admit we'd been talking about dogs. No one who spends any time with Justin fails to note that he doesn't think much of dogs or, more correctly, their owners, after a lifetime of trying to protect nesting birds. I loved our old-dog chat, but I also love nightjars and vowed to return to hear them sing.

Nightjars are strange-looking birds. Grey-brown and mottled, they blend easily by day with tree bark or lower down in heather. They are found in woodland, moorland and on heath, spend the summer in the UK breeding, then return to Africa around August. Their song, like that of the chiffchaff, the swift and swallow squeak, is the sound of summer. Uncommon these days, for, like many, their habitat is increasingly scarce, but if you know their song, you'll find every opportunity to seek it out.

The writer Kate Bradbury once described it as like a washing-machine whirr, as good a description as any. It certainly allows you to identify it for the first time if you wake in a tent in a wood and wonder who's washing at that hour. It churrs along, mechanically; at the beginning of the season, there's the added clap of the male's wings. It can be quite jarring, hence the name nightjar. I'd like to think if they were into electronic dance music, they'd be gabber fans, that dark, fast hardcore with distorted drumbeat that made for late-late nights.

The day after the solstice Kate and I meet for dinner at hers, then go for an evening stroll onto the bog to listen out for the nightjars. At ten, unsurprisingly, it's still light and we can't hear any nightjars. After strolling round the public boardwalk I suggest we go onto the monitoring one as it's still bright enough to do so without torches. Kate has never been on this boardwalk, perhaps because she is the sort of person who heeds authority but also, I think, because she fell into the bog once. She was looking for wildflowers on the south side, near the coastal path, and veered off it, as you do when you're nose-to-the-ground hunting. She fell into a cut full of water and found herself suddenly lost. It would have been embarrassing if all of Borth knew she'd had to be airlifted out, so she kept pulling until she had freed herself, then picked her way back to the path with her dog. The worst of it, she says, was to be sunk in water and thirsty – it was a blisteringly hot day. I pointed out that it's quite possible to drink bog water: it's the same acidity as weak cider vinegar and actually quite pleasant if you don't think about all the drowned bugs.

It was lovely to take Kate to the middle of the bog and hear her delight at seeing it from the inside rather than the edge. The bog disorients everyone initially. We pieced together the landscape, then realised we had to turn back quickly before it became too dark to see the boardwalk. As we scurried along, the slats slapping the peat, we heard the first churr of the nightjar from the woods, quickly followed by another from Llangynfelyn way, then a third from somewhere on the bog, and then yet another. From our central position we were bounded by their whirr and churr. I had previously only ever heard a single nightjar call into the night, but to hear a refrain was magical.

Nightjars don't just sing at night: they hunt too. They eat insects, mostly moths and some beetles, so heath, moorland and bogs are excellent places for them. They may call from trees but they nest on the ground, their eggs camouflaged to resemble dead wood or logs and often found on dry ground between heather. They need open habitats to find plenty of food.

A strange superstition surrounds European nightjars, born of their odd-looking mouths. Their Latin name, *Caprimulgus euroaeus*, translates as goat-milker. Aristotle wrote,

> The so-called goat-sucker lives on mountains; it is a little larger than the ousel, and less than the cuckoo; it lays two eggs, or three at the most, and is of a sluggish disposition. It flies up to the she-goat and sucks its milk, from which habit it derives its name; it is said that, after it has sucked the teat of the animal, the teat dries up and the animal goes blind. It is dim-sighted in the day-time, but sees well enough by night.*

They don't suck goats' teats, but wherever there were herds of grazing animals there are insects, so it's likely that the herder either saw or captured nightjars and took their strange mouth

---

* *History of Animals*, translated by D'Arcy Wentworth Thompson (The Clarendon Press, 1910).

for sucking rather than snatching. Misconception seems to follow these poor birds: they were also known as lich-fowle, which translates from middle English as 'corpse-bird' and some believed that the nightjar held the souls of unbaptised children, doomed to the wild night sky. Like many nocturnal beings of wild places, their evasiveness – their strange night songs and courtship displays, and their camouflaged colours which make them so hard to find in daylight – mean they have been misunderstood. Their big eyes have large numbers of rod cells allowing them to see well at night, their strange vocalisations occur when few others are singing, meaning the sound carries further, and their ability to disappear during the day means they can avoid predators.

As we left the edge of the bog, we caught one in flight, its heavy body and long tail giving it away against the inky night sky. Nightjars thrive in undisturbed habitats; they are easily flushed from their nests by dogs or humans. Another reason, then, why the bog is so special: its edges and margins are a perfect habitat for this elusive bird.

A few weeks later, Ele and I went to listen to the nightjars after we'd been to the cinema. We left the highly saturated world of Wes Anderson and ventured into the gloaming to Borth. As we pulled up over the hill to see the bog we were met by an evening of steely blues and greys that looked so fresh and alive after the saccharine pastels of the film. I couldn't help sliding back into my usual refrain: wouldn't she like to move here? Those hills, the length of the beach, the bog . . . No, she wouldn't: she still thought Borth was a bit depressing, odd, beguiling, but ultimately it made her sad. 'What about behind the bog, in Dôl-y-bont or up on the rocky outcroppings?' I knew I wasn't winning her over, but I had to keep asking.

We pulled up the road to the bog, the pot holes satisfyingly full of rain water. I could sense the bog was happier. Even if the ditches gurgled with all the hidden leaks, the surface would be wet and everyone on the bog would be thriving because of it. As we parked the car and debated which way to go, we were met by the swoop and dart of bats. So fast and silent, so near, fractions away from us, bending at the last moment and veering off to miss us. Ele saw one catch a moth mid-flight, but I was slightly anxious we'd meet an adder, which would be the final and biggest nail in the coffin for ever moving closer to the bog as Ele is phobic of snakes. I figured I'd walk ahead, and if I found one, I could scare it off.

We didn't have to walk long before we heard the first nightjar whirr away – it seemed some distance to the east side of the bog. Then, from the west side of the woods, we heard another. A few high-pitched notes, then some loud claps, much closer, over one of the ponds. I knew immediately the claps had come from a male. I'd always imagined it happened when the bird was perched on a branch and was taken aback to witness it happen in flight. There, just in front of us, were two nightjars. The male flashed his wings and we saw clearly, even in the late light, the white tips. Then he and a female circled and spiralled around us for several minutes, coming so low and near, it might have been possible to reach up and touch one. I could hardly believe they were so unbothered by our presence, but I could see that no one had been on the bog path for some time now. There were tell-tale upturned divots in the bark mulch that suggested someone had been hunting for grubs or worms, and the bracken had fallen completely over the path in places and no one had pushed it aside.

I spend so much time thinking about how we all need to visit our peatlands more to bring them back into our lexicon as places we cherish, but I also relish that so few people come here. That I can choose any hour to visit and meet maybe two people is one of its delights.

As we watched those magical birds, other nightjars took up their evening song, a whole chorus of high-speed techno whirring. I realised how little we know of the intricacies of the night. A whole world was coming into flight as it darkened: moths fluttered around, something crept into the water and something else shifted on a branch. The midges nibbled at our ears and along our hairline. Ele drew up her hood, but I had come out with nothing suitable to keep them at bay and they chased us off the bog.

*   *   *

It was late summer when Kate and I next went to the bog together. We met up to look for the Irish lady's tresses orchids that were just coming to the end of their flowering. Justin had shown them to me the week before, so when Kate texted a few days later, I knew I had to take her. Nothing pleases Kate more than wild flowers being where they want to be. It was only as we were driving along that I remembered we had to vault an electric fence.

The more I got to know Justin, the more I loved his boyish side, which slipped out between the serious business of caring for the Dyfi National Nature Reserve. It came with twinkling eyes at the least expected moment. And there was his glee at high jumping an electric fence, which he did balletically from a stand-still. The orchids are so rare in Britain, with just a handful of sites across the country, mostly in western Scotland, that the population is strictly monitored. The wild ponies that graze the bog aren't aware of this, of course: the fence is principally there to keep them out, perhaps us too. I couldn't imagine Kate, Ele or me vaulting it.

We walked out across the wet meadow edge to see them. The land is still thick with peat, part of the dome of raised bog, but it had been drained for agriculture, washed at various points with seawater from the flooded Leri, drained again, and is a marginally fen-flushed edgeland of the once-bog. I have come to see these edgelands as ghost spaces, haunted by what should be, inhabited by all sorts of lost things that have wandered in and found they could make a home if they wanted to. Further along that edge, earlier in the summer, Justin had shown me swathes of lesser butterfly orchid, heath spotted orchids, early marsh and northern marsh orchid dotted among blunt-flowered rushes and, along the edges, narrow and broad leaf buckler ferns, all plants that are there only because fen-flush adds enough minerality to the acid peat for them to eke out a living.

These are complicated edges, like the woodland that now butts up to the site. They are not supposed to be there, and true restoration would grub out the trees and wash the fen-flush clean, but where would the whinchats and the orchids go? No one is suggesting either of these things should happen, but the philosophical question of what makes a bog such is always fraught with it. Cors Fochno as its truest self, the version unchanged by human hands, would be a vast raised dome that had eaten the scrub woodland and all of the marginal fields in metres of peat. But the nightjars and the great tits, the owls, the moles, the adders, newts, toads and the rest that have been hounded from other habitats need the scrubby edges. To restore the bog completely would make them homeless.

Classification is tricky, there to create building blocks of knowledge, but often stuck in binary notions. Cors Fochno on paper is a classic raised bog, but in reality it is a peatland complex in an ever-evolving, even more complex landscape of land, sea and human desire.

Ele, Kate and I stood by the electric fence and I pointed out the diminutive orchids sparsely dotted between the eyebright and the bog pimpernel. Irish lady's tresses are slight, with three whorls of white flowers on a stem that is no more than 15 centimetres high and not much to look at from a distance. We needed to get around the electric fence, without vaulting it. Then I realised there was an easier way to go in. We dropped and rolled commando-style under the fence, carefully making sure there was nothing precious we'd roll onto. The spring had been so dry that nearly everything was weeks ahead. The orchid flowers were quickly turning to seedpods, but there were enough still out that we could sniff their hawthorn scent and admire their flower-whorls and fleshy leaves before dropping again and rolling out. Once their seed is set, the fence is taken away and the ponies keep the landscape shorn enough for them to reappear next year.

We decided to take an evening stroll around the boardwalk to see if we could find some sundews as we were too early in the evening to hear nightjars. Walking past one of the larger ponds, peering at early mushrooms and other finds, Kate spotted something moving in the bark mulch on the path. 'What's that?' We crouched. It was a baby toad, marvellous with its rusted orange markings around its eyes. I gently picked it up to take a look. 'Well, there she is,' said Kate, and I looked at her, puzzled. 'Our toad! Or at least evidence that she lives here.' Seven months later we had finally found a toad, not a giant one from the folklore tales, but better: a next generation. We watched it amble off into the rushes. Before we left, we stood in the early dusk watching the soldier beetles bonk like mad amid a drift of ragwort and wild angelica.

Part Two

11

Recorded Places

All soils have a memory. Caught in their layers are the effects of the elements: the many waters and winds that pelt down, run over and move through them, the heat of the sun or the earth erupting through them. Added to this are the effects of things that live in and off the soil, of all who call this place home. Everything makes its mark on soils.

Many soils, though, are not necessarily good storytellers. Hidden in their depths are fragments of tales, a word here, a phrase there, more rarely a chapter and a verse. Mud has its own way of recounting: it can encase a relic in its clay and keep it there for future finders; sandy soils may desiccate their memories but their shifting nature means they can wear them away; alluvial soils are traditional poets, writing in lines and creating the odd stanza, but no soil can recount all of its past better than peat.

Peatlands are found all over the world and have a history far deeper and older than you might imagine. Thick seams of peat don't exist without life: the formation of abundant peat was impossible before the spread of plants. Our most ancient peatlands appeared during the Devonian period, around 372 million years ago. These peatlands have hardened with the weight of time pressed on them. The deeper the peat is buried, the more the core of the earth can heat it and turn it gradually into lignite. With more time and more cooking, the carbon is concentrated and converted to almost 84 per cent pure carbon. In these hard lumps of energy, peat's story is hard to read: it has been beaten out of it by the weight of the new world above. Which is interesting, but not much use if you want the story told. The young peats, those up to ten thousand years old, give the best renditions. These peats are portals to distant worlds, other realms and other times, where there were many gods to appease and worship, and bogs were deep places to cross boundaries.

The catotelm layer of peat has the memory of a good librarian. Everything has its place: stacks are kept neat, artefacts carefully ordered from day one, so that a history of not only the peatland but the wider world is captured in its layers. It is known as the peat archive, a term coined by the botanist Harry Godwin in the 1980s, and is a common metaphor for anyone telling a bog's story. There is a fossilised record of change in any peat's profile through the vegetation that built it, the pollen and spores released, but also the animals, everything from the microscopic to the giant Irish elks and, in the Americas, Pleistocene bison, dire wolves and sloths, as well as archaeological remains. From our Stone Age ancestors onwards we've been leaving and losing things in bogs, thus adding to the layers of history put down in peatlands.

Exposed peatlands have revealed the earliest flint tools, flint flakes fashioned by hands four hundred thousand years ago, stone spearheads and rapiers (simple thin sword-like instruments) and blunt tools to make such things. Depending on where you were in the world, around ten thousand years ago farming practices started to appear. The hunter-gatherers were successful and early farmers were by no means superior in knowledge or lifestyle, but the change brought a huge shift in tool-making and other art forms. So, we go from elegant rapiers and spears to large numbers of polished stone axes that bear witness to huge clearances of woodlands, then the chisels and adzes used to create more specialist works. Occasionally the axes were made of exotic stones that had no reference to where they were found: jadeites from Piedmont in Italy have been found in Donegal and Scotland, indicating that trade routes were appearing.

The bog is such an exceptional protector of memories that it has even kept safe examples of fragile-material culture: prehistoric basketry, early examples of bags made with a coiling technique, fishing nets and even some textiles, shawls, blankets, many fastenings and beads that hint at what they were once attached to. There are amulets, necklaces of periwinkle and other shells beautifully strung together in opposing asymmetrical rows. Archaeologists working on dry land expect to see 10 per cent of material culture from any given dig, but wetland archaeologists, particularly those digging in peat, can find up to 90 per cent still intact. Peat holds on to the fabric of our life in many different ways.

The Bell Beaker people, named after the distinctive upside-down bell-shaped vessels they produced, expanded across western Europe carrying new technology to relatively isolated places, like Britain and Ireland. They didn't just change the shape of the pottery, but brought with them knowledge of metalworking and thus the possibility of producing a whole new range of tools and weapons. Peatlands have thrown up metal axe heads, but also cauldrons, the earliest made from pure copper. Soon miners were digging out alluvial deposits of gold to be hammered into sheets and fashioned into everything from neck ornaments, known as *lunulae*, to bands and discs that were used as jewellery, often incised with geometric patterns. By any standard these pieces are as intricate and breath-taking as any modern jewellery.

Metallurgy continued through the Bronze Age and was not confined to bronze. Gold mining increased and with it the smiths' capabilities. Minute amounts of gold were used as fine foil to cover *bullae*, a type of early locket, and to fashion rings and discs, dress-fastenings, collars and bracelets. These objects are not found with the dead, but were disposed of in bogs and on dry land, sometimes under rocks. Many such ornaments could not have been for everyday use, either too fine or too heavy and bulky, but were rather used to symbolise rank and authority; they were restricted to certain areas, where societies had greater access to raw material for metal work or goods of high value to trade for them.

Many of these artefacts and details about our ancestors come from bogs, not from sand or silt or clay, but peat.

The talent for detailed work wasn't just demonstrated in finery: axe heads, spearheads and daggers became increasingly sophisticated. Then chisels, gouges, punches, tweezers, sickles and knives started to appear in great quantities, produced through sophisticated casting techniques. Their appearance, as well as many more hilltop enclosures particularly in the late Bronze Age, suggests times of violent uncertainty, and during this period, there was an increase in spears and swords, too.

Metal tools allowed our societies to expand. Farming was on its slow but steady ascent to being our major production of food, but hunting and gathering still ruled as a way of life. Yet we were altering the landscape too.

Peatlands are formed by climate and informed by the geology of place. And we have been influencing our climate from the minute we started to fashion tools. The Neolithic, the new Stone Age, was heavily forested, but the advent of tools, particularly early metal ones, changed everything. When you have a spear, you still have to chase much of your supper, but you don't have to maul it. A good spear, which flies silently through the air, allows you to creep up on and kill all sorts of animals, which supply more fats, more hides, more bones to turn into other tools, toothpicks and needles, tallows and glues.

From very early on as hunter-gatherers, we not only used tools to change our landscape, we also had fire. A great deal of evidence shows that hunters corralled animals in bogs and wet places where they could be immobilised and easily killed. Fire was used to clear land and open the canopy. Many large herbivores need to graze on nitrogen-rich plants and grasses that won't grow in dense woods, and fire created a good hunting landscape. At some point the fire-hunters turned into fire-farmers, using flames to concentrate subsistence resources – desirable plants to eat and use as building materials, textiles, dyes and medicines and animals that would do well for them – in a sort of garden area around a camp that made hunting and gathering easier.

Why and when we stopped hunting and gathering and turned into farmers isn't easy to pinpoint, but all this activity influenced the landscape and climate. Vast amounts of forest were lost through this slow-motion landscape engineering, burning woods to open them up, burning fires to cook meat, cutting trees to make fires, burning fires to keep warm, cutting trees to make tools, burning fires to melt metals. We made fires to create tools to fight with, to farm with, to fish with, and cut trees to sail across oceans. This is our history; it is also that of the bogs.

Cutting down and burning created deforestation, particularly over the better-draining hill landscapes, which lay just below the hill forts. And mass deforestation appeared as the climate was changing. The late Holocene (between five thousand and two thousand years before the present) saw a shift to a damper, cooler climate, and the loss of tree cover exposed the brown earth soils, which developed beneath forests. Forest soils are rich in organic matter; they are soft, well aerated, from all the leaves that fall onto them. In short, they were easy to cultivate, once the trees were removed. Our ancestors would have realised that every time they took down trees they were left with fertile soils.

But brown earth soils that are exposed to a cool, wet climate can't cling to all this goodness: weathering through erosion would have meant they started to podzolise, the process of the beginning of soil formation. When this happens, the clays are broken down, lowering the pH and affecting the relationship between organic molecules and metals, the latter leaching into the water. With increasing rain, cool days and nights, the once rich forest floor starts to acidify, losing its minerals and fertility. And when this happens, bogs are born. One theory is that the development of peatlands during this period, in the UK at least, is thought to be strongly linked to past human activity, a direct result of early forest clearance leading to wetter soils.* Just as we were starting our journey as a farming civilisation, the once forested uplands were turning into vast peatlands and covering all the tools and treasures we had left there.

Bogs are many things, but they are not easy places to live. No one knows why so many things were buried in bogs, but perhaps it is no coincidence that so many hoards and single objects, from the late Bronze Age onwards, have been found in rivers and bogs. The climate was deteriorating, and the cool conditions encouraged the formation of peat as bogs swallowed the landscape and covered it with a damp blanket of soft mosses and cotton grasses. The growth of bogs was so rapid that Bronze Age people needed continually to build wooden trackways to get across them. As the bogs grew, the trackways, and the wooden wheels that rolled over them, were preserved under new layers of peat. We know that bogs had spiritual significance from the objects buried in them and that they were crossed on paths left behind. Some scientists believe that Neolithic deforestation brought about the bog-forming climate change; others say that models suggest the climate was shifting regardless. Either way it has left us soils full of stories.

Many of these stories are now housed in the National Museum of Ireland, in Dublin. Ele and I spent a wet March morning peering into glass boxes filled with such treasures. The plan had been to explore the blanket bog over the Wicklow mountains. We'd spent the previous day walking up Tondruff peak next to Lough Tay, then gone to see some bog restoration work. Bog

* Charman, D. J., *Peatlands and Environmental Change*, (John Wiley & Sons, 2002).

hopping is not for everyone. It is slow and you can't get anywhere directly: you have to like the untrodden path and understand that you may have to go back on yourself before you can go forward. The Wicklow mountains have had years of interventions, of cutting peat for fuel, in part because Ireland had no coal seams, and a colonial history of its woods and forests being exploited and controlled. Its people were left with little but peat to burn during Ireland's occupation by the British. Added to this there was a colonial history of systematic burning for grouse shoots and to create better grazing for sheep. This has left the bogs very damaged, with exposed peat spilling into paths and washing away with rain. These damaged bogs have been taken over by moorland and heathland vegetation, dominated by heather, deer grass and purple moor grass, all a sure sign that they have dried out.

There are pockets of hope, mature grey heather stems splayed to expose nursery crops of Magellanic bog moss, bog rosemary, scatterings of bog asphodel seed heads, and pools are slowly being colonised again by *Sphagnum cuspidatum*. But the overall picture is pretty bleak. We drove over to the Sally Gap and back along the Military Road, where in the distance we could see domestic peat-cutting plots scarred into the landscape like gravestones. The Wicklow mountains are a huge granite range that has been eroded into smoothly rounded hills capped on the upper part with hard mica-schist rock jutting out. They owe their present topography of deep glens, valleys and corries to the last cold snap of the Ice Age, between 11,600 and 12,600 years ago, but as the earth warmed, the mountains were covered with pine forest. As the climate changed again, and human activity grew, many of the trees were cut down and the conditions were wetter, milder, the ground became waterlogged, the soil leached and the hard granite below became ripe for peat to grow.

Four thousand years or so ago, the uplands started to grow peat into a soft blanket that covered all but the most rugged of granite outcroppings. Now, though, instead of being the deep olive green it should be in winter, it is largely purple, brown and orange, as the heather, deer grass, purple moor grass and bracken take over. From the distance, the deep purple-brown of the winter heather, contrasting against its silver-grey stems, reminded me of ripe bullace plums just before they're about to drop and are still covered with their grey-white bloom. The deep purples, the copper of the bracken and bleached blond of grasses made a patchwork quilt that was deeply arresting. But I now understood it was damaged peatland. We drove home in near silence, taking it all in.

*   *   *

Later, over a pint of Guinness, Ele admitted that her overall feeling of the mountains, and in particular the bog, was that we were not supposed to be there, that we were trampling on things best left alone. While I had been wrapped up in spotting mosses and reading different depths of exposed peat, Ele hadn't relished the walk. Once you understand the plants you can quickly read where you may find solid ground or end up knee deep in a murky pool of peat, and which plants have roots enough for you to stand so you don't slide off the mountain's edge.

When I saw that rain was predicted for the next day, I gave up my plans for botanising and compromised on a visit to Dublin. 'We can go and see the bog bodies together,' I suggested optimistically. Ele plumped for some modern art, to which I retorted, 'If we have time. It wouldn't be polite to rush looking at the dead.' Which was how we ended up in room after room of exquisite axe heads, early tools and so much gold. In fact, my lasting memory of the museum is of a golden glow.

12

Buried Places

Just a handful of the buried treasures deep in the peat were neither lost nor forgotten, but buried on purpose precisely because the bog was a good place to keep something. They were buried in the knowledge that they might never rot. The Irish Neolithic bog bodies are housed in their own wing at the museum, with the light turned low, each behind a screen. It is an attempt at respect but, rather, it adds an air of crime-scene investigation, perhaps not inappropriate, but odd.

In truth, after I'd said we shouldn't rush, it was me, not Ele, who whirled around the bodies. Perhaps I had read too much about them, or perhaps it was the hordes of Spanish teenagers who had gathered around them, or just that they were too strange, but I ended up spending most of my time looking at axes and fishing nets. Ele had more staying power, and when we got home to Wales, I found her, one evening, uploading the beautiful photographs she'd taken of all the bodies so she could make drawings of them. I realised that she had looked at them entirely differently from me.

Ele saw them not as their stories but as who they were, people who had been injured. She is a doctor and peered at them carefully rather than curiously. Despite the noise of the teenagers, she studied them calmly, allowing the rush around her to dissipate until only she remained with them. Her pictures are replicas of many others – it doesn't take a doctor to find the space and silence necessary to honour them – but seeing those bodies through her eyes shifted my own curiosity about them.

Those bodies are spiritual beings because of and despite their violent ends; they were chosen to remain between worlds, not allowed to disappear, to rot away. Most people visit them out of curiosity, but also to pay respect, to meet our ancestors, to imagine their lives, their loved ones, their language, their values and honours. And, to some extent, that is what the rest of the museum is there to teach. I found Ele's pictures moving because they allowed me to see the bodies in a different way, but also to see her, one of those fleeting moments when you see afresh someone you love. Strange, then, to experience all of these emotions for leathery skin pulled taut by the weight of time.

Those who interred the poor souls could not have imagined that one day they would lie in stone buildings, under magical lights, away from their waters, that a whole industry would spring up to understand them, their hairstyles, clothes, teeth, their manicured fingernails, their last meal of gruel, the psychedelics used to alter their perception of the violent ways their bodies would be slashed, bent, broken, stabbed and, finally, pinned down in watery graves.

It is thought that many Irish bog bodies were boundary markers, denoting territories of kingdoms, placed very specifically so that they could disturb neither this world nor the next. Some might have been captives of other tribes, others from their own people. Some bodies were found with bog butter placed nearby, others near gold hoards. Bog butter is not butter as we know it: it is a huge wooden bucket of fermented milk, thought to be an offering to the gods for future years of fertility. The

114

butter bucket is a foot or so wide and that again deep, a lot of milk for a society that has only just started to domesticate cattle. It represented as great a gift as any gold necklace and is a glimpse into how tenuous life was: only the gods could predict good seasons and large stored harvests. You might sacrifice butter, men and even children to appease the unknown.

At least five hundred bog bodies have been found across Europe, many from the Iron Age. There must be more still buried and countless others lost over time. There are accounts from the fourteenth century onwards of people digging up various body parts and occasionally whole bodies. A document from the eighteenth century noted that 'sometimes in the mosses are found human bodies entire and uncorrupted'. But superstition meant many were reburied in the peat or elsewhere, never to be seen again. And many of those buried things, once uncovered from their waterlogged world, immediately began to disintegrate.

There's a Danish account of peat-cutters in 1823 finding a whole Iron Age wagon, completely with wheels, which 'fell to pieces once exposed to air'. Some accounts are a little fanciful, such as J. Wentworth Day's claim to have found the body of a man buried deep in the peat, 'clad in a long leather jacket, belted with garrets round his legs and the right arm was raised as though about to cast a spear. The body of an unknown hunter, a nameless warrior . . . It crumbled to dust in the sharp Fen air'. But there are many more accounts of found objects, so numerous that locals were blasé. Of barn floors littered with 'large and miscellaneous collections of antiquities', of great quantities of bones, ancient stockades, ruins of huts and more, but as most of these materials were organic, they were often ignored for the more desirable axe and spear heads, pins and brooches, other jewellery, early metal and stone objects that were display-cabinet worthy or could be sold to dealers.

Some of the more fantastical finds include the Deskford carnyx, an early type of trumpet fashioned with the head of a wild boar. Found in Scotland, it is made of Roman metal, brass and bronze.

A handful or so of European carnyces have survived, but many pictures and reliefs show what they would have looked like. The animal head would have been mounted on a very long tube that would have been played upright or horizontal. Initially it was thought they were war horns, partly because the reliefs tend to show carnyces leading troops into battle, but the musician John Kenny, who has played a reconstructed Deskford carnyx, thinks their range, which is finest when played low and quiet, is better suited to ritual.

The Deskford carnyx, like many bog burials, was 'killed' before being buried in the bog; its head was ripped from its tube body. As with so many hidden treasures of the bog, it was important for those burying it to decommission it. Much of what is buried in the bog was sacrificed on some level. If the bog is a portal to another world where the gods live, then whatever was entombed in peat was not left whole in case it came back.

That was the Deskford carnyx's fate, buried in a time of great change. I watched a video of Kenny playing the strange instrument. The sounds varied: deep and rich, mournful, haunting. Kerry said of playing it that it was 'like being able to put your hand back through the curtain of time and touching something you can't see, but you can feel'.

*   *   *

All peat had a life before it sank into its dark places. Many mires and bogs were once lakes, marshes, lochs and ponds, places that many Neolithic and Palaeolithic people chose to live in because wetlands were such good places to forage from. Wetlands are rich in food, medicines, pigments and materials for housing, clothes and tools. They are also surprisingly safe places: it is possible to retreat and protect yourselves on water perhaps more easily than on a hilltop.

The early Palaeolithic wetland-dwellers were almost entirely ignored by antiquarians of the eighteenth and nineteenth centuries, whose education still focused on Grand Tours of classical Greece and Rome, their literature and mythology. The idealisation of a classical past often meant those scholars measured everything else against this: Greek and Roman archaeology was high morality and pagan rather low.

It was left to just a few curious peat archaeologists to start piecing together the artefacts found in bogs, peatlands, riverbanks and lakes to begin to understand the habits and ways of early wetland people, about pile-dwellings, crannogs and other human-made islands. Pile-dwellings are islands, sometimes floating, sometimes not, built on tree trunks that made crude, but effective homes in wet places. They could be on the edge of the wetland or, if more safety was required, in the middle. To these places roadways were sometimes purposely sunk just below the water so that they were passable but invisible to the uninitiated. Where lakes and rivers barred such passage, rafts, logs, bridges, dugouts and eventually primitive canoes and paddles were used. It was finding these things that led scholars not only to re-examine prehistory, but for wetlands to become the focus of great interest in archaeology.

Wetland archaeology was still in its infancy in the nineteenth century, and most in the scientific community paid it little attention: it was an eccentric sideline to the fairly recent subject of archaeology, barely acknowledged in literature until the winter of 1853–4. There had been a long drought in Europe, and extreme cold that winter meant that the rivers feeding Lake Zürich shrank; the lake water receded to its lowest recorded level. From what was left of the water, piles of oak, beech, birch and fir became visible in rows parallel to the shore. They formed a whole pile-dwelling village, piles that held platforms supporting huts where people lived, dropping their debris into the lake mud below. Once these finds were made public, collectors, antiquarians and the wealthy started to hunt lakes all over Switzerland looking for similar early settlements.

In Lake Geneva, a geologist donned a bucket with a glass

window and a supply of air via a pump in a rowing boat, then stalked the bottom of the lake with a pickaxe looking for finds among the piles. He wrote, 'It was strikingly poetical to stand amid those ancient posts in the bluish twilight.' Others followed suit and the alpine lakes of northern Italy and Germany were soon under investigation. It wasn't long before the lake explorers became bog examiners on moors in Austria, peat-filled marshlands around the Jura lakes and peat beds around Lake Pfäffikon, in Switzerland, were soon throwing up discoveries through the use of steam-driven mud-dredgers.

These finds persuaded others to look further afield than the Alps. Soon there was a craze for prehistory as antiquarians and newly initiated wetland archaeologists joined with turf cutters to expose bogs, tarns and swamps in Ireland, Britain, Sweden, Florida, the Netherlands and almost anywhere there was peat. Many were keen to make their mark on the new discipline of wetland archaeology and there was much to explore.

It happened against a backdrop of the industrial revolution, which changed our landscape like nothing else that had come before it. Land was owned in a way it had never been before; it was drained; forests were cut down; rivers rerouted and mountains blasted. Although mires – fens, marshes and bogs – had been drained, mined and dug into, they had never been exploited in quite the same way as the industrial revolution saw fit.

It was easy to understand why the soft, dark sponge of peat might appeal to the farmer if it was drained a little. It would also benefit industrialists if they could cross it on the railway or by a canal, but for ordinary folk, increasingly, moved from subsistence farming into factories, the bogs offered the last common land, where they might still afford to forage, farm a little and cut turf.

13

Metal Places

Some bogs grow more than peat and plants. They also grow iron, albeit in very small amounts. Our planet has an iron-rich core, which attracted the planetary embryo to crash into us, so iron is one of the most abundant metals on earth. It is easily found in rocks, such as magnetite, hematite, goethite and limonite. The iron in the bogs is not as pure as that found in rocks, but it is fairly readily available. The minute humans found bog iron, they started to utilise it.

How the bogs form iron is complicated, but essentially the metal bubbles to the surface; the acidic nature of bogs dissolves it; water transports and concentrates it in pockets of bog iron. These pockets are often found where iron-rich waters flow close to the surface of the bog. Here the iron oxidises, either because it is brought to the surface but more usually because there's an abundance of bacteria that eat iron. They derive energy from oxidising it and spit out iron minerals as their waste product. When there is an abundance of the bacteria, the waste product is often visible on the surface of the water as a slimy, slightly gelatinous reddish-orange slime. It may coat the vegetation and rocks, but sometimes it's just an iridescent sheen on the water's surface that hints at what's happening below. It's easy to assume it's some sort of pollution rather than the earth's metallurgy magic.

I say all this as if I've seen it. I haven't. I've looked and asked, gone to specialist gem and rock shops, hunted on eBay, but bog iron remains hidden. From that it sounds obscure, but before modern iron production, bog iron was *the* way to make tools and swords. 'Iron hunter' was a genuine job title, and if you found a source, you could dig it up. Because of the bacteria, it grew back, so you could return periodically and dig up more. It must have been a messy, time-consuming task because you don't get huge amounts, nuggets rather than footballs, but hunting it amounted to a living. Bog iron was utilised around the world wherever it appeared. The first smelting attempts are dated to sometime in the second millennium BCE around Egypt, though China has similar smelting tales. Over the next two millennia the Arabian technology quickly spread throughout Europe, and iron production reached Scandinavia around 800 to 500 BCE. The Vikings (a vague term, I know) loved bog iron, and iron farms were founded in bogs in Iceland. They loved the iron because they loved swords and nobody made better, shinier swords then they did.

Bog iron, because of its impurities, polishes exceptionally well and some of the most striking swords contain bog iron, but the same impurities also made them brittle. I read, on one of my internet hunts, that Vikings mixed bog iron with the bones of their ancestors when forging their swords, believing that their ancestors would protect them. Adding bone turned the brittle bog iron into something far more solid, so the swords indeed protected them better.

Bog-iron use continued long after the Vikings, and made up a large percentage of peasant tools well into the twentieth century in Russia. Swords are the glamorous end of bog iron, but it could be hammered into spears, arrow heads, axes and daggers. It wasn't all about violence, though: iron workers also made cauldrons, cooking knives, utensils, spades and adzes. But mastering metallurgy was seen as changing a world ordained by gods, and those who achieved it were thought to have mastered a ritual that was unnatural. It is thought that this was why residual products of the smithy, fragments of blast and tongues of tools used to forge metal, are found in burial sites or ritual settings.

I gave up hunting for bog iron on the bog and turned back to the internet. Maybe I could buy some . . . But whenever I found a seller, they were always sold out. I was not alone in finding bog iron fascinating. I wondered if I could get a little closer to it by talking to someone who'd found it. Eventually I received a voice message from Reece Foster, a blacksmith based in a 270-year-old forge in Mount Shannon, Ireland, wondering whether I would like to know more about bog iron. I jumped at the chance.

A day later I got a glimpse of his world. He and his friends were making Ireland's first bog hammer in what he thought must be eight hundred years and in the summer they would make a sword. The next hour was a rapid lesson in bloomery furnace, fold of metals, turning iron into rudimentary steel, of Japanese blade-smithing (a still extant traditional process that gave insight into how early swords were made) and smelting. I learnt that you didn't have to look for great lumps: the slime and nuggets could be collected and mixed with clay and sand; in the furnace they turned into bog-iron dust that was then charged with charcoal till you got an iron bloom. This was then refined: from ten kilograms of bog-iron dust you might get three kilos of bloom iron. The art of turning it into workable iron was all in the white heat of blacksmithing, folding it onto itself to push out the slag until you had something of worth. The folding process gives the iron a grain like wood: 'The bog iron has a low carbon content and a linear granular structure that makes brilliant patterns,' Reece told me. He lifted his bog-iron hammer head to his phone so I could peer at it.

I asked if he knew about Vikings burning the bones of their ancestors into their swords for strength and he laughed. Of course he did. Bog iron's low carbon content means it's a soft material and carbon is introduced to make rudimentary steel; usually wood ash was added to act like a flux, but bonemeal too. So, yes, when they added their ancestors, they naturally made stronger swords because they were producing rudimentary steel. Unlike other iron, bog iron resists rust and can be polished to a very high sheen. I suddenly understood why Reece's bog-iron pendants sold out in seconds: it was a surprisingly seductive pitch.

We talked about hunting for bog iron and the renaissance of native bog-iron products. He said it took up to a hundred years for bog iron to regenerate and that, like foraging for wild food, bog iron could be over-collected. There was a need for sustainable practices to avoid 'over-consumption'. But he left me with a clue of what to look for: if I saw the characteristic oil slick on the water, I should tap it with a stick. If it was bog iron, it would shatter rather than spread like oil. He gave me a list of bog-iron blacksmiths to look into and sent on a flurry of Instagram reels explaining various furnacing processes, and finally invited me to a festival that summer to watch the first Irish bog-iron sword being made in a thousand years. I pitched it as our summer-holiday jaunt to Ele when she came home, but her response was a rather hard no.

I told Jody, my acupuncturist, of my bog-iron forays and she asked why I hadn't just contacted an academic metallurgy specialist, as if everyone had a couple of those in their address book. I quipped that I liked the hunt of the internet. I played a game now each session to see how long we'd last before we talked about bogs. She told me that early Bronze Age pottery often had human bones added for ritual reasons and we talked of how we used to keep our ancestors close. I thought of the Christian graveyard and what it meant to bury your people somewhere else.

Then we talked about foraging and blacksmithing. Reece had

said that the bog-iron hunters would have been very low in the pecking order, but the blacksmith was of a much higher class. One of the reasons it was so hard to figure out the processes of ancient blacksmithing was that little if anything was written down or recorded. It paid to keep your alchemy secret. 'Not just secret but away from the village,' Jody said. It made sense, with all the fire, to put the forge just outside of the village because it was dangerous, but this also put the forge on the edge of society, she explained, because then people couldn't see how the magic happened.

She once told me about the hoard from Llyn Cerrig Bach on Anglesey, a bog hoard of chains, swords, spear heads, even a mouthpiece and length of horn that might have been a 'trumpa', an early instrument used much like the carnyx. The swords, like many offerings, were bent to decommission them. She said, as she handled an imaginary sword, 'You could see how it had been bent over the knee of some warrior,' making the gesture over her own knee. The bent sword perhaps was a desperate offering to the gods of someone fleeing the Roman legions as they marched relentlessly on.

The hoard also contains a slave chain and a beautiful crescent-shaped plaque, a precious offering to a sacred place. 'Imagine,' Jody said, as she packed up her needles, 'you knew if you buried a body in the ground that the flesh would disappear and you'd be left with bones, but if you buried it in the bog, the bones would disappear and the body would be left perfectly preserved. Imagine how upside down that is. You are passing from one world to the next.' Despite days of reading about bog bodies I'd not made the leap that the bog was a parallel dimension, the upside-down in near pitch darkness where the laws of the human universe seemingly played out very differently. It made sense to offer something to appease the gods of that realm.

The most common form of bog iron, goethite, can also be processed as a pigment. It makes a form of brown ochre, itself a useful dye that, when added to other pigments, could create a golden sheen. Goethite is found in the shroud of King Midas, and one theory is that Midas's golden touch came from this material.

Once heated, goethite turns a brilliant red, and red ochre was an important dye from Palaeolithic times onwards. The Celtic Picts, often thought of as dyeing themselves blue with woad, are equally thought to have dyed themselves red with goethite from bogs. It's thought that this was where the Irish Fer Dearg, or Red Men, came from. The Fer Dearg are small, red-clothed fairies that tend to mischief. Red ochre can also be used in more prosaic applications from glues to food preservation, tanning of hides and even insect repellent.

The peatland plants offered colour, but also fibres, from birch, nettle, various rushes and grasses, flag irises and bracken. From the rich biodiverse lagg, the drier margins to the deep centre, the bog provided a great deal of material. Even the peat fibre could be woven into textiles. Once carded, peat fibre is soft and the hollow structure, particularly of peat that is made from hare's tail cotton grass, *Eriophorum vaginatum*, creates a deeply insulating layer, which makes garments woven with peat warmer. Peat fibres could also be felted and turned into paper, though it must have been quite a task whitening the result enough to read anything on it.

The live mosses were used too: there's evidence of sphagnum moss as packing or padding material in early Bronze Age funerary contexts and the haircap moss, *Polytrichum commune*, which is not a sphagnum moss but another moss commonly found on bog and other wet places, was woven in cordage, string and even cloth.

14

Present Places

Peatlands are such interesting places of physical and meta-phorical appositions: when they are wet, they are good; when they are dry, they are bad, but also useful. It would be amiss not to recognise that we have benefited from extracting our peatlands, whether that's draining and drying them to grow food or timber, for grazing, but also mining them for fuel and compost. Of course, some of us have benefited much more than others.

Peatlands also produce a lot of our food. The fens in eastern England, all four hundred thousand acres, still represent some of our most profitable farming lands, but you'd be surprised by what else was once wet. Many of the UK's vegetables and cereals are grown on drained peatlands, including salads, carrots, pota-toes, onions, leeks, beans and cut flowers. The fens are rich land because their geology and waters make them alkali. The history of drainage is long and well documented. Draining acid bogs doesn't increase yield in vegetables, but it does in fuel, compost and better grazing.

In the UK we haven't dug up all our bogs, as has happened in

Ireland, because we have a different form of carbon to dig up: coal. We dug up plenty of peat for fuel until we found coal. We also dug plenty of our peat for compost and still do in England, mostly in Somerset and Cumbria, Scotland and Northern Ireland. Roughly 170,000 cubic metres of peat is extracted from the UK alone, each year, every year. Peat is still dug up in Estonia, Poland, Belarus, Russia, Canada and China for domestic and global markets. The vast majority of this goes to horticultural compost.

From the 1960s onwards, garden centres have relied heavily on peat-based composts. Once mixed with a little fertiliser, peat makes a very good growing medium for young plants, ericaceous plants (heathers, proteas), carnivorous plants, houseplants, pot-grown herbs for supermarkets and crops such as blueberries and mush-rooms. There's an amateur and a commercial market for it. After it has been removed from its land and is dried out, peat is rather a bland but pleasing canvas from which to build a compost: it is stable, consistent and light (so easy to transport); it is porous, low in nutrients, but easy to add to, and is now coupled with an industry that has invested heavily in mechanisation for peat-based potting machines and automated watering-systems. They are surprisingly hard to recalibrate for non-peat composts that tend to be heavier and remain wetter for longer. We use around 1.7 million cubic tonnes of peat every year to grow plants. This is being phased out by our government, though painfully slowly: many exemptions and licences are still in place. The price of peat is also kept artificially low, too low for a non-renewable product, in part because of the continued licences for extraction, which affects the market for peat alternatives, which are always considerably more expensive. As long as peat is extracted, it not a level playing field and stalls a genuine move to alternative growing practices.

I've been involved in campaigns for banning peat-based composts for the entirety of my horticultural career. A ban is now in place for the amateur market, then the professional, which means that by 2028 peat extraction should have ended. But a ban isn't effective without legislation, which is still being drawn up and requires parliamentary time to debate and implement it. Plus, the ban covers UK plants grown in peat, not necessarily imports. As long as peat is extracted globally, and China is a huge growth market, plants will be grown in it and imported because they are cheap. Houseplants are an obvious example – the market is dominated by peat composts – but also landscaping plants for public and private spaces, for show gardens, new housing estates, car parks and shopping centres, as well as commercial plug plants. As with every other industry, the supply chain is global and it's easy to buy a plant that was sown in one country, grown on in another, imported elsewhere. You'd be surprised how many plants have passports. So, we have a current, recent and past history of wrongdoing to these habitats.

But the damage we have done is not just from the physical act of draining or milling: we have also affected bogs through atmospheric pollution, chiefly from industry. The coal-fired factories of the industrial revolution belched epic amounts of sulphur dioxide and continued to do so for the next century. When sulphur dioxide meets the atmosphere it dissolves into acid rain, which is injurious to plants, but particularly bad for sphagnum moss: it has a direct toxic effect on the species.

When factory production slowed in the 1970s, the sulphur-dioxide level reduced, but was overtaken by nitrogenous air pollutants, chiefly nitrogen oxide, mostly from vehicle emissions. When it hits the atmosphere nitrogen oxide also dissolves into acid rain. By the 1990s catalytic converters for vehicle exhausts had been brought in and levels dropped, but we've filled the space with ammonium pollutants for intensive livestock farming.

Nowhere in England could the rain of this barrage of pollutants be witnessed more than in the north, the cradle of the industrial revolution, with textile mills and factories in Manchester and Huddersfield, steel in Sheffield, coal mining and pottery around Stoke-on-Trent, and in the middle of these lie bustling conurbations, which sit below the southern Pennines, a series of sweeping hills covered with blanket bog. For at least two hundred and fifty years these hills were pelted with acid rain and subjected to poor landscape management practices, overgrazing, historic turf cutting, drainage, commercial afforestation and human-induced fires. Hills were denuded of moss and, with the keystone species gone, the steadfast drying out of peat followed, with all that comes from it: surface erosion channels, peat pipes (cracks deep in the catotelm that release the water), the loss of vegetation, until one day there was nothing but the moonlike surface of bare peat. What was once soft and blanketed green became wind-whipped black dust flecked with the glint of the mineral layer. It was bad for walkers, for the sheep, the waterways and drinking water, the atmosphere, and truly awful for the bog ecosystem.

I met Chris Dean, then head of the Moors for the Future partnership, in the Peak District National Park on top of Holmes Moss on a hot, bright day. I was early and, it turned out, at the wrong car-parking spot, but with little knowledge of that and time on my hands I did some litter picking. I collected three disposable barbecues, an empty motorcycle-oil container, several cigarette packets, half a pizza, a burnt black burger and numerous empty plastic bottles. Plenty of others were stopping for the view – it's a popular spot, but the rubbish tells you that. When Chris called I drove back on myself to find a very tall man in a very small Smart car.

If there's one thing, I've learnt about the peatland community it is that they take their emissions seriously. Where once the atmospheric pollution came from the factories of the industrial revolution pumping out sulphur dioxide, now it comes from the spread of cities – more than 16 million people live within forty miles of the Peak District emitting all sorts of pollutants: oxidised nitrogen from vehicle exhausts, reduced nitrogen used as fertiliser in agriculture, nitrogen and sulphur from electricity generation, volatile organic compounds (VOCs) from industrial and combustion processes and, last, ozone, created from the oxidised nitrogen of vehicles and VOCs. The latter are increasingly appearing in high concentration on the Pennines.

Bare peat erodes and releases its stored carbon to the atmosphere, but it is not just the increased carbon dioxide levels that matter. Bare peat doesn't hold on to its water, and rain falling onto it runs off quicker. Increased carbon dioxide in the atmosphere has a direct effect on our weather patterns: it means more uncertainty, longer periods of drought in the summer, more storms and rain in the winter. The blanket bogs of our uplands are fundamental to the health of our rivers and drinking water. They are the beginning of the catchment areas: they filter and slow down the waters that reach the tributaries that enter our major rivers. Bare peat erodes into these water sources infilling reservoirs and discolouring the water. (Streams and tributaries running off peat should be at best the palest orange, never deep orange or brown, a sign the water is filled with peat particles.) One of the Moors for the Future remits is to deal with this issue, to restore the peat so that it can keep our waters clean.

Chris suggested we walk onto Holmes Moss, then to the Black Hill trig point. The Black Hill is named after its dark peaty soils and from the 1950s onwards had become so degraded that by the early 2000s the moss was peat soup in winter, almost impassable or certainly a sticky trap to fall into, and by summer was a dustbowl of blown peat.

The transformation from bare peat to vegetation is remarkable and Chris is rightly proud of the speed of the regeneration, but it took a while for this to sink in with me. As we went up onto Holmes Moss, we walked through small grassy valleys bordered by high exposed peat haggs covered with a toupee of heathers. They looked like dried-out stream beds with a new regrowth of grass and the haggs that rose above my head in places. I stopped Chris, confused by this landscape: 'What was it?'

'These,' he explained, 'were the erosion gullies,' that had swept through the landscape. Their height and depth were testament to just how much peat had been lost.

The polluted bare peat was an inhospitable environment to any plant life and it wasn't just the moss that had gone, but everything else. The sulphur and nitrogen had made the peat too acidic to support life. It wasn't a case of just reintroducing the mosses and waiting for the rest to appear. A much more drastic approach was needed because for two hundred years the peat had lain bare and nothing, not even a lichen, had tried to make a home there. So, Chris said, they had done something deeply controversial at the time. They had limed the rare and important acid habitat and sown it with grass. In short, they had sown a lawn on top of the bog.

The lime had raised the pH just a little, so the grasses would germinate and act as a nursery crop for the heather brash that was laid on top. A nursery crop nurses young seedlings into maturity. The grasses, a mixture of sheep's fescues, brown-top bentgrass, rye and wavy hair grass, stabilised the peat and created humid conditions for heather seed to germinate. Eventually the grasses were outcompeted by other moorland and blanket-bog species. After seven years the bare peat had disappeared, the grasses had stabilised to predominately wavy hair grass, *Deschampsia flexuosa*, a native of dry heathlands, cotton and hare grasses (bog species) and heathers – common, bell and cross-leaved.

The peatlands were coming back to life, and not just the soil, but all life above it. The vegetation introduced food and cover for insects, mammals and birds. It started to slow the carbon emissions associated with bare peat as erosion from the wind and rain reduced and slowed the production of sediment. The vegetation also slowed the movement of water. The denser and more varied it became, the more surface roughness it added, slowing the flow of water from storms and reducing the impact of flooding below by increasing the lag time from peak rainfall to peak stream discharge.

The vegetation cooled the peat surface. Dark peat heats very quickly compared to the cool greens of grasses and heathers, which helped keep the top layer of peat wetter and in turn allowed the water table to rise: the high water table meant that neither purple moor grass, *Molinia caerulea*, nor common heather, *Calluna vulgaris*, came to dominate any of the restored sites.

But one thing was still missing. Seventeen years after restoration no sphagnum mosses were present. Others had moved in – pioneer acrocarpous mosses, the upright cushion mosses, the same group as those mound-forming mosses you see in cities, on roofs and stonework, species such as star moss, *Polytrichum commune*, later taken over by the pleurocarpous mosses, the feather mosses that sprawl along the ground – but never the keystone bog mosses.

It appeared the sphagnum mosses would not naturally recolonise as part of a short-term succession process. The bog would only start to sequester carbon with anaerobic surface conditions, and that can't happen without extensive sphagnum cover. If they wanted the blanket bog back in good health, they would have to plant the mosses.

I heard tales about these plantings. Moors for the Future had a reputation for getting on with things and Chris, with his wide-brimmed hat and long lolloping strides, his no-nonsense storytelling and determination, had an air of John Wayne. The areas of bare peat were extensive, remote, high up and perhaps a little bewildering to the team: some of their approaches were novel and included chucking 2.8 million gel capsules full of sphagnum plantlets out of a helicopter across the remote moorlands. We plodded to one such spot and, lo and behold, tiny mosses were present. Chris told me their distribution and time to establish were uneven and slow. In the end they had returned to hand planting.

A moss plug plant is actually a bunch of little plantlets rolled together to the thickness of a walnut. Depending on the budget, the plugs are planted at densities of four to 100 per metre squared. Each plug costs somewhere between 50p and a pound. They had more than three hundred hectares to restore.

Almost two decades later, they have achieved 85 per cent sphagnum cover in flow pathways – that's in places where they have created blocked gullies – and 25 per cent on undulating ground. Once the gullies are blocked, the flow pathways quickly fill with water, which makes an agreeable spot for many sphagnum species. The undulating terrain is a little more difficult because it suffers more from weather patterns and water-table depth. Also, the sphagnum species that live on the hummocks take longer to establish because they grow more slowly.

We carried on up towards Black Hill, wandering through erosion gullies, until we were at the top and could see Kinder Scout on the other side and over to Manchester, Huddersfield and the many places between. There is something profound about being up high, not just for the obvious thrills, the heady climb, the view, the sense of satisfaction of getting to a trig point, but to see where you have come from, both visually and metaphorically, what you stand for, what you occupy, what you have left behind.

This landscape is wild and damaged, but also very beautiful. It is easy to understand why so many people come here. It's a space away. There is another threat to this landscape, which was visible in the rubbish at the car-parking spot. I had the impression that it haunted Chris and many other peatland practitioners.

Although the peatlands are regenerating slowly, they are still a landscape that is far too dry, and when peat dries out, it burns. It could be a stray cigarette butt thrown from a car, a smouldering barbecue, a discarded oilcan leaking over the soil, accidental sparks from machinery . . . Or, at the other end of the spectrum, it is deliberately set ablaze, either by someone with a grudge or simply to encourage new shoots of heather to grow and keep the land suitable for grazing by sheep, deer and adult grouse. A study from the National Trust of Scotland identified the main source of wildfires on their estates as coming from burning that had got out of control.

Increasingly our unpredictable weather patterns support fires. If the summer or winter is too wet one year and too dry the next, this causes a fluctuating water table. The period of dry weather means the peat is exposed to air: it starts to degrade, to sink and compact, particularly around the margins, which makes a pocket within the peat that is capable of burning and pulling the fire in deeper.

In land-management burning for grazing and grouse, it's argued that good practice is possible. This might include measures such as a reduction in the frequency of fires and in the proportion of areas burnt, creating and maintaining fire-free buffers by restoring woodlands around stream systems for instance. Many argue that burning is a part of this landscape, that the moors have a two-hundred-year history of grouse shooting, that it is part of the culture of people living there.

Muirburn, or moor burning, tends to happen either on a ten- or twenty-year cycle. It can and does happen more frequently, but for traditional management this is the norm. After the initial burn, over the next decade or so the heather slowly grows taller and more leggy, exposing its grey-stemmed mature wood, with fewer healthy, tender new shoots for deer and grouse to eat. It looks a bit like the lavender in your garden that never got pruned, all old wood and just a fringe of short new growth. It has developed in that way because the once wet, healthy peat-forming bog has been turned into something that resembles a dry-heath ecosystem.

The wet, bog-rich sphagnum has gone and all that remains is a dominance of heather (and usually purple moor grass to boot). It's an unfortunate treadmill because the more you burn to rejuvenate the heather, the more the bog dries out and the drier the heath it becomes. In a healthy bog the sphagnum carpets make sure that the heather never becomes leggy or grey-stemmed, continually wrapping its wet sponge of growth round the stems, forcing the heather to grow upwards and in the process layering it. Layering is a natural process of propagation, in which stems produce roots where they touch soil or, in this case, sphagnum moss. Rather than drowning in moss, the heather takes advantage of the soft, wet environment to put down new roots.

When I first started training as a gardener, we still used this method for propagating. We took stems of plants we knew would layer and wrapped them in sphagnum moss rolls covered with plastic so that the moss wouldn't dry out and would allow the roots to develop. A month or so later we'd unwrap the roll to find healthy new roots all the way down the cuttings. I assume some observant gardener noticed this method in heather growing in a bog.

Anyway, a healthy bog grows delightful heather for adult red grouse and, better still, a wet bog has just the right conditions for the insects that form the diet of the week-old chicks. A happy, healthy bog had evolved a great management plan for red grouse, but we are currently stuck in an endless cycle of burning to rejuvenate old heather, further drying it out. There is now a move towards cutting rather than burning the heather, but all of these methods are costly in effort, time and money, when the bog alone would do all the work if left to its own devices.

The surface of a bog burns quickly if it is dry: the heathers and myrtles are rich in essential oils and act like tinder. Extensive damage is done and carbon dioxide is released through surface burns, but if the fire is left unchecked for any amount of time, the conditions are dry enough and the water table is low, it may spread rapidly down through the acrotelm and, in the worst case, into the catotelm.

This is a huge fuel source, as it is where all the carbon is stored. An embedded catotelm burn is very hard to extinguish. On the surface, the fire may appear to have burnt out yet a metre below it smoulders, creeps and burns for days, months even. Chris told me of one fire that started in the summer and was still going the following spring.

You wouldn't imagine it but peatland, damp, soggy, saturated peat, has a lifelong relationship with fire. In fact, a healthy peatland can use fire to its advantage, and wherever there is peat, you can find a history of fire somewhere in its layers. Down in the peat archive there are layers of charcoal, where trees and shrubs that grew on the peat were burnt and slowly consumed into the layers below. Often, they are just fragments, but they add to the carbon bank: charcoal is a very stable form of carbon that takes a long time to break down. The peat archive tells us that the fires tend to occur roughly every 150 years and the vegetation steadily recovers in the intervening period. On near-natural or natural peatlands most burns take hold only in the top one to seven centimetres. There may be deeper pockets, but on the whole it's just the surface and so remains of low severity.

Deep burns are much more common on degraded bogs and at their worst can reach down several metres. Their damage is much more profound to the habitat, with emissions from lost carbon resulting in climate impact. The nature of the catotelm means that fire acts very differently the lower it gets in the peatland. It's not a fire of flames, but of smouldering, like the embers of a campfire. Instead of naturally dying out, these fires are self-sustaining because there's so much fuel to burn, particularly if the catotelm is degraded and dried out. If the water table is high, the fire can't creep down into the lower layers and instead remains on the surface.

Many peatland plants show fire adaptations, heathers sprouting regrowth from the base of burnt stems. The Venus fly trap (found on acid bogs in Northern and Southern Carolina) grows so low to the moist soil that the fire just passes over it but catches taller herbaceous material. This benefits the fly trap, which doesn't do well in shade. None perhaps show a better adaptation than the marvellous sphagnum mosses. Their ability to hold water means they have a high gravimetric water content: they are more water than moss and any fire that reaches them has to expend energy in driving off the water to get to the combustible material, which saps the fire's momentum and ensures it can't go deep. Sphagnum mosses also show a remarkable ability to repropagate from fragments after a fire.

In wooded bogs, the kind you find in North America or Russia, the sphagnum's ability to spring back is part of a refined regeneration cycle. As the trees grow and the wood thickens the mosses are shaded, which slows peat growth as well as drying out the bog. Perfect conditions for wildfires, which eventually appear and take out the trees, but not the mosses, which spring back from fragments, dominating the bogs, until the trees reappear and the cycle starts again.

Degraded tropical peatlands are just as susceptible to burning as their northern kin. Many tropical-peatlands forests have been drained for agriculture, particularly for palm oil. Also, the traditional practice of slash-and-burn agriculture is affecting the peatlands. The climate is changing in the tropics with greater periods of drier weather when such techniques can easily get out of hand and the fires are particularly hard to put out. The peat in these places can be very deep, and if the fire gets in, it can rage on a scale that's hard to fathom as there's just so much fuel to burn. A thick haze may affect air quality for huge swathes of South East Asia. One of the most studied peatland fires took place on Borneo in 1997. The fires burnt furiously for several months and caused a haze that travelled as far as Australia and China. It was thought that the event accounted for somewhere between 15 and 40 per cent of global human-made emissions that year and caused a surge of respiratory emergencies in populations across South East Asia.

If peatlands are burning more frequently or more severely, whether that's human-induced fires or natural ones, without time to reaccumulate the lost carbon, this poses a huge challenge to us and our climate. We now know that one of the biggest drivers of peatland fire severity is how wet the system is. As our atmosphere warms globally, it holds more moisture. A wet atmosphere means more heavy rain, more storms, more hurricanes, but also, paradoxically, more intensely dry spells as water evaporates from the land.

You may think more heavy rain would be good for peatlands as they like it wet, right? Peatlands are good at storing water, but not at maintaining their evapotranspiration rates – a plant version of sweating. The hotter the conditions, the more evapotranspiration rises. Vascular plants, which include nearly all plants other than bryophytes – the mosses and lichen – have a system to deal with it. They have spores known as stomata mostly on the underside of their leaves and can open or close them to regulate evapotranspiration. Mosses have no vascular system, just the balloon-like cells that are either full of water or not: they can't open or close them. Evidence shows that as the atmosphere warms and the demand for water vapour increases, the peatlands lose more of their surface water to the atmosphere. If demand increases and there is no rain, the ombrotrophic, or cloud-fed, bogs, are having their manna sucked back from them.

Like all of these tales, the near-natural and natural bogs have ways of coping with this. They seem to be able to compress their peat column with a lowering water table. Then the demand for atmospheric water vapour and the evapotranspiration rates can remain in balance, even in periods of long-lasting drought.

Peatlands have weathered many changes and have ways to survive. But over the long term a lowered water table means that more vascular plants, particularly trees and shrubs, can move in, dominate the moss and start to dry out the bogs. Natural or near-natural peatlands have resilience built into them, but the degraded bogs are only just holding on. A world that sucks out their last moist breath will spiral us all into more lost carbon.

15

Cool Places

I love bogs as much as I do because I am best suited to their cool, clouded climates. I am just too pale for most sun. I walk down to my local river and plunge into a pool that lies on the curve of one of its many bends to swim back and forth while the dippers and the kingfishers dive for minnows that school around the eddies. This is the river Rheidol and its source is in the Cambrian mountains, on the western flanks of Pumlumon deep in blanket bog. It has not always run clean as a river – it was heavily polluted from silver and lead mines and industries of the past and, like all of our rivers, it has sewage-outlet problems, but now it is cleaning itself as it is a little more respected.

The more I learnt about blanket bogs the more I wondered about those that are the source of my summer dips and my winter walks. By the time the Rheidol gets to me it spreads, like fingers, through a wet carr woodland before coming back together to rush to the sea.

It's a typical carr made up mostly of alder, grey and crack willows, oaks, downy birch and the odd hazel in drier spots. In winter much of this woodland is either completely submerged or made up of pools littered among fallen and rotting logs. On a bright winter's day they glint and entice but you can't get to them: the soils are saturated and the landscape shifts under your weight. What might have been passable muddy ground in summer, now becomes a trap of half-rotten timber. Only the wild things can play here. On high flood days the heron picks her way through to look for tasty morsels, with the ducks, willow warblers, willow tits, long-tailed tits, wrens, robins, dippers and kingfishers. I once saw an otter at dusk dip into one of the pools and swim off down the river.

If this all sounds idyllic, let me add to the picture the shopping trolleys, the litter, the teenage camps, the entire workout bench plus weights, and on cold days the often overpowering stench of the nearby sewage works. It is like many riverine carr woodlands, a little scrappy, overlooked by most, even though it is doing a hugely important job. Not all wet woodlands build peat, but many do, particularly if they are submerged during the growing season. Then their rate of growth will be faster than their rate of decomposition, thus turning them from a carbon store to a carbon sink. Wet woodlands are perhaps the most neglected and misunderstood of all the peatlands, most likely to be drained and built on. They make up the rarest type of woodland across the UK and Europe. Primary carr woodlands are hard to come by, but the scrubby sort, made up of regrowth, perhaps a couple of hundred years old at most, are found everywhere. I think of every city I've lived in and can point to many examples, pockets of scrub along streams, rivers and canals, at the edges of playing fields and industrial estates. I can also think of the versions I've seen lost to housing developments, car parks and shopping centres.

With their tangle of trunks, stems and branches, they tend to be shallow-rooted and that, plus very wet soil, means they are as likely to be horizontal as upright; their intermittent wet and dry cycles mean they are full of dead wood, which brings many mosses, fungi and, importantly, insects. That's why they are rich habitats for so many song birds. Plus the semi-rotting layers of the woodland floor act like a strangely woven cloth that slows and attenuates all of the water running down from the mountains above. They also reduce agricultural nutrient run-off and other pollutants so that by the time the water reaches the sea, it is a little clearer and cleaner.

I wanted to see this beginning and ending better to understand the role that peat plays with water in and outside its landscapes. The Afon Rheidol (*afon* is Welsh for 'river') is not a long river, running nineteen miles from start to finish, but as it lies in a very wet part of the world, it receives a lot of water in a year, 1.02 metres of it. No one knows exactly where it starts, but the waters that run off Pumlumon Fawr flow into Llyn Llygad Rheidol, the river's eye lake. From there they proceed through a thick layer of deep peat, first into a basin of blanket bog and smaller pools, then across an acidic upland grassland, rushing down a fair few waterfalls into the steep valley of sessile oak woodland. At the lead mine it widens into a very handsome river that swirls and sweeps through the agricultural lowlands, then races past the industrial estate to the carr woodland and my bend, where I take a dip, then through the town till it meets the Ystwyth and finds its home in the sea.

I asked my friend Clare if she wanted to come to find the source of my river – she's long been a collaborator in my slightly whimsical adventures and is someone whose company and views I never tire of.

We got up late, but this adventure was near to home and the weather the day before had been terrible so we were in no hurry to see how the day would pan out. We didn't get onto the mountain till late morning, but by then the sun, a tentative yellow of early winter, had turned the grassland into white gold. It shimmered and squelched underfoot as we picked our way up the side of a headwater stream and slowly through the lethal tussocks of purple moor grass. Anyone who goes hill-walking in Scotland

and Wales in winter will know of the slow progress that is walking through this sort of landscape. The mounds of purple moor grass are surprisingly high and the valleys are boggy, often hiding rivulets that you sink into.

I thought back to Richard Lindsay's plea that I should think of this landscape as mire complexes, mosaics of systems sitting on top of deep peat. The hollow in front of the Llyn Llygad Rheidol was typical shrub-dominate bog with crowberries, Magellanic bog moss and papillose bog moss, hare's tail, common cotton grass and ling heather: good bog land. Then, as the landscape swept over the mountain, it started to change and was dominated by purple moor grass, *Molinia caerulea*, turning the scene a dull dun brown when the milky sun got lost behind some cloud cover. Some tormentil, *Potentilla erecta*, popped up between the tussocks, making use of a flush of minerals, and sometimes bog myrtles and common cotton grass, but it was a pretty uniform landscape of purple moor grass.

'*Molinia*' has become shorthand for a bog that's routinely been either overgrazed or burnt too often, so seeing it prompts derision but, like all things, it has its place, particularly in Wales, Galloway, the western Highlands and the Inner Hebrides, places of shallow peat on concave slopes, where just enough peat can get hold or on other wet, clayey soils, which is why the walking can be such hard work. If there are other species among the purple moor grass, it may be doing exactly what it should in covering the ill-drained hillsides and carpeting the floors of glens and valleys. It's an incredibly important habitat for field voles and I have walked over hills covered with the sweet, swirled tunnels they make to hide in the long grass.

Where field voles appear so do their predators: short-eared owls, kestrels and hen harriers.

But when purple moor grass is the only plant present, it's most likely to be on degraded land. The over-burning and -grazing cycle can convert wet heath and blanket bog to this *Molinia* mire, particularly if it happens with artificial drainage. Which certainly happened here after the Second World War. If you burn this sort of landscape, the shrub layer is quickly gone and takes time to regrow, particularly if it is grazed after the fire. *Molinia*, with its thick layer of dead, damp leaves, can spring back unchecked. Its living buds are hidden deep within the fibrous depths of the tussocks and thus are well insulated from fire. Sheep, red deer and cattle will eat *Molinia* when it's very young, but it's certainly not their favourite. Llamas and ponies are a better bet, but for now, at least, these hills are covered with sheep. All of this area is part of the Pumlumon Project, which is slowly restoring the hydrology so that the landscape will dip back to more sphagnum mosses and peatlands shrubs, to wetter ways.

We walked up to the lake, debated going to the summit, then sat on its edge and ate our packed lunch, discussing plants, people, life directions, and argued about the best way back to the car, which was now well out of sight. I am wayward with maps, drawn to preposterous routes and flinging myself down steep slopes. Clare, who has spent months alone in these land-scapes surveying plant communities, was having none of it. 'Let's just walk directly back and see what happens.' We wound back down the side of the mountain past two pretty pools, with tiny island hummocks of sphagnum and heathers. Suddenly I sensed what that landscape must have looked like two hundred years ago and where it might return. It was almost dark by the time we got back and we'd seen no one but the farmers at the house we passed on our way up.

You often read that these mountains are empty and bleak, biological deserts with nothing but purple moor grass in summer and windswept tussocks in winter, when they should be covered with trees and absent of sheep. None of this is true. They are very much inhabited, you just need to know where to find the occupants. The landscape is not supposed to be entirely covered with trees, but wet with bog, and this is happening, slowly but surely, and the trees are happening too, in the cloughs and river gullies where they should be. More importantly, remember who asked for these lands to be drained, overgrazed or afforested. It wasn't those who call them home. It was ill-fated decisions by ministries and governments, driven by different fears post-war, of feeding future populations, of GDP, of declining empires and changing global positions. The more time I spend in wet places, the more I understand that large-scale drainage is nearly always politically motivated.

We walked back past Devil's Bridge, drove home along the A44, stopping off to have a Russian pancake at a roadside canteen. Now I had seen both ends of the river and the extensive deep peat that occurs in its headwaters. Like many of our rivers, the Rheidol can flood dramatically affecting homes and roads.

Peatlands respond to heavy rainstorms very differently from mineral upland soils. Blanket bogs are naturally flashy systems and a common misconception suggests that they should act like a sponge and soak up excess water. But a sponge only does that when it is wrung dry: a saturated sponge can't hold extra water, so a healthy wet bog with a high water table won't suddenly have extra space for more water. But a healthy bog will also have varied vegetation, shrubs, grasses and many mosses with all their hummocks, lawns and pools, which creates a rough and varied surface. Every leaf in the system has a different way of holding onto and moving water across its body. Even the relatively smooth hare's tail cotton grass has a clump-forming, fibrous base that water can cling to. The heathers with their tiny leaves don't look as if they could hold much, but smaller, rougher leaves slow water. Plants have spent millennia working on this problem and minute details on the leaf structure can have a profound effect. The time it takes for a hydrological system to release the water from peak rainfall intensity is known as the lag time, and if you are in charge of the drains, you want a landscape that has as long a lag time as possible, and a restored near-natural or natural peatland will do that.

The water will leave the peatland at some point and when that happens you want it to have gained as little particulate as possible.

whether that's DOCs (dissolved organic compounds), which give rise to the peaty-coloured water syndrome, or actual particles (POCs),because either has to be removed before it can be classed as drinking water. Healthy bogs do not turn the water bright orange, red or brown. There may be a slight tinge depending on time of year, but when the headwaters have met the tributaries it should be running clear.

Every time the Rheidol swelled over the winter I'd peer as closely as I could to see what colour it was running. It's not just my river that matters. Pumlumon Project covers the headwaters of the rivers Severn and Wye; 70 per cent of our drinking water comes from upland catchments, or the home of peat. The Peak District peatlands provide four million people with water. It's thought that globally peatland catchment areas provide 71.4 million people with drinking water. Yet only 28 per cent of these peatlands are either pristine or protected globally.

If you're in a city you may feel far from an upland, but there's a good chance that if these upland peats don't supply your water (and you'd be surprised how far water travels to get to your tap), something you ate or drank was irrigated with peat-filtered water. Clean water is a basic right for humans and peatlands alike.

16

Saturated Places

I'd spent much of the summer darting round the complexity of mire hydrology. You can't spend time on any sort of bog or peatland and not be deeply affected by its ability to hold its water or not. My phone memory was rapidly used up on videos of peat pipes or gullies. Peat pipes are underground cracks deep in the peat that run like pipes drawing water off the system so it gushes out somewhere. Along with gullies and haggs, these are a result of peatland degradation and erosion and cause water to leak from the system. Anything from a constant drip to unintentional waterfalls and streams that eddied from the edges of bogs.

When I started, I often mistook these waters, particularly if they resembled a ditch, for some remnant of the lagg, the mineral flushed, biologically diverse edge that ran around the bog where it met the surrounding geology. But when I eventually saw intact natural lagg, I realised what I had been counting as such was often a ditch, an imitation of that mineral-rich edge, taking water off the bog rather than acting as a holding pool.

Standing in the car park next to Cors Fochno after one of

many visits, in which I pestered Justin with too many questions while he looked at botanical finds (this time butterfly orchids in the far north-western corner), he invited me to follow him again, this time with the bog's hydrologist, Rob Low, to measure the dip wells, which are dotted throughout the bog.

Justin told me Rob was brilliant on the complexities of where ecology meets hydrology. 'You can ask him your questions,' he said. That might have been an invitation to quieten down. Justin is a measured man. He thinks long and hard before he answers, quite the opposite of my scattergun approach. I wondered if he thought I needed to study more and say less, but he kept inviting me out. I said yes that day to hopping over the bog, mostly because it meant leaving the boardwalk and going across the bog with someone who knew the way: I wouldn't fall into the deep and lethal cutaways.

It was a bright, hot day and we started early. Criss-crossing a bog is not swift work. The first few dip wells were near the scientific boardwalk and thus fairly easy to get to, but after that it was a case of following the GPS until you could actually see a dip well, which sits a few inches above the surface of the bog. It was tough going, that sort of walking: you have to look at each potential step to assess how solid it is and there's a great deal of leaping over pools and hidden dips.

As we crossed from one corner to the next, I saw the bog from whole new vistas. It became much easier to read where it had been cut over in the past, where huge channels and ditches had been dug in various attempts to drain it for either turf cutting or agriculture. But what was more heartening was how marvellous the central dome is. The hummock and hollows that I couldn't pick out from the boardwalk gave way to beautiful lawns, and the whole thing rose in certain places so I gained height, then flopped down again. It undulated in unexpected ways. It was immense fun to walk on. The heathers and the odd myrtle smelt delicious as I brushed over them and the peat below its thick covering of mosses had an equally satisfying resistance that eventually gave way to a spongy texture.

I was pretty redundant for doing anything useful, so l followed the men and spent my time looking at moths, bush crickets or the many shield bugs, allowing my eyes to chase bumblebees, peering at spiders and obsessing over what the peat reminded me of. I decided it felt like walking across a really huge slab of brownie, a good one. That led me to think of Neapolitan rum babas that are really best eaten while walking around in the shade of the close-packed streets of Naples. The way the saturated sponge can only just hold the syrup, and how it oozes out when you bite into it, is akin to how healthy peat holds water, giving it back under any pressure.

Our pace was relentless. Each step was unknown. I had to lift my feet high enough to clear the heather and the taller myrtles, but I often couldn't see beyond them to what the next step might hold, although it was certain it would never be solid. Because of this I couldn't linger, had to keep moving in case I might start to sink. It was exhausting and after a while I could think of nothing but sugar.

There were a lot of dip wells to get to, to take readings from, make sure they were working properly, and all the time we were chased by huge horseflies with their beautiful but violent green eyes. If you kept moving, they seemed happy enough to follow you around, but if you stayed still, they took this as an invitation to come closer, rarely landing to bite, but dancing and darting incessantly. We were curious beings to those whose livelihoods are played out on the bog, and many small strange eyes were looking to see why we had appeared.

There was no respite from the sun or, at the edge of the bog where the river Pwll Du ran, the humidity – the air was thick with it. Here, the bog's acid met a fen flush of nutrients from the river and was thick with grey-green leaves of the common reed, *Phragmites australis*, just coming into flower. I picked a few as a fly swat and tried to concentrate on what Justin and Rob were talking about. In a month or so the dark purple plumes of the reed would have silvered and the whole plant would start to

147

turn its golden autumn colours. It's handsome, but I had only ever seen the other side from the coastal path that veers away from the sea and comes round the back of the bog. I often met twitchers there: the reeds make a perfect habitat for many small birds, such as reed bunting, reed and sedge warbler. I'd not paid much attention to the Pwll Du, which looked more a ditch than a river. Which is what it is, these days: it was canalised in 1820 to drain the south side of the bog.

We parted enough reed to gaze down into it and it wasn't exactly running fast, but if it had been, it would have been draining the bog. We looked to the other side of the field, which had tell-tale signs of being very wet, with stands of rushes here and there. It hadn't always been a field: way back it had been part of the bog. Rob pointed to its far edge and said that was where the original lagg was. Canalising the river had drained the field, but only so far, and there was tension between parties and land: fields are better drained, bogs aren't.

Rob pointed out that if the far edge of the field was once the lagg you could draw an imaginary arch to the centre of the bog and work out what had been lost. He pointed above his head, and he is very tall: 'This is how much higher the bog would once have stood,' he said. It had lost so much peat. Its arching dome would have been magnificent in the landscape, visible for miles.

It was kind of hard to fathom on many different levels. The great expanse of bog that I had come to love was a fragment of what would have been a much larger bog complex that would have run up to the brackish waters of the estuary and down to the sea. Nearly all of the fields that surround Cors Fochno are a bit of the bog, turned over to grazing, and they all sit on a thick layer of peat. You wouldn't know it because the peat has sunk considerably as it degraded and is continuing to sink because a bog without water can only go in one direction.

Water is like oxygen to a peatland. It is its breath and it is only truly alive when water and peat act as one. When the peat is wet and intact it moves with its water, like lungs. The surface is not fixed and the peat moves up and down. The shift can be slight, a diurnal inhalation, as it breathes in and out over the course of a day, and seasonal, as it lets out a summer-long sigh, and its belly swells with autumn and winter rain. It's known as *mooratmung* or bog breathing. It's so regular that it can be measured remotely with a satellite and used to measure the health of peatlands. That beast again, hiding under a landscape blanket of mosses, sighing in and out, drawing in the clouds with its breath.

Peatlands are happiest when they're wet, but a resilient system can draw down its waters and perform a number of amazing tricks to weather the drier spells. The water table drops, which causes the peat to lose volume and results in the bog surface also falling, which ensures that sphagnum mosses are still in close contact with the water table. When the mosses are damp, the bog remains content. But in periods of extreme drought, of hot, dry summers, the mosses may lose water and batten down into their resting state. Then the water table will drop even lower, any pools may dry out to their mud bottoms, and the surface becomes decidedly crisp. This can look drastic but a resilient peatland can sit this out.

The Flow Country in Scotland has shown that, during a prolonged heat wave, the pools may run dry, but in the following years they can recover, even if there's no excess rain. It turns out that the drier margins of the Flow Country, which might once have been seen as less interesting than the deeper, wetter peat, are playing a vital role. In a period of prolonged drought, they collapse somewhat, compacting their peat. This could be read as the peat degrading but it is thought now that it acts like a seal around the edge of the bog against losing any more water to lateral flow.

The more bogs are studied, the more we learn that it is the whole that matters: they tell us clearly that we need all of them or nothing. It has taken a long time, with many extreme weather cycles, to perfect its ways, and the bog knows what it's doing far better than we do. On one level bog breathing is a biogeochemical response, another cog in the earth's system, but it is also its way of speaking to us about who the bog is. You learn that at the end of summer the bog sighs to expand for the first rain of autumn; in summer it takes a breath and pulls its mosses closer to its water, and the warming sun charges the mosses into photosynthesis. Even the moon plays a role: the growth of the mosses accelerates towards the new moon and slows when the moon is full. That this supposedly flat and bleak space is constantly shifting and shimmering, like a magical cloak, keeping invisible the creature below, would you not want to know the bog a little better, not just the alchemy of how it works, but who this being is?

When I think back over my summer of visits, I have such a strong sense of each peatland as an individual that I can almost smell their breath, hear their winds moan, feel their spirit. When their lands are ravaged and dug over, the spaces hold something, even if it is just a fragment of its former self. You learn to read how they once were. How they once rose over the landscape, these ancient slumbering beasts. And how they might again.

Once you understand the importance of water to peat, anything that disrupts this relationship is suspect. The obvious is removing the peat for fuel or compost, but then you learn about trees or, more importantly, afforestation. I heard about the issues of planting trees on bogs at a peatland conference at Aberystwyth University.

A vast amount of our peat is under conifer plantations. First the bogs are drained, then planted with row upon straight row of conifers, which grow, are harvested and, if the value of the harvest is considered successful, they are replanted. In some cases, the margins are not profitable or successful, particularly in light of the damage trees do to the peat below. Trees growing on peat dry it out.

It's tricky: if the trees are profitable, and many argue they are, the profit is a short-term gain against the ancient carbon lost through degraded peat. The crop could never suck up in its life-time the carbon lost through the soil. Those forests are an industrial landscape in which the vagaries of economics drive decisions. A conservationist described the many plantations that dot the Flow country as 'the sore thumb in the landscape'. I know a Welshman whose hills were once soft with blanket bog. He refers to the afforested sites as 'green slime', a description so apt of how those trees slink over their landscape.

I've heard every side of the argument from foresters, investment bankers, conservationists, but there is one stark reality: the trees are planted on peat because the value of that land is perceived as far cheaper than mineral agricultural soils. You can still pick up a bog for a song.

But there are other damages: roads, railways, windfarms, these infrastructures all disrupt the hydrology of peatlands, slicing once whole landscapes into less than the sum of their parts. Whenever you pour concrete, make footings, put something hard into some-where soft, the hard thing creates dry edges, channels oxygen into the deep, starts the process of decomposition again. Water has to find new ways, some of which are exits. The peatland that was once entire is now fragmented and vulnerable.

It is not just about peatlands in the UK. The huge blades that run wind turbines are made in part with balsa wood, famed for its lightness. Peru and Ecuador are some of the world's largest exporters of balsa wood, much of it grown in planta-tions, some cut from rainforests. One of the centres for this production is the Pastaza-Maranon river basin. The Pastaza river's headwaters start in Ecuador, slicing down through the north-western Amazon basin to the Maranon, the main stem of the Amazon river. The Pastaza-Maranon foreland basin is made of peat, ombrotrophic raised bogs and nutrient-rich swamp, the tropical version of Cors Fochno down the road from me. Professor Sue Page and Outi Lahteenoja wrote that the Pastaza-Maranon basin harbours a considerable diversity of previously undescribed peat-lands ecosystem . . . Their existence affects the habitat diversity, carbon dynamics and hydrology of the Amazonian lowlands . . . Considering the factors threatening the Amazonian lowlands, there is an urgent need to investigate and conserve these peatland ecosystems which may in the near future be among the few undisturbed tropical ombrotrophic bogs remaining in the world.

There is a boom in balsa-wood production to meet demand from the explosion of wind farms as we rush to find ways to create sustainable energy. Perhaps I seem against wind farms. I am not but we need to see the whole picture and understand where the intersections lie. Again and again, it comes back to our relationship with carbon, of the near and the far, of ancestors past and future, of timescales we find hard to fathom.

17

Restored Places

Restoring bogs, on one level, is very simple: you 'just add water'. You find the cracks, the peat pipes, map the gullies and haggs, block the gaps, re-profile the exposed edges and wait for the rain. There are many ingenious methods to dam gullies and block cracks: heather bales, coir or coconut fibre bales, peat bales, wool bales, wooden sluices, plastic sheets, stones, banks and weirs, anything to slow down the movement of water so the peat can re-wet.

On less damaged areas it is possible to use contour bunds, low mounds of peat from the bog that follow the contours of under-lying topography so that water backs up behind them. This method is so successful that after a few years it is very hard to spot where the intervention happened: the bog just looks delight-fully wet.

The bunds are made using excavators that scrape back the surface of the bog over a prescribed area to expose the catotelm peat. Then from a nearby area, more peat is removed, scraping back the surface, then digging into the catotelm and using this peat to create a mounded bund. Here, two peats are keyed together so that, with time and weight, they will form a bund. Then the surface vegetation is layered over it. For the first winter it looks like a badly stitched scar, but if rain comes and the contour is in the right place, behind it the water rises: the bog and its restorers sigh with relief. A summer or two later, to the untrained eye, it is barely visible.

I think of the mini-digger operators as invisible darners. They take the tattered moth-eaten jumper that is the living surface and work the bund as if weaving threads over a damaged area to make it as near perfect as possible.

I stood on top of Hartley Fells in the hazy mist of a December day with Kate, a senior field officer, and Andrew, a support officer with the North Pennine National Landscape team (part of the Great North Bog gang), to watch one of their operators in almost stunned silence as he re-contoured the cliff face of the hagg into a gentle slope, then picked up a piece of living peat bog and laid it down over the exposed area, adding more until the fragments made up a carpet. It was tender work from a hulking great machine. The mist settled and enveloped the rest of the landscape, so everything seemed suspended. We stood and watched for some time as man and machine wove resilience back into the landscape.

Then we went to look at the coast-to-coast path restoration: many feet on degraded bog can cause as much erosion as many sheep. Then we went on to the Nine Standard Riggs, nine giant cairns: they sit on the edge of the escarpment just north of the summit. No one knows who built them, though apparently an old Welsh document talks of a sixth-century defeat of the Saxons by the Britons on a 'toothed mountain' in North Yorkshire and includes an accurate description of them. That said, they are most likely to actually be Victorian.

Time takes its toll on the cairns. They have fallen and risen again, as many different generations have rebuilt them, hence their strange shapes. There's one story that the Romans built them to look like an approaching army of giants. Anyway, I loved walking to them as they loomed out of the mist surrounded by blanket bog. The erosion is quite bad – down to the mineral layer, the very bottom of any bog, in places – and there were exposed pools of peat across the path, so restoration is urgent.

We walked and talked about restoration, the path, the wider landscape, but I could barely keep up, striding and asking questions, so I followed, watching them take in their landscape, as they paused to discuss restoration techniques and trials, catching sight of a raptor on the wing. By the time we reached the bottom the mist had disappeared, sun and clouds raced across the swales, and we went to have lunch at a local tea room. I asked them what had drawn them to this work. Kate had fallen for bogs while studying at Bangor University. A peatland field officer is a planner and facilitator of restoration: where and how the peat will be dammed and stitched back together, when it will happen, how the machines will get there, the airlifting of mat-erials to remote sites. Considerable negotiations with landowners, estate managers, gamekeepers and farmers must take place for anything to happen.

This work, they said, is satisfying, but the cherry is the time out on the land, monitoring, checking on progress, the days when it's just them, the GPS and the wild, huge skies, the birds, the mosses taking hold, repairing the land. Kate and Andrew are rooted in the landscape, grew up in the area, tactful and thoughtful about how the land is managed for just a handful of people. Which is another of the tricky things about bogs.

Peatland restoration costs a lot of money. It is actually quite cheap, relatively speaking, for restoration work and fairly fast to repair, but it still takes billions to return our peatlands to a place where they are not emitting carbon dioxide. And I had come up there to ask the difficult question: how do you pay for all this?

I first heard about these bogs when I heard Paul Leadbitter, from the North Pennines National Landscape team, talk at the IUCN UK peatland conference in Aberystwyth in 2022. He's a charismatic Canadian, easy-going and direct: peatlands won't be restored in time without private investment, he said. The peatland code IUCN is a robust attempt to make a voluntary standard for UK peatland projects wishing to market the climate benefits of restoration. It's another form of carbon credits for private finance. And that's tricky for all sorts of reasons, because it's complicated to make sure emissions are truly cut by the businesses that are buying the credits, or to somehow put a monetary price on the future and float that on the stock market.

And yet the more time I spent on bogs the more I saw how much money was needed, more than any government was going to give. And, as Paul said to me, is any money completely ethically or morally clean? I thought a lot about this as I took the long drive back from meeting him and the team in County Durham to Wales and I thought about the peat archive, the hidden information in the layers, how our past and present behaviour with bogs informs our future.

The peatland carbon code aims to be different from just another carbon offsetting scheme, in which carbon is generated, calculated and a figure is arrived at on how much it would cost to remove it from the atmosphere and charge for it through a carbon-capturing scheme. Tree planting is the best-known form of carbon offsetting and recent history has shown that it can be a flawed model. The trees aren't planted; the trees die; the trees burn down; the trees are planted in the wrong place.

Offsetting is a financial tool used to limit or eliminate liabilities in business and banking. This is loaded language, but it is a trick to balance the books. In late capitalism, we are forced to inch forward in imperfect ways. Right now, we have to work within the existing system, while at the same time working towards dismantling it. It's complicated, the interdependence between our fraught past, our present and what lies ahead. It's as if the peat has been telling us all along. The peatland code is rigorous in its demands of what it expects. Currently the code is stuck because it is not easy to work out how to link it to the inflationary index – in short, how to profit from it. Governments are putting a lot of money behind restoration, but not nearly enough, so when the peatland community came up with the idea of creating a code for carbon credits, they took the flawed system and made it work as best it can.

The peatland code supports investment by purchasing carbon credits to help restore peatland and the services it delivers for society, including clean water, reducing flood peaks in vulnerable areas, biodiversity, habitats, recreation and well-being, while helping landowners to move towards better and more sustainable land use and management. The carbon credit pays the farmer, the estate or landowner to restore and maintain the bog and in return receives a demonstrable and accredited system to show that the buyer is committed to reducing their impact on the global climate and compensates for their UK-based emissions.

The earliest initiation of this model was in 'green washing': companies and individuals bought some trees, assumed they were planted and carried on as usual with no change for the environment. However, some people got wise to this and suggested that a truly nature-based investment market had to offer more than just compensation for what was being ruined. Also, it should be regulated: investors would have to show they were making changes to their business models to reduce emissions and comply with sustainability demands. They couldn't just buy their way out of bad practice. Standards, codes and regulations were introduced.

One such was the Science Based Targets Initiatives (SBTI), now one of the most influential climate-change bodies advising large corporations about decarbonising. Currently it promotes emissions removal (removing carbon after it has entered the atmosphere – through direct air capture, for instance). Peatland restoration leads primarily to active emissions reduction rather than removal, which leaves the bogs in a grey area for carbon credits. Some say this puts companies off investing. The STBI says it encourages companies to invest in peatland restoration, but encouraging is not quite the same as recognising, so much-needed financing is lost.

Currently the decarbonisation market stands at around $900 billion annually. There are two main markets: compliance and voluntary. At the moment it is almost all voluntary and strictly green portfolios are uncommon, but compliance markets will grow because the climate is getting hotter: every month we break some record for the hottest recorded temperatures.

On top of the current shortfall in public funding for peatland restoration, there is another issue. The majority of financing goes to initial restoration; there's a lack of funds for peatlands that are privately owned and for ongoing maintenance and monitoring once the capital works are complete. And to put that into perspective, a million acres of England's peat are owned by 124 people.* That amounts to 60 per cent of the total peat soils in England. Putting aside the debate about how and why so few people own so much of our land, the sharp reality is that, however wealthy the landowners are, few will pay for the monitoring, maintenance, reporting and independent verification that are key to successful restoration.

I don't want bogs or any of those who work so hard to restore them to have to market themselves as a solution. There's enough work ahead without that, but time is short, if not for the bogs, then for us. Paul Leadbitter, and others like him, didn't want to waste any more time so they got to work on creating a code. Now we need it to be widely adopted. Peatlands restoration is crucial to tackling climate change.

* Shrubsole, Guy, 'Who Owns our Carbon?' in *Who Owns England?*, (William Collins, 2021).

Part Three

18

All Roads Lead to Ireland

It was inevitable that I would end up in Ireland at some point on this journey. When I think of Ireland, I think of many things, of friends and food, of wild beaches and wild ponies but, of course, also of bogs. When I picture Ireland, it is saturated in the dark browns, purples and deep greens of bogs, of whistling past them on long drives, of roadside cups of tea staring across their vast spaces, of piles of cut turf and distant hills smoky with the purples of heathers.

There's 1.2 million hectares of bog, a whole sixth of the land mass, which, surprisingly, doesn't put Ireland particularly high on the bog list. A single bog complex, the western Siberian lowland, covers a million hectares making Russia the king of bogs, with Finland, Sweden and Norway following suit. These places are covered, sometimes frozen, with peat, but Ireland, because of its history of turf-cutting, seems synonymous with bogs. And because I'd spent a great deal of time in Irish bogs, I craved to go back with all I'd learnt about peat.

Clifton Bain, author of *The Peatlands of Britain and Ireland*, the guide for peat heads, had suggested to me that, other than the Flow Country in Scotland, the Atlantic raised bogs of north-west Ireland were really the bees' knees for truly good-quality bogs. I drew up a plan. I'd start in the Wicklow mountains, an area I knew was not in good heart for its upland blanket bogs, but had interesting work going on, then drive up through the heartlands of peat cutting, the Midlands, with their extensive raised bogs, and end up on the Atlantic Ocean blanket-bog complex of Roundstone Bog, with the sea lapping at its many inlets and peninsulas.

I had planned to do this with Ele, but I could see spending every day in wellington boots, knee deep in peat, was not her idea of a summer holiday and our small, very old dog agreed; she didn't want to be hauled across another bog, so I decided to go alone.

I spent the first few days in the Wicklow mountains, though this time I was more concerned with looking at upland grazing than mosses. I went back to the Sally Gap, this time to go around the small lake that Ele and I had looked down on when we went walking to see what mosses were there. I sat on a rock and ate some banana cake Ele had packed me off with, and spotted a beautiful ground beetle hunting. The hills looked parched, beautiful but desolate, over-trampled. I was starting to find these spaces difficult to be in: not enough mosses, too much leggy heather, which was turning them into hard places. I was beginning to resent dominant heather cover. It's not the fault of the heather, of course, but it's hard to see it when you know too much of it means only one thing: damaged peatlands.

I drove down, up and around through the undulating mountain forms, looking at conifer plantations, restoration work, sheep, more restoration work, cutover areas, more conifers. I saw a lot of peat pipes. They are almost mythical in the peatland community, in that everyone knows of one or many on areas they are conserving and restoring, but the how and why of a pipe is still unknown. Although they are human-induced, they are not human made. There's no clay or plastic pipe, but an underground channel that peat water flows through. They tend to appear out of the vegetation at an exposed gully, either as a small inlet from the head or from the side of a straight gully. No one is sure why they occur where they do, or what effect they have, though they are more present, it seems, on degraded blanket bog and often after fire damage. They can run for some length and, like any pipe, if they are at the right angle, they create a path for water, specifically as an escape route for water held in the catotelm, the old, compacted peat, which is doing all the carbon storage. Their effect is to lower the water table, which is not a good thing, but also to export more carbon, both dissolved organic carbon (DOC) and particulate organic carbon (POC). This affects water quality lower down the mountains. Both the Liffey and the Avonberg rivers have their sources but also their headwaters, the first and second tributaries that eventually make up larger streams that feed rivers, in these mountains, and both are important salmon and trout rivers.

Peat pipe exit points can be rather beautiful if you don't know what's happening, like magic pools with deep orange waters that spring out of the vegetation, but they are wounds, pouring out the life blood of the bogs. Also, they tend not to respond well to being blocked: they can't be dammed easily because this often exacerbates further pipe redevelopment. Something complex is happening beneath the surface that's not easily identified, but the peat pipes seem to lessen if the vegetation is restored so that surface run-off is limited and so that the gullies they spring from are also re-vegetated or re-profiled. A gully, an exposed bank of peat, is susceptible to drying out and when it does so it cracks, which seems to lead to peat pipe formation. The solution is more mosses: just as sphagnum makes an excellent dressing for our wounds, so it does for the peat. It softens and knits together, which allows other vegetation to move in. In diversity is found resilience.

After a morning of looking, I was ready to try to understand this landscape better, so I went to have tea with the ecologist Faith Wilson, who lives just above the Avoca river. She has a wonderful house with a beautiful wild garden and stunning views. I would have found it hard to talk if the views weren't what I was interested in. Faith loves the wild: nature runs right up to her front door and wraps itself around her home. In 2007 she surveyed the rare mountain flora, the obligate alpine species, those that cannot survive anywhere but the highest parts of the mountain and thus are susceptible to climate change: if the summit gets warmer there's no higher for the plants to go to keep cool. This survey was a follow-on to *The Flora of Wicklow*, a 1950s publication that mapped the flowers of these mountains. The contrast between the two was strikingly sad: we are losing habitats and species at an alarming rate.

The Wicklow mountains are dry to the east, but their west aspects are decidedly damp. It's here that the blanket bog is favoured, particularly in the hollows between the mountains. Peat cutting for fuel has a long history, but the introduction of the Great Military Road that runs to the Sally Gap meant greater and easier access for local people. The mountains run past Bray and all the way to Dublin, and many needed this fuel source. By the 1980s this had gone from hand cutting for home use to large expanses of commercial mechanised cutting, and drainage that threatened the very existence of the blanket bog. The government acquired a large area to turn into the Wicklow National Park, which houses the famous Glendalough with its ancient churches. You can see the effect of all this cutting pretty much everywhere. Anything suitable was extracted.

Like nearly every other upland area, farming here is not easy or particularly profitable. Years ago, when the famous Avoca hand-weavers, using a mill powered by the fast-flowing river Faith's home overlooks, created their rugs, blankets and later tweed (Elsa Schiaparelli was a fan), there was a market for sheep, but less so now. Faith told me, 'These mountains don't offer a living, so all the farmers here are part time. Most farmers aren't walking the mountains, they're looking after their sheep.' And for a very long time the way to keep those sheep was to burn the moors. Upland burning gives you a brief spell of new heather that the sheep will eat. It has implications for the flora, for the peat, for the atmosphere, for the water quality, but 'until farmers get paid for carbon sequestration and water quality,' said Faith, 'burning will continue.'

She decided to look at what was actually going on with the farmers, a group of people who can effect change. 'The first thing to do was to walk the hills with them and say, "Here is what good condition means ecologically. This is what it should look like. And this is what good ecological habitat can do for upland farming, so this is what we need to aim for."' They walked and talked, and she listened to what worked for them.

Like many other places, subsidies for farming are changing in Ireland. 'Farmers need to be paid for the uplands being in good condition and they need to be paid properly. So, it's important that everyone understands what they get the money for. That means diversity, mosses, all parts of the ecosystem functioning.'

The problem, however, is not grazing *per se*. Grazing and bogs have a very long history: 'the spring bite' of the bog, the first sweet tender new growth, has been documented since before the medieval period. But the grazing animals were not exclusively sheep: goats, pigs, cattle, horses, deer, even moose had their fill. The problem with sheep, particularly in large numbers, is that they don't graze in a manner that benefits the bog plants. Sheep under-graze, which allows coarse grass and heathers to dominate, and they hang about too much, compacting the soil.

'Sheep have only really been on the upland landscape since the wool boom in the eighteenth century. On top of that they are large lowland sheep that are stuck out after weaning and mostly not shepherded about the mountains. There's a few old lads who like to go walking with the sheep and the dog, but the young farmers don't have to time to do that. They've got another job to get to,' Faith explained. So, the burning is driven by what the sheep like, which is tender young heather stems. But with any short-term fix not only do you get leggier heather but, because the peat is degrading and drying out, purple moor grass and bracken spread, two things no one wants to eat.

It is almost unilaterally agreed that eventually the burning will stop, but what will be left by the time that happens? Restoration is a very different business from preservation and what is lost in between is often hard to get back.

But the blame does not rest at the hoofs of the sheep. There are too many deer, there's the issue of artificial grouse numbers for shooting, and then there's us. The Wicklow mountains, like parts of the Lake District, the Pennines and the moors around Manchester, are under enormous pressure from recreation. 'The upland-path study landed last week and there's four years' worth of work just to deal with the current level of erosion on the paths on the Wicklow Way,' Faith explained.

It was a sobering conversation. Faith does not mince her words: she is direct, deliberate, indomitable in her passion for equity for all things more-than-human, but compassionate for the culture of farming such hard hills.

We took a walk through her garden, which was thick with insects, butterflies fluttering, birds warbling, things creeping, all here because her approach was as gentle as possible, a few paths, a swing, a place to sit sheltered from the rain, a small pond to look at from the sitting room, the rest a wild riot of life.

Faith suggested I come to a talk on water quality being given that evening at the national park by Professor Mary Kelly-Quinn, a leading expert on the subject. We grabbed something to eat and wound our way back up the mountain.

Peatlands are their waters. The relationship is so intertwined, so essential, that when you think of peat you must imagine it saturated, heavy with water, cool to the touch. Dry peat is dead peat, wet peat is alive.

If your life is so steeped in water, it makes sense that you might play a part in its quality. In northern Europe, many of our rivers' sources and headwaters are found in peatlands. The way the water flows through these areas and the rate at which it does so affects the water quality further downstream. The headwaters are the most vulnerable part of the network and are 'crucial to the biodiversity and water quality further downstream,' explained Professor Kelly-Quinn. If the forests are the lungs of the world, the peatlands are the kidneys of the landscape, holding and cleaning our water. 'Wetlands are degrading or disappearing three times faster than forests. Fresh waters are among the most depleted habitats worldwide,' she added. This is partly because water consumption in developed countries is at least twice the rate of population growth.

In both the UK and Ireland, peatlands, in particular blanket bog landscapes, form major catchment areas for surface water. It's the peatlands that keep the rivers clean and full. Yet in the last thirty years there has been a doubling in levels of dissolved organic compounds (DOCs) in water. This discolours it: it's responsible for those peaty-coloured orange waters that rush off the hills and mountains. We often see those waters as almost emblematic of a place, but they're not supposed to be that colour.

Dissolved organic compounds are natural, very much part of the carbon cycle. They move from fresh water to the oceans and play a huge part in the health of our soils, but when the DOCs that make up our soils, and in this case our peat, end up in elevated levels in our waters this is not good. A DOC is tiny, a particle that can pass through 0.7 micrometres. A single micrometre is too small to see, a strand of human hair is 80 micrometres thick. It seems that most of the DOCs come from the top living layers, the acrotelm, and degraded peatlands tend to have high levels of DOCs. Since the 1980s, levels have doubled in uplands, representing a huge change to water quality in areas known for their clean, clear waters.

There are many factors as to why this is happening. There's

a relationship between atmospheric sulphur creating acid rain. Much has been done to reduce sulphur emissions for this reason, but peat has a long memory for things that fall on it and sulphur pollution is still playing out. There also seems to be a relationship between the amount of DOCs, peat pipes and gully erosions: bare peat has higher levels of water run-off with DOCs than peat that is covered with vegetation. Moss is good at slowing down discharge rate, cotton grasses, heathers and other plants less so. Moss with its intricate layers of rough leaves has more surface area and a great propensity to hold on to water; it acts like a physical filter. The relatively shiny leaves of cotton grass, heathers, various *Vaccinium* berries, *Arctostaphylos* species: bearberries, Arctic berries and bog myrtle all have leaves that water runs off more quickly. A diverse mixture of them ultimately will slow down run-off, which is particularly important in storms and periods of high rainfall that can lead to flash flooding.

Another factor is temperature; the warmer the peat then the more DOC that ends up in the head waters. This is because bare peat being dark in colour has a low albedo effect, meaning it absorbs the sun rather than reflecting it back and thus warms up. All of these things can lead to sedimentation, which, in turn, can increase the pH of the water, which over a long time affects the macro-invertebrates.

Professor Kelly-Quinn calls macro-invertebrates 'the canaries in the river'. If you want to know how clean your local river is go looking for them. She set up microscopes so we could learn the difference and we discovered there was a hierarchy: if you find mayfly, stonefly and caddis-fly in your water, that's a good sign of high water quality. Mayfly, three prongs to their tail, won't live in polluted waters. They live up to a year as nymph (larval stage) before they hatch to their brief adult lives, which happens as their name suggests. Stonefly, with two prongs to their tail, can stand a little pollution, and caddis-fly, which look like little caterpillars and often cover themselves with tiny stones, leaves and twigs to make a shelter to live in, are the toughest of the lot. If you don't have any, your water is degraded.

The Wicklow mountains are home to the Arctic, alpine or upland summer mayfly. It is one of those alpine obligates, and needs very cold, clean headwaters to thrive. It is also found in the uplands of north England and to the far north of Scotland. It is obligated to live where it does. As climate change warms our rivers, there is no higher for it to go: 20 to 30 per cent of assessed freshwater biodiversity is vulnerable or at conservation status in Ireland, and that figure is more or less the same across the globe. As Professor Kelly-Quinn emphasised, it is still unknown whether restoration efforts can take damaged habitats back to a pristine condition. We don't know if certain species are lost or whether they can be returned.

I found myself thinking of that as I trudged over restoration sites. Peat has a remarkable ability to heal an open wound; sphagnum mosses, particularly those of the hollows and pools, can make good progress. Their neon greens are such a vibrant delight among the felled bleached limbs of plantation Sitka spruces or in cutover ditches, but peatland restoration is still very young. The oldest restoration projects started in the 1980s on peatlands that are thousands of years old.

Once the moss layer is restored, many of the other ecosystem players seem to move back, but little is understood about the minor species and whether in fact they can be described as minor: they may not appear so frequently but they may be important in the ecosystem's ability to be resilient. There is so much to learn about this world, the fungal communities, the microbes that live in the top layer, even the mosses and how they will respond to changing weather patterns.

The sticky truth is that climate change will affect peatlands to their very core. It already seems likely that temperate peatlands will move further north as permafrost thaws. Mosses are often the first plants to move in after glaciers melt. New peatlands sound like a good thing, but it will take them a long while, centuries perhaps, to come to a place of resilience.

Tropical peatlands are just as vulnerable, perhaps more so. It seems inevitable that, due to fires, droughts and land-use changes – palm oil plantations sit on tropical peat – tropical peatlands will release much more carbon in the near future, affecting wetland sites and watercourses.

I left the talk as fired up as the sunset I drove into, winding my way higher and higher into the mountain to whistle down it into the Midlands, whispering, 'Bogs matter,' to the creeping night. I felt validated by the good conversation with Faith and the room full of concerned citizens who had come to hear the talk. The landscape I left is in a very fragile state but there's a sea-change in attitudes, recognition, interest, understanding: the peat is revealing itself in our stories as a life force. We're coming back to our ancestors' understanding that these liminal spaces, these deep places, are truly special.

The Midlands

My meeting with Douglas MacMillan was quite by chance. Part of my Irish road trip had included a delightful detour to the Carlow Garden Festival to do a talk, and because my brain was mostly occupied with peat, I asked Eileen, the festival co-ordinator, if she knew of any bog people. That was how I came to be driving through sheeting rain and considerable wind with Doug to visit some bogs. When I think of how coincidental this beginning was – a friend of a friend type of thing – and how fulfilling the next five hours would be, I marvel: were the bog gods at play?

What perhaps was more remarkable was that Doug had brought his entire family. His mum and dad, his wife and delightful children were all coming in the pouring rain to look at the bogs too (I think in retrospect several of them had been bribed with the promise of rhubarb pie). When I acted a little surprised that they might be willing join in, he brushed it off: his work was seven days a week, it was a chance for them all to be together and a nice day out (in the rain). It turned out later that it was his wife's birthday.

The bog gods looked kindly on us because although the road to Donie and Colette Reegan's farm in County Offaly was littered with fallen trees, blown down by the wind, by the time we were up on the bog the clouds were lifting and the day would end in glorious sunshine.

Doug started the Green Restoration Ireland Cooperative with his friends and wife in 2019 as a proactive solution to restoring biodiversity and to fight climate change, working with farmers and communities in whatever way was most practical. Doug wants to get things done, which means looking at everything on the farm, not just whether it sits on peat, but the hedgerows, woodlands, ditches, fields, the whole shebang. This is crucial because even if the peat is just a slice of the farm, peat grassland makes up a third of the pasture Donie and Colette use to raise suckler cows and their offspring; the way the whole farm is managed will affect that section. And in turn how that peat fares will affect nearby watercourses, biodiversity and the overall carbon footprint of the farm.

You can enact any number of other agro-ecological, environmentally friendly approaches, plant up woodlands, use no fertiliser, sow multispecies swards in your pasture, mob graze, but if your peat is degrading and your fields are physically dropping in height year by year as the peat decomposes, the rest will never balance out the carbon dioxide emitted by that loss. Peat trumps everything and because of that it matters to see it holistically integrated into the whole farm system.

Doug had already filled me in on a number of innovative approaches to putting peat at the heart of the work as we drove through the heartland of Irish farming. He pointed out how much of what you might assume was just rolling green pasture in the Midlands is actually drained peatlands. It was once a vast complex of raised bogs that sat on a depression left as the glaciers melted around twelve thousand years ago. It's classic raised-bog territory. The depression turned into small lakes filled with melt- and rainwater, but the conditions quickly turned anaerobic: any plant material that fell partially decomposed and a thick layer of peat began to fill in and rise to the surface of the lake. This was ideal for sedges to grow on and the lake became a fen, fed by the calcium-rich groundwater that ran into lakes from the surrounding areas. The sedges thrived and the peat formed a thicker layer. Eventually the peat was too thick for the sedges' roots to penetrate to get to the mineral-rich waters below so the plants died. The only source of minerals was now the rainwater, and in these increasingly poor conditions the only plants that could survive were the acid-loving sphagnum mosses, cotton grasses and the like. The fens had become bogs.

Many of the raised bogs aren't visible because they are under grass. Centuries of fuel cutting has meant that much of the sphagnum peat layers have gone and the fields are sitting on the fen peat layers, which are rich enough in calcium, making it good pasture for cows. But the little peat left is still degrading and some of those fen peat fields are now down to their mineral layer, the last vestige of peat before you hit marl and granite bedrock.

I'd got very good at spotting peatlands at a glance, even very degraded ones, but that landscape baffled me. Doug pointed out that a certain sort of pioneer woodland of birch, alder and willow at the edges of fields was a good indicator there was peat below. Likewise a very straight but undulating road with fields much lower at either side was a sure sign you were driving over peat. The road was raised because it was sitting on top of the old bog, and the fields' lower levels were a sign of how much peat had been lost through cutting, decomposition and erosion. 'People think the stones are rising out of their fields, when actually it's just huge amounts of peat shrinkage,' Doug said. Once the peat is drained and exposed to air, it rapidly breaks down and is lost to rain and wind, releasing carbon dioxide to the atmosphere and dissolved organic carbon to the rivers.

Once one of these roads had been pointed out, I started to see them everywhere, and those birch-dominated young woodlands.

Donie and Colette's farm doesn't just sit on peat grassland: it butts up to a raised bog, which is communally owned by a group of surrounding farms, each farm with turbary rights to cut a section of bog for fuel. Doug's project has twenty-three farmers signed up for its Farm Carbon Initiative, mostly beef farms, big and smaller ones, like Donie's: his herd is twenty-five or so suckler cows, as well as two organic dairy farms with larger herds. Each farm has some peat grassland and is in a catchment area for nearby rivers. Some, like Donie's, have sections of intact raised or blanket bog.

But before we set off to see the bog, Colette ushered us into her dining room for mountains of scones, thick cream and jam with tea – such warm hospitality that I was bowled over. I'd only come to see their bog! But I learnt I was not alone: the *Irish Times* was there a few weeks ago. The word was getting out. Their farm is doing something truly innovative, where others are selling up (or, more accurately, renting) to potential wind farms, Donie and Colette are heading to the least visited corner of their farm, the bog, to find a solution. Like all farmers, they love their land. They have grandchildren and want to leave it in the best of health for whoever comes next.

Doug and the Regans are not re-wetting the peat. Re-wetting farmed peatland is highly controversial and was recently removed from European nature restoration laws. Peatland drains are dammed up and the land is re-wetted. A field can often look flooded, especially after heavy rains, and that's a hard sell to a cattle farmer. One of Donie's previous jobs was as an agricultural adviser and he spent much of the 1970s working on land-drainage schemes, so he understands farmers' hesitancy about losing reclaimed land. It's a story you hear over and over again: people's forebears spent lifetimes digging in drains; they were being asked to feed hungry, growing populations.

Instead of re-wetting they are raising the water table by partially re-wetting. You can't tell immediately as there's no surface water, but below the surface the water table is inched up, which better protects the peat from degradation, but still allows for farmers to graze their animals. Much of this work comes out of the Netherlands, where research has shown it is possible to have a higher water table and a sward that can be grazed, not all year round, for sure, but the notion of any field being grazed year-round without severe degradation, whether it's on peat or not, is largely fiction. This isn't full restoration of the peatlands: these fields will never again become active mires, in the sense of building peat, but they can significantly reduce their emissions, protect the existing peat and water catchment, and provide an additional income stream for farmers. While the debate for carbon credits of peatlands continues, this offers a feasible alternative to farmers.

We walk across the land to look at the peat grassland, which is predictably lower than the surrounding landscape. Once we eventually get onto the raised bog it is a climb up, showing starkly how much soil has been lost to harvesting, peat shrinkage and degradation.

Doug explained that peat grassland emits up to ten times more carbon dioxide than a bog because the water table on peat grasslands is so low, due to drainage. The higher the water table, the less oxygen is available, which has a substantial effect on how much carbon dioxide is released. But if you disturb that water table with drainage so that the bog can become agricultural land, carbon-dioxide emissions will go through the roof as you trigger the mineralisation process. It sounds quite nice, no? Releasing minerals into the soil? But the process involves microbes doing recycling work and they release the carbon dioxide. After that, if there's fertilisation involved, that can speed up the degradation even further as it stimulates bacteria which break down the peat.

Raising the water table is a proven method of reducing greenhouse-gas emissions, but raising a water table to its near-natural condition, around ten centimetres below the surface, is incompatible with anything besides summer grazing. So, you cannot just raise the water table because that would take peatlands out of agricultural use for dairy (and most other conventional crops and livestock). Unless the farmer has developed a steady and stable income, you are robbing them of their livelihood and your coffee of milk. To anyone muttering about oat milk, it's not that simple: current oat production requires ploughing and nitrogen . . .

There has to be a middle ground that takes in the needs of the farmer and the preservation of peat. Doug is offering a gentle transition into restoration. If the water table is 100 centimetres or more below the field surface, they'll block the drains so it is raised to 40 centimetres. A pristine bog will have a raised water table that sits almost on the surface of the bog and is no lower than five centimetres year-round; 40 centimetres is a long way from that, but it makes a difference to the amount of emission, slow peat degradation, and it doesn't affect grazing. If the field becomes over-saturated with water, after heavy rains, for instance, the drains can be temporarily unblocked. The farmer decides how much they want to raise the water table on their land. This farmer-led solution is a long way off full restoration, but it's a start.

Raised water tables offer opportunities for food growing, which was where the rhubarb pie came in. Growing crops on wet or re-wetted peatlands is known as paludiculture and is not new: Indigenous communities around the world have been using it as a semi-pastoral technique for food production for thousands of years. In tropical peatlands, including the Congo basin, Malaysia and Peru, various methods of hunting, fishing and gathering take place on peat, much as our ancestors once did. But, apart from traditional reed harvesting for thatch and summer grazing of wet meadows, paludiculture is new to European peatlands that are currently drained for agricultural purposes. Is it possible to re-wet them and still produce food?

Doug isn't trying to make intact bogs productive, but to work with the peat that remains under grass and in cutover bogs. Paludiculture is a key tool to bridge the gap between conservation and agriculture with the right crops that can cope with high water tables. It is a buffer zone between more conventional agricultural practices and peatlands. Perhaps as importantly, it can lower the cost of re-wetting and create an income stream. It also answers Doug's most asked question: 'What can you do with wet peat?'

Doug and Donie's have-a-go attitude is much suited to the experimental nature of this new form of paludiculture. They've created a number of small plots that allow them to trial different wetlands species and vegetable cultivars known to tolerate some level of waterlogging. Blueberries and cranberries, both bog-species, are an obvious choice; mint and watercress make sense as do rhubarb and celery, which thrive in damp conditions. I was surprised to find cabbage, broccoli and cauliflower, thirsty vegetables, for sure, but fond of damp feet? The broccoli wasn't faring so well, but the cabbages were impressive. There were also true wetland plants, like bulrushes: their dense chocolate-brown seed heads are comprised of fluff, a viable alternative to feather down in padded jackets. Not only that: the stalks can be chopped, dried and compressed into a mould-resistant, light, durable, highly insulating building panel: a genuinely exciting alternative to expanded polystyrene, which is famed for having a potentially unlimited lifespan. That's great if it stays in a building, but not if it ends up in landfill.

It doesn't stop there. Doug, Donie and forester Bernard Carey have created trial plots for wetland trees, including Dawn redwood, swamp cypress, American sweetgum, alder, black poplar and willow. About forty per cent of all forestry in Ireland is on drained peatlands (this accounts for 20 per cent of peatlands), Doug explained. You can't just re-wet forested peatlands with trees growing on them because that would kill the trees. Forestry on peatlands is controversial. Without doubt, it further degrades the peat, yet the debate rumbles on as to whether the carbon taken up in the trees outweighs the carbon lost through peat degradation. It doesn't, but it's a tricky equation: in the short-term trees can capture more carbon than the mosses and other bog plants can sequester in the same period. Trees just grow much quicker than mosses and cotton grasses, but long-term afforested peatlands lose more carbon than the tree can sequester in its lifetime.

On top of that there is the end product of those trees and how carbon is stored in them. Peatland forests can be of fairly poor quality, so those trees are not used in housing or anything that might stand for some time, but as chipboard, biomass fuel, compressed logs, cheap wood: all states in which the carbon has a short stay before the product degrades.

Currently, in the UK you are not allowed new forests on deep peatlands that have a depth of 50 centimetres; on shallow peats, between ten and 40 centimetres, replanting is allowed. The debate of trees versus peat is heated and contested. The foresters believe passionately in their trees for carbon sequestration, but even they would be the first to say that not all forests are equal. Trees grow better timber that will store carbon for longer when planted off bogs, but the trees-versus-bog debate throws two much-needed climate solutions against each other and currently compromises both.

But what if, asks Doug, there was another way, one in which the peat is not drained but was replanted with trees that grow in wetland conditions? Wetland forestry could be a real possibility for degraded peat, providing an income from the forested crop and carbon sequestration on the re-wetted peatland. Doug is making it one of his many missions to find out if this is a possibility. His enthusiasm and drive are infectious, Donie is on board, and so, towards the end of the tour, was I.

My travels had shown me plenty of places where the notion

of getting degraded, particularly milled peat sites back to a functioning bog was just too far-fetched in any timescale to mitigate climate change. These little plots, the wildlife ponds around them, the ditches returning to wetlands have created a mosaic landscape that was thriving with life, huge dragonflies and speedy common darters, bees, butterflies, bird of prey, ducks, warblers: life was pouring back in. It is just a dip of a toe into the raised waters of peat, but there's nothing like seeing something growing.

The plots are small and it is still early days, with a lot of learning ahead, but they offer a glimmer of hope. Wetter farming could be the future of lowland agricultural peat soils in central Ireland, the fens of Norfolk, or the great areas of drained land of Bedfordshire, greater Cambridgeshire, Suffolk and the Mosses of Manchester. The truth is that much of this land is currently steadily declining in depth and in yields as the last layers of its peat are turning to dust. Land that would cry out, if it could, to be re-wetted. Farming on lowland peat is becoming more complicated as weather patterns change with the climate crisis: wetter winters, drier summers, wet summers, dry winters. It will be harder to turn a profit on such soils. But a raised water table could provide a very different picture for everyone, including the last vestige of the bogs and fens beneath.

Before we left, we went up to see Donie and Colette's bog, the belly of the beast that still lay intact to the west of the land. While Doug and his daughter probed the soil to find out how deep the peat was – an impressive eight metres – his son ran over the heathered landscape looking for bog asphodels. Donie showed me his lock spit: the demarcation on the bog cut out centuries ago to identify each farm's section for cutting fuel. These lines are still visible, criss-crossing the bog. Almost no one cuts turf, these days – as Donie said, 'It's too much work.' He hopes their efforts to re-wet their land below the bog will entice other farmers to do the same and that in time they can restore this relic of what was once a mighty bog that covered the landscape.

It was lunchtime and I'd packed a bag empty of food. I needn't have worried: Colette had us return to her dining room where she'd laid on a huge Sunday lunch, lasagne, more tea, and rhubarb pie, which was everything Doug's son had been raving about all morning. Irish hospitality goes as deep as its peat.

Our day wasn't finished: we had one more farm to go to in County Offaly. This one butts right up to Bord Na Mona-owned land. Bord Na Mona is the Irish peat board and was founded as a state-owned (now semi-state-owned) company with statutory responsibilities to produce fuel from Irish bogs. By the 1960s, it had another role in creating a market for Midlands peat outside Ireland, as a fuel but also as a horti-cultural product in the form of compost. Bord Na Mona is synonymous with peat cutting in Ireland, and if you're in the UK, you most likely know it as a stamp on a bag of potting compost for the garden.

In June 2020 Bord Na Mona stopped harvesting peat and is now in the business of Irish-bog rehabilitation. This is not without its controversies: a lot of the cutover peat is being re-wetted so fast that the land looks flooded and this is doing Doug no favours in persuading the farmers to come on board, which is why the demonstration farms are so valuable.

The second farm is owned by part-time farmer Adrian Egan, who was away for the day so we explored alone. We walked down to the bog along a dappled lane thick with a resplendent hedgerow in full summer glory. On the far side is afforested land full of Sitka spruce, then the flat plane of bog. Over the past couple of years, Donie and Adrian have blocked the drains and the land has re-wetted considerably. The blocked drains bowed under with the weight of the water and the pools behind them are starting to teem with life – we saw plenty of frogs.

This was not pristine bog by any means yet it was still full of life: dragonflies, amphibians, birds. There's something so diamet-rically opposite to all the dark folklore of these places when you're actually on them. They are places of fascination, of reflection, of endless interest. There was a large bog pine, blackened and preserved by the peat, at the depth of cutover, which was more than a metre. That tree could have stood for a thousand years but now it lay as a resting spot so that anyone could sit and peer into the pools and watch frogs reclaim the space. Bogs, given the chance, are ready to jump back into life, eager to cover their wounds and get on again with being.

Doug showed me several plots sown with multispecies sward so that I could see what kinds of mixes made suitable grazing if a pasture is re-wetted to just below the surface – essentially wetland grazing. If the re-wetting of pastures is to happen at scale, farmers should stick to what they know best, namely raising cattle. Two problems need to be addressed in order to solve this: replacing nitrates which are no longer released from the degrading peat; and providing a thick enough sward that stops livestock from sinking into the peat made soft from re-wetting. There's great hope for the strawberry clover, *Trifolium fragiferum*, a species that is gaining wide recognition around the world, particularly in North America and Australia, for its use as a perennial grassland species that is tolerant of waterlogged conditions while able to withstand periods of drought. That would make it invaluable to re-wetted grassland peat.

It's actually a species native to Ireland and the UK, a legume, which means it can fix its own nitrogen from the atmosphere due to its relationship with soil bacteria that live in its root nodules. It releases the nitrogen back into the soil, making it available for other plants, which, with its waterlogging tolerance, makes a champion for perennial swards: as we know, peat is notoriously low in nutrients. We hunted for signs of the clover among the mix, Doug thrilled with every plant that was surviving.

As interesting as these plots were, I couldn't help but be drawn to the other side. The land was split by a small railway, one side belonging to Adrian Egan, the other to Bord Na Mona. The railway is one of many thousands of miles of bog trains, narrow-gauge tracks that once took the millions of tonnes of extracted peat to markets elsewhere. It is said that from the 1970s onwards, around five million tonnes of peat were moved annually by those trains. It's a staggering figure, but in terms of the landscape's height, most of the Midlands was once vastly above our heads.

Both sides had been considerably cut over. The far side was dominated by heather, and in the distance I saw what I was beginning to recognise as the typical regenerated woodland of birch and willow that grows on dried-out peat. On Adrian Egan's side there was a huge hagg where peat harvesting had stopped, its exposed side like a stratigraphic map of the past, a layer cake of centuries of knowledge. The top acrotelm ran down from light brown to fudge colour, a sure sign it was degrading to the wind; the catotelm was more fudgy, dark and richer-looking but with many crags and pipes, so at various points the water poured off the upper bog into Adrian's pools. If it had been a designed water feature you might have said it was beautiful in a strange sort of way, but it was a stark example of what happens to degraded peat: it can't hold on to water and whole sides of the hagg were collapsing.

It was a sobering sight. Peat cutting for fuel never became a big industry in the UK because of our coal reserves, so we don't see an extracted, milled peatland landscape often in the UK, although there are sites dotted all over the country. Some are still cutting peat commercially for horticultural composts.

On Cors Fochno, cutting for fuel stopped in the mid-1950s, which is why the middle is so intact. Land drainage for the fields around it, for sure, but extraction less so. In Scotland there was a much bigger tradition of peat cutting for fuel and for whisky, particularly on the islands and for horticultural use, and there are active licensed sites for milled peat dotted across the UK. But this landscape of wounded peat is not something we see so much. Burnt, polluted, overgrazed, or all three, yes, but not this.

But there were kittens to see at the farmhouse, a greater

attraction even than the frogs, so we went back to admire them, sunning themselves around their mother. I had hours of driving ahead to get to where I was staying, so I left Doug trying to negotiate with his daughter over how many kittens were too many to adopt, and I hit the road.

19

Other Places

I was leaving the heart of the country to drive west, right out to the edge. Since I'd got to Ireland, everyone had a bog they thought I should see, a really good, pristine bog that no one else knew about, that was magical and truly the essence of a bog. And each offer sounded more tempting than the last, a bog owned by a Bulgarian prince who'd forbidden anyone to cut it, a fragment high up in the mountains that no one knew about, down a track too remote to be commercial, on the edge of a brother's friend's neighbour's land, on an uninhabited island off the coast. In the end, I ignored everyone and headed to Connemara to Roundstone Bog.

Connemara is famous for having some of the best examples of Atlantic raised bogs, but I was travelling back to make amends. I'd driven right across the country to go to Roundstone once before, when I was heartbroken and no one knew what to do with me. My friend Andrew, at a loss to deal with any more tears, had sent me to the edge of the world to meet a man called Ronnie in a tiny cottage on a white beach. Ronnie and I drank an entire bottle of 1920s whiskey, and with each measure he told me exactly why my heartache would never go if I stayed in that relationship. I left, exceedingly hung-over, the next day and drove back across the bog. I don't remember much of the trip, but I do remember the bog. Seared in my memory is how good it felt to cry somewhere so soft and wet, the bog mirroring my emotions, giving space and sky to them. When you're that kind of sad a bog's emptiness is quite lovely. There's no shame in howling on a bog when you feel miserable. But you can't linger too long either.

So, I decided to return, driving up and up the map till I hit the Atlantic coast. I stopped at Maam valley under the guise of needing fuel, but really desperate for a pee. I couldn't figure out why there were so many people there on a Monday, until it dawned on me that it was an Irish public holiday. If the queue to the one dismal Portaloo wasn't bad enough, the smell was.

You don't have to head to Roundstone to be deep in bog territory: everywhere in Connemara, if it isn't granite, is bog. Which means there's not so many bushes to pee behind, but I found a scrub of willow growing out of a ditch on the other side of the road and saw a path worn enough to suggest I wasn't the first with this idea. As I squatted to pee, hidden, I hoped, by the willow, I started to sink. I looked around: a rich carpet of sphagnum moss, a little bog myrtle, some heathers and a smattering of bog asphodel, a few of which were having one last fling at flowering. I took this to be a good sign for my return and got swiftly back on the road to find my bog.

Roundstone is one of the prettiest villages you can imagine. It sits on the water's edge with mountains just behind it, the folded coastline all sea-tangled with wrack and granite rocks. Between the mountains and the sea is the bog, a large, encircling flat blanket bog that makes up part of the Connemara bog complex. Roundstone Bog has been spared from forestry and commercial turf cutting, thus leaving it impressively intact.

Now, at this low altitude you might expect these bogs to be

raised because blanket bogs are famously of high places, of mountains and upland hills. But here, on the wettest side of Ireland, where the rain rarely ceases, particularly in winter, you can find low-lying blanket bog, often referred to as Atlantic blanket bog.

Like everywhere else in Ireland, much has been cut over for fuel, particularly the edges and along the sides of the famous bog road (it's haunted), but the heart of Roundstone Bog beats strongly. There is deep peat to be found here among the rocks. The whole bog lies on very old bedrock made up of volcanic lava that bubbled up and out of the earth, then metamorphosed through pressure and heat into basalt sometime in the Ordovician period (470 million years ago). A period when the very first land plants were taking hold, the earliest ancestors of the sphagnum mosses that now dominate this landscape.

Of course, the bog wasn't around then. Before the bog there were marshes, woodlands, lakes and fens. This mosaic of other landscapes is still visible across the Connemara bog complex. There are the familiar hummocks and hollows of the blanket bogs and vast lawns between; there are many bog pools, flushes, transitions and quaking mires, freshwater marshes and lake-shores, lakes and river systems and, where the granite rises and the bog can't stay wet, dry heathland appears. This gives the bog a unique flora. Where the relic-base-rich landscape of fen persists, black bog rush, *Schoenus nigricans*, appears and becomes a key indicator plant of this landscape, dotted between the more familiar purple moor grass, common cotton grass, cross-leaved heath and deer grass. Beneath these are vast stands of bog asphodels, white beak-sedges and many sphagnum species. Carnivorous sundews are so common that in certain areas the bog sparkles with their jewelled leaves, ready to dine on the smallest insects that flit by.

Famously, at least in botany circles, the dry heath that runs up between rock knolls and into the mountains grows St Dabeoc's heath, *Daboecia cantabrica*, and even more obscure, Mackay's heath, *Erica mackaiana* and Dorset heath, *Erica ciliaris*. Though as writer and cartographer Tim Robinson, capturer of Connemara magic, points out in his essay 'Botany – A Roundstone View' to the untrained eye all three look exactly alike. After reading this essay while nursing a pint in a local pub I briefly thought about dedicating the rest of my trip to finding all three. But the folly of such botanical rambles would have meant missing out on what I'd come for: all of the water.

The bog complex is famous for its many bog pools, ponds and lakes. Robinson describes them as a 'bewildering topography of lakes lost in bogs'. You could see the largest of these from the bog road, but many more only appear as you pick your way carefully across the landscape and you find yourself in a place of more water than earth. If you can find an outcropping to climb, more often than not a pattern arises from all this water. There's a system to these pools, and different types of mires create different patterns. There's a science to the patterns that are formed in part by the surface of the peat creating waves as it grows and is weighed down by all its water.

The easiest way to grasp this is to think of the setting point of jam. When you want to know if your jam is set, you take a tiny blob of the molten liquid, set it on a cold plate, wait a beat, then push your finger into it to test its viscosity. If it's ready, it wrinkles, creating a set of wave formations. The peat is doing the same thing, not driven by sugar and heat but by the compression and tension of the acrotelm (the living layer), the shape of the slope the peat is growing on, and then a relationship between the wave produced and its amplitude creating movement – the skin wrinkles with age just like ours. Behind these wrinkles hollows form that turn into pools that eventually become ponds. They are often too deep for mosses to grow over but, perhaps more importantly, once they enlarge too wide, mosses won't take hold on windy water.

The largest of these pools become dystrophic. With the same etymology as dystrophy of muscles, its meaning is poor nutrition, and the pools are coloured a deep, peaty brown because of the high levels of humic matter and acids in them. This makes them so eerily clear that you can peer right to the bottom. To call them not productive is loaded: they may not be rich in nutrients, but that doesn't mean they are without life. Characteristic plankton, zoobenthos (tiny insects and crustaceans that live on the bottom layer of the water), aquatic plants and some fish communities love this acidic, peat-infused water. They are among the least disturbed aquatic assemblages.

Where the pools pass to lakes, they are known as oligotrophic, again nutrient-poor water with very low productivity, which results again in very clear, deep waters. There are many of these lakes or loughs, which have historically been used for fishing and shooting, of brown trout and Greenland geese. These bodies of water, particularly the small pools, are often known as the moor or bog eye. Caught on a bright day of brilliant blue sky, their often elliptical shape appears as the bog's blue eyes peering back at you.

The hollow-loving *Sphagnum cuspidatum* and the wonderfully named cow-horn bog moss, *Sphagnum auriculatum,* will grow in the smaller pools. In the large ponds and lakes, you find bog beans taking hold and along the edges water lobelia, pipewort, shoreweed and some waterlilies if the edges meet a base-rich moment. Occasionally, the very rare slender naiad (named after the water nymph) is found, as is the lesser bladderwort.

I've always been fascinated by dark pools of water. As a child I had a hidden pool on the bend of my local stream that you could only get to either by tiptoeing around lethal, leg-smashing deer traps that had been rusting in the wood since the 1960s, or by wading upstream. I spent a whole summer when I was ten or eleven, going to swim alone in this pool suffused by golden dappled light and full of big brown trout. It wasn't a large pool and the trout were essentially trapped in it till the higher waters of autumn came. Initially they'd balked at my company, but we adapted to each other and would swim round in unison. The trout were there because a neighbour had tried to stock his section of river for fishing and he'd tell my father about his 'lost' fish at every opportunity. I'd stay silent, knowing they were growing fat in their secret lair.

I'd think of these fish and that silted, soft-bottomed pool as I peered in and wonder if I should take a dip, but something about those bog pools terrified me. Perhaps because I'd read too much about the interment of bog bodies: their graves would have been pools like these, but time has filled them in and buried them deeper.

My friend Fionnula told me of jumping into a particularly enticing deep bog pool. Fionnula is one of the strongest, most fearless swimmers I know. She grew up on the coast of Donegal, with a fisherman for a father and a wild expanse of bog loughs to explore, so she's not someone to jump without thought into deep waters. She said the minute she went under she realised her mistake and opened her eyes to discover she couldn't tell in that peat-infused water which way was up; no light was penetrating through to guide her back. As she tumbled round, she had to trust her lungs to guide her back, knowing that they were infused with enough oxygen and, if she relaxed, would naturally draw her body upwards. She stopped kicking and began to rise. This is the abiding image I have of this story; her strong, capable body bent over, foetal-like, suspended in a soup of peat, concentrating all of herself into the lightness of her lungs to reach the sun again. A birthing of sorts.

Seamus Heaney's first collection of prose, *Preoccupations*, is, in part, a vivid account of his early life on his father's farm in rural Northern Ireland. It is also about the beginning of his lifelong obsession with bogs:

> I believe my betrothal happened one summer evening, thirty years ago, when another boy and myself stripped to the white country skin and bathed in a moss-hole, treading the liver-thick mud, unsettling a smoky muck off the bottom and coming out

smeared and weedy and darkened. We dressed again and went home in our wet clothes, smelling of the ground and the standing pool, somehow initiated.*

I sat on the edge of the pool in Roundstone debating whether I should take the plunge. There was no one around to see me so I could strip and truly taste the bog, but I couldn't quite bring myself to do it alone on the bog. I felt spooked by those waters.

*   *   *

I knew of a lay-by halfway along the Roundstone Bog road that would be fine for one night at least. It is said that that road is haunted, that a local brother and sister who ran the Halfway House, near the bog, would regularly rob and murder travellers, then dump their bodies in those lakes, that those lost souls are condemned to wander the road trying to get away. In daylight, it is a straight enough road with miles of good view of the soft, undulating cover of the bog and the distant bens beyond, but by dusk and then dark, it is easy to see where these stories come from.

There's something deeply unsettling about knowing the single slice of road is the only solid ground to cross. I had to steel myself a little even to imagine sleeping beside it. I need not have worried: it was the height of summer and I wasn't the only one with romantic notions of a free night on the side of the bog: two campervans were already settled on a lay-by nestled into a rise of granite rock. It was late enough for me to pull in and go straight to sleep to rise early for the dawn and the call of the waters.

*   *   *

* Heaney, Seamus, *Preoccupations: Selected Prose 1967–1978*, (Faber, 1984).

As the other campers slept, I tiptoed past their vans, then climbed up and over a granite outcropping to greet the bog in morning light, each pool and pond shimmering a steely blue-grey to reflect the clouded sky. I picked my way off the rock outcropping to wobble across lawns of sphagnum mosses. Until that moment I had seen only smaller versions at Cors Fochno, but here they expanded like a lawn in enticing yellow-greens. But unlike a grass lawn, they quaked and rippled with any sort of weight placed on them and, in places, they sank to quite some depth.

Before I started my bog adventures my father insisted that I inherit his wading staff for fishing. It is a wooden six-foot pole with a huge loop of string that you could sling over your shoulder to allow you to measure the depth of what you are wading into. I thought it was a little bit over the top, but I promised my mother I would take it with me, particularly if I was going alone onto a bog. I gingerly prodded the ground ahead and the whole pole seamlessly vanished, with me teetering behind trying to keep my balance. I looked for a different route and found it was possible, as long as I didn't linger on anything flat, jumping either to the grasses or anything remotely hummock like.

The neon yellow-green of the distant view was much more varied close up. There were soft pink hummocks of moss, and bright orange ones; greens slowly melted into lighter browns; sundews, greater and rounded, sparkled on top of hummocks, but also on peat haggs and old cutaways nearer the road.

Making my way from one lawn to another, I glimpsed something large among the grasses. I bent down tentatively to see if my weight would be supported by the hummock I was wobbling on. There at my feet, large watchful eyes looked back at me: a cricket. Initially I thought it must be a bog bush cricket, merely because it was the only cricket I knew about, Justin having introduced me to one on Cors Fochno, but this one looked different, more vivid green, with brilliant vivid red stripes to the hind legs.

Like many true naturalists Justin's eye for detail is exacting, a little intimidating even, but that is how he's able to spot differences. He'd never mentioned red stripes on the bog bush cricket, so I stayed as still as I could: he had mentioned that all crickets are very good at noticing you and will drop down and hide so well that you can never find them again. I pulled out my phone and searched for my bog bush cricket, hoping this one gesture wouldn't scare her away. I was looking at something very different. The large marsh grasshopper is the biggest of all grasshoppers at 36 millimetres long, but is so rare in the UK that it is restricted to just two sites in the south. At Roundstone, I read, the species is doing very well. They favour quaking bogs rich in sphagnum and the female lays her eggs at the base of grassy tussocks, like the one I was standing on. We eyeballed each other a little longer. I wanted to take a picture, but in the second I let our eyes part, she did exactly as Justin predicted and disappeared.

I carefully stood up, aware that my weight was leaving a lasting impression in the beautiful carpet and moved on. All through the day I heard the grasshoppers sing. They have a very particular set of clicks that come in threes, a pause between each one and then a long pause before the grasshopper starts again.

One thing you read over and over again about bogs is that they are silent spaces, upholding the idea that they are empty of all but the wind, but if you go carefully and quietly, there's plenty of song. It's not the easy melodies of the woods or scrubs: it's more electronic, with the synth tones of the winds as backdrop, but it's a song for sure. I guess it's another of the bog's secrets: only there for those who seek it.

I spent the day hopping across the bog, marvelling at its vast lawns. They often form on the wettest part of the bog and are made up mostly of mosses, often dominated by feathery bog moss and cow-horn bog moss hollow, which are quick-growing in pool conditions, and later other mosses establish themselves. Other plants, such as bog rosemary, sundews, cotton grass and beak-rushes, move in but they make up less than a quarter of the overall vegetation of the lawns, and the shrubs are always very dwarfed because of the waterlogged conditions. This gives the lawns their distinctive appearance of an English country garden lawn, bright green from *S. cuspidatum*, with a scattering of daisies – bog rosemary, sundew and the rest. This is particularly true from a distance where, amid the more muted browns and dark greens, these vast flat surfaces look welcoming. Like much else on a bog, though, they may be flat, but they are peat soup below, and you always sink in them, sometimes to your knees, often much deeper.

Just like a patterning of bog pools, regular mossy mats of lawn are an indicator that the bog is in good health. Heathers, purple moor grass and shrubs don't do well in these spots, which helps to contribute to a wetter surface area. I was entranced by them from a distance and up close. I was impressed by how varied they were, how they rippled and buckled as you approached their edges, how vibrant they were, with their neon yellow-green searing joy into my vision. If I looked away, I had to look back, and I would have stayed all day if not for one flaw. My trusty wellington boots, which had seen me through almost twenty years of gardening, had decided the bog was one journey too far and the left boot was cracking. There was a tiny fracture in the plastic: it must have been there for weeks, but now was growing and my foot was sodden.

I made my way carefully back to the campervan and brewed some coffee while I ransacked all the pockets and spaces under the seats to see if there was something useful to fix my boot. I found some gaffer tape, some electrical tape and, while the water boiled, I mended the hole. I downed the coffee and went back onto the bog. I walked for about thirty minutes, trying to pretend that my replacement sock wasn't getting wet.

I retreated to the van and fumed. I'd waited so long to get there and now a growing hole was defeating my adventure. I changed into walking boots and made a new plan. I'd spend the rest of the afternoon visiting what was left of the Marconi wireless station in the middle of Derrigimlagh Bog, which sits on the north-west corner of Roundstone Bog.

Derrigimlagh translates from Irish as 'the red marshy shore or strath' and is a fitting name for a place that must once have glowed with red sphagnum in the late setting sun. It's still very beautiful, but this is a bog that has been extensively cut over and is still being harvested despite all the optimistic information boards telling of its importance in biodiversity and carbon capturing. There were piles of mechanically cut turf (unlike hand-cut turf it bends as its dries) in various stages of drying and several young men loading tractor trailers with it.

I don't pretend to know much about burning turf, but I know enough of the bog and its layers to see that this was of pretty poor quality. Much of it was falling apart, decomposing, as it dried. I stared at several piles, trying to make out what the roots poking out here and there might be (I decided mostly heathers), when a brightly dressed walker stopped to tell me wistfully in a broad American accent that this was a pile of the homeland's finest fuel. I must have appeared truly horrified because she looked swiftly at her feet and marched on.

The Marconi ruins were interesting, though they had mostly been foremen's houses, not for telecommunication, but for the long history of peat extraction. The real ruin was the bog. There has been some attempt to re-wet cutover areas. There was some colonisation of *Sphagnum cuspidatum*, many sundews twinkling in the afternoon light and some lesser bladderwort. This I was pleased to see because it was on 'my list' – the secret bucket list that all wannabe botanists carry of plants I want to see, or see again, before I die.

Bladderworts are tiny hair-like plants that float in shallow pools. Between the olive-brown leaves there are tiny, oval bladder traps that suck in prey under a trigger mechanism. They dissolve, extract the nutrients, and set a new trap for their next meal. All of this is happening underwater and often all you can see of the plant from a distance is their tiny butter-yellow flowers on slender, reddish-brown stems that rise just a few centimetres above the surface water. Several re-wetted ditches and pools were covered with ethereal drifts of them. Their bladder trap allows them to make the most of the nutrient-poor acidic waters. They favour re-wetted pools because there is barely any competition: little else can do well there. With the ditch banks covered with sundews, those shimmering yellow mirages were a delight amid the ravaged earth.

Compared to Roundstone Bog, Derrigimlagh was heavily visited. There were runners, speed walkers, curious tourists and a fair few sheep wandering about. I walked back through more piles of turf ready for collection to a backdrop of Connemara's mountains, huddled together in late-afternoon sun.

One night on the bog had been enough, particularly with a damp foot. I needed somewhere to wash my socks so I found a campsite just above the incredible white sands of Dog's Bay. I spent the evening floating in the crystal-clear waters of the sea between bouts of exploring the machair grasslands that cover the sand dunes between Gorteen Bay and Dog's Bay. To get to them you cross a tombolo, a spit of sand that connects the dunes to the mainland. All of it was covered with machair, dancing harebells and the last few hot pink flowers of the early marsh orchid (confusing name because it's almost exclusively found in sand dunes). All day the roads and beaches had been packed with bank-holiday folk, but now the long weekend was ending: it was just me and few others from the campsite.

I wondered briefly about trying to climb Errisbeg, the lone peak this side of the bog to catch the sunset, but a local farmer told me it would take more time than was left in the day, so I spent what was left of the light exploring the coast, which was a mixture of rocky shorelines, dune slacks, brackish pools, salt-marsh, freshwater marsh, fen and grasslands.

Oscar Wilde described Connemara as having a 'savage beauty' and it's true of this wild, sparse landscape of foaming sea that gives way to hard, crystalline rocks that rise out of the vast, spreading bog with a labyrinth of cloud-racing pools and lakes that eventually give way to distant mountains. It's one of those places where you can watch the weather coming for you, the Atlantic winds racing rain to one side while on the other there are columns of sunshine between low ceilings of cloud. Twenty minutes later it is all blazing blue. It's a transformative landscape, physically in the way that one ecotone rolls into another, meta-phorically because it is a glimpse of what much of Ireland might look like when the bogs are allowed to grow again and start their slow process to becoming whole.

The following day I got up early to drive back to catch the evening ferry at Rosslare. On the way, I could swing past Clara Bog, a very large raised bog in County Offaly. There were once 310,000 hectares of raised bog in Ireland. Now around 7 per cent remain intact. Clara is one of the largest, relatively intact raised bogs left in Ireland and is famous for having a bit of intact lag (the fen-flushed moat that surrounds a raised bog), which I was fascinated to see. The state owns about half of the bog on the eastern side. It is open as a nature reserve with a trackway and boardwalk. The other half is owned privately, but is still protected.

The eastern half was going to be drained for industrial peat extraction in the 1980s, but it was saved after an international campaign. It was in part spearheaded by Dutch peatland scien-tists, who raised considerable interest and money to persuade the Dutch and Irish governments to sign a technical agreement to cooperate on the bog's restoration and management. It's an inter-esting side note in Dutch engineering and colonial history: Dutch drainage engineering changed the world from the seventeenth century onwards and not for the better. It's a complicated history that saw their technological advances ravage many wetlands around the world. Clara Bog brings the story full circle, as the drainers became ditch blockers.

I'd read a lot about this intervention, which at the time had been quite radical, to get two governments together to save a bog. I was keen to see what a bog that had been restored quite some time ago looked like, and to find the intact lagg. I'm not sure what I was expecting, but as pretty as bits of it were, it was also a pretty standard bog. I saw a few more carnivorous butter-worts with their fly-sticking leaves and I met a lot of lunchtime joggers on the boardwalk, but I couldn't tell how healthy the rest of the bog was. It certainly wasn't Roundstone and I left the beaten track to try to find the lagg.

I came to the conclusion that it must be on a privately owned corner because the flushed edge I could get to was heavily treed, but when I pushed through I found a suspiciously straight ditch; I couldn't imagine it was the original lagg, which would have circled the raised dome of the bog. I took a few photos and paused to eat in the shade of the trees.

When I eventually got onto the ferry that night, I decided it was time to peel off my damp sock and examine my bog foot. I pretty much cleared out the lounge just taking off my shoe, the smell was so bad, and my foot looked little better. It was time for a new pair of wellington boots.

20

The Flow Country

Even thinking about the Flow Country does something to me. I swell inside, just like it does, and I'm not embarrassed to admit that I cried when I left it. In the last half-hour of driving off it, as I wound alongside the River Helmsdale, I caught a hillside ablaze with little silvered flags dancing amid the russets and burnt umbers of the heathers. I abandoned my car, scrambling over a ditch to lie among the flags. Each belonged to a spider that had hoisted its web to a single blade of grass that rose above the heather and embroidered a sail that had caught the morning dew. Hundreds of spiders spinning light and water into magic. It was too much. It burst out of me as tears.

That sort of enchantment is what the bog up there is all about. It is a land of incalculable distance, available all at once . . . if the sun shines. You can see your future coming at you, the near hills golden, the far hills darkened, the furthest hills the colour of distance, a milky blue-grey.

At its closest, it is brown, but also golden and green; it is orange and purple, wine red, pink, mirrored silver; it is everything, all the colour, all the light; it is all sky; it is vast and miniature. When it rains it does so in waves; when it shines, it is heaven on earth. It is so ancient and still growing. It is so very local and, of course, global: 400 million tonnes of carbon are stored beneath its mossy layers. That's double the amount stored by all the trees in Britain.

The tapestry is so intricate and the patterns so varied and so detailed that after hours of viewing, you cannot tire of it. Just when you think you can predict what will appear next, it surprises you with a nest of speckled eggshells or an ancient club moss, a jewelled insect, a pair of nibbled antlers, a whole fawn skeleton, a pool, a shattered mirror of sky on the ground, and beneath it an underworld of bog beans, a red kind of mud that seems suspended from weight in its water, and above, a smell so sweet and clear, a breath of landscape.

But what is this place? The Flow Country is wild, perhaps our wildest place in the UK. It sits in Sutherland, edges into Caithness and runs from across the top of the north-east corner of Scotland in either direction spreading out into 400,000 hectares. It is the largest and most intact blanket bog complex in the world. In 2024, it was designated a UNESCO World Heritage Site.

Like all bogs, it was once much bigger. But like anywhere and everywhere, however seemingly remote or difficult to get to, much of the more accessible areas has been cut away for fuel or drained for agriculture. If you take a look on Google Earth the distance view is a never-ending pinkish brown, but zoom in and you can see tell-tale strips removed for fuel and herringbone patterns for drainage. It is not empty of human settlements: along the rivers there are farms and green fields for grazing sheep, but venture past the edges of roads or rivers and this disappears. In this land of soft organic shapes, there are some startling lines. In the middle I see surprising dense green blocks with neat edges: forestry plantations. There have been peat-fired power stations, commercial peat cutting for the malting of barley to flavour whisky, and recently the advent of wind energy, the forest not of trees but of turbines, which litter the edges of the bog. So, it is vast and wild, but scarred by our misunderstanding of its value as a wet place.

I read someone's post on the internet because they were talking about the Camster Cairn, a Neolithic tomb on the eastern side of the Flow Country. They want their audience to go there, but they described the chambered cairn as sitting in the tundra-like wastes of north-east Scotland. The only wastes of this landscape are the scars we've left upon it.

Despite all that has been thrown at the Flow Country to make it 'productive' for growing crops, it still remains largely intact and is one of the best examples of what a blanket bog should look like at this scale. In terms of its hydrology, it's really wet, with many thousands of pools as testament to this, and its constant wetness promotes one of the most diverse living layers. If you want to find rare mosses, you have to come here: there are at least thirty-five species of sphagnum moss found across the UK, and the Flow Country is home to twenty-nine.

From the very beginning of this adventure, the Flow Country sat at the top of my wish list to visit. Initially, I thought I'd try to walk across as much of it as I could (ha!) and even persuaded my friend Mel that this was an adventure she wanted in on. Mel agreed, if I came with her on a tour of significant sites of the Bell Beaker people on the west coast of Scotland. This seemed a fair and suitably odd transaction. She sent me screen grabs of army boots specially designed to walk across wetlands with a strange drainage channel in the soles. We would have finished both expeditions by now, if it hadn't slowly dawned on me how arrogant it would have been to try to conquer the bog with such a walk. Yes, you can walk on water, but I'm not sure you should, at least not just so you can say, 'I went from here to there.'

Large parts of the Flow Country are privately owned by huge shooting estates. This is deer-stalking, loch-trout-skulking, salmon-leaping-to-the-fly country, and I wanted to see something of the bog's beating heart without too many permissions. The right to roam is treacherous: you might get stuck thigh high in bog because you veered left rather than right. When I was still chasing a walk, I emailed the RSPB to see if I could walk across Forsinard Flows, their largest nature reserve in the UK.

They said, 'Yes, of course. Come!' and pointed to some drovers' routes that would make walking easy. I left it at that. It was deep winter when I spoke to Milly Revill Hayward, the peatland engagement and communication officer for Forsinard Flow, on Zoom. The rain was pelting down as hard there as it was at home, so I put off summer adventures to go back to learning peatland terminology.

Later in the year Milly emailed: was I still coming? What was my plan for walking? I could still stay at the field centre if I wanted. I was tardy in replying because Mel and I hadn't found a date between us and I was beginning to question the sanity of walking across a bog. I had much more experience in bog-walking by then and was aware of how painfully slow this attempt would be.

It turned out that I didn't have much of plan, but Milly did. She said she had one spare space on the RSPB working-holiday week. I could do some surveying and peat-probing, help with restoration, talk to the RSPB staff and meet other volunteers. I could do as little or as much volunteering as I wanted. They were easy; I just had to say yes.

Who on earth goes on a bog-restoration holiday? Seven days in wellington boots, potentially never drying out, to sleep in a bunk in the middle of nowhere? Milly said people came from all over the country. Some would be returning, others coming for the first time. I was steeped in people who did this work for a living, but what about those who did it just for love? The idea of meeting my kind was suddenly irresistible.

Late in August, I found myself on the twelve-hour, 600-mile round trip to the furthest northern tip of this isle. It's possible to do the entire journey to Forsinard by train but I'd left it too late to get a cheap ticket, so I drove. I also drove because I had a slight fear that perhaps people who loved bogs were all mad and I might need an escape plan. It made me laugh when Lo, one of the working-holiday volunteers, admitted several days into the holiday that she had had the same thought. No one was mad, unreasonable or even odd; the majority came for the birds and to gain practical experience in burgeoning ecology careers. Three of our team were under sixteen; four were old friends who had met through Scottish dancing; one member got a sundew tattoo after he left the Flow Country; two quiet, kind men stayed on for another month; and all of them by the end of the week felt like bog family.

It was one of the best holidays I've ever had. Yes, I got wet, so wet that waterproofs stopped working and the rain pooled into my gloves and ran down my arms into my armpits as I tried to measure quadrats, and I was bone tired by the time I hit my bunk (which had an amazing mattress and fine pillows: you certainly don't lose sleep at Forsinard), and there was plenty of walking across the bog, sometimes very slowly as we picked a way between pools and hollows. I would be lying too if I didn't point out that you have to do many of these tasks behind mesh netting: the midges really do come in clouds. But the sunsets were something else, and the full moon so large and bright in that land of all sky where the stars reached down around me. And now as I sit here in the dry, I even remember the rain fondly. And the midges, well, they bring out the bats that haunt the twilight sky, followed by the family of owls that lives in a disused building just opposite the field centre and gets up to hunt. A whole other world comes out to play.

Plus, the Forsinard team are great. Milly, Claire and the long-term volunteers made even the duller tasks joyful. The days had a nice rhythm: they started with simple, informative lectures on what you would be doing and why, how to dam a bog with a piece of corrugated plastic, the point of peat-probing and ground-truthing – essentially confirming that a satellite or digital image is what it says it is on the actual ground – why you might measure how much a deer has nibbled a heather plant, how to pull out a regenerated conifer sapling. And then you were off out and between tasks there was plenty of tea and biscuits. The young folk, a trio of siblings who came with their dad and were well used to working holidays, leapt, jumped, tagged and tumbled down hills, throwing themselves into each task with such vim that it inspired the rest of us to action. The days flew past as we got to know each other and a little of the bog.

By late August, the many birds that nest there have raised their broods and are getting ready to migrate or move on, and the winter tasks start again. For volunteers this is largely one of two things: pulling out or putting in trees.

The trees that need to be removed are natural regeneration from afforested conifer plantations – if there was ever a sentence caught up in the contradictions of modern nature there it is. These trees were planted as a crop, for use as timber, paper, fibre, for absorbing carbon dioxide, carbon offsetting, flood mitigation, recreation. There are many reasons, but nearly always a concealed politics in them. The relationship between humans and plants is complicated: afforestation is never a forest for a forest's sake. It's a forest for our needs.

Our history is interwoven with forests and trees, particularly with wars. It's hard to imagine now, but for centuries trees fuelled war: you couldn't go to war if you didn't have a vast supply for warships, cannon, planes, aircraft carriers, for the mundane, wooden disposable forks and knives, pit props and folding utility furniture. In recent history, the Second World War left us with many anxieties, and forest cover was one. We planted trees to replace what we had taken down, but also to future-proof our uncertainties. We started planting particular forests of non-native conifers. Those plantations make up 7 per cent of our landmass today, 1.5 million hectares of dark lines of Sitka spruce, lodgepole pine, western hemlock, Norwegian fir and spruce, and hybrid larch.

Forestry's relationship with bogs is seismic, often catastrophic and still in the grip of how we see and think about these spaces. Mineral agriculture soils are seen as too valuable for tree planting, and to past generations peat was fair game: it was valueless land that was drained to be more productive. It's important to remember that the depth of peat that defines an area as a peatland (more than 30 centimetres) was set by foresters rather than ecologists. Our peatlands definition has been set by people who think in terms of trees rather than soils. It's the same skewed logic that sees mass tree planting in treeless habitats worldwide, in grasslands, prairies and dry lands, for instance, and has similarly disastrous effects. We habitually think of trees as an ecological way out of our carbon problem. They often aren't.

There was a time when the Flow Country was at risk of disappearing under trees. In the late 1970s and 1980s huge blocks were planted with pine and Sitka spruce, not because anyone thought the Flow Country would grow good timber – there was plenty of evidence that such soils would be hard for trees – but because forestry had any number of government tax incentives, particularly for inheritance tax.

Many wealthy and famous people, including the late Terry Wogan, many professional golfers and some rock musicians, bought into the scheme to plant the bog with trees. It was a terrible plan that made a few people richer. The trickiness of money and investments means that most of us aren't aware of where our pensions, mortgages, loans and savings end up, but the result was near disastrous.

To plant trees on bogs, you must drain the land, carve it up into rows of peaks to plant the trees on and valleys to create drainage ditches. The trees further drain the soil as they grow, wicking away moisture and releasing the stored carbon. The idea here is that the trees take up the carbon in growing and thus the equation is balanced out.

The carbon budget for afforestation on drained peatland compared to wet peatland is complicated, and as one scientist pointed out, you can find data to suit either side. However, a comprehensive study on the state of current scientific evidence of climate mitigation of peatland under forestry (looking at afforested and naturally forested peatlands) highlights several key issues with afforestation of drained peatlands.* First, without restored waters the ecosystem cannot fully recover its functions. Thus, it is likely that long-term carbon losses from drained peatlands will be larger than the amount of carbon stored in forest biomass. There's a lack of evidence to show otherwise, and the added loss of other ecosystem functions, polluted waters, loss of habitat for wildlife and more, means it's a bad punt to put your money into trees on drained peat.

Also, the trees make for poor timber grown on such nutrient-deficient soils, so the end product is generally turned into short-term carbon, mashed and pulped in biofuels, cheap composite woods or paper. Long-lasting harvested wood products are quite rare. As one forester said to me, 'If we were growing our timber to turn into cathedrals or homes that would stand for hundreds of years it would be one thing, but we're mostly growing for chipboard that won't live out the century.' There's a general rule that for a timber product to be truly climate cooling (to take in more carbon than it releases in its entire lifecycle, including growing, watering, fertilising, time between harvests, processing), it needs to last for half of its growing life. So, a product from an eighty-year-old tree needs to spend more than forty years in use. Most of this timber doesn't last half that. The reality is that trees are planted on thin peat (less than 30 centimetres) because the land is cheap and no good for agriculture.

Peatland scientist Richard Lindsay led the team that surveyed and reported on the global significance of the Flow Country in the 1990s. His study highlighted that it wasn't miles of emptiness but a highly diverse, valuable ecosystem that needed to be preserved. He and many other conservationists fought hard for this landscape to be truly seen. As swiftly as the inheritance-tax scheme was brought in, it was dropped, but by then hundreds of acres of trees had been planted across the middle of the Flow.

* Jurasinski, G., Barthelmes, A., Byrne, K.A. *et al.* 'Active afforestation of drained peatlands is not a viable option under the EU Nature Restoration Law', *Ambio* 53, 970–983 (2024).

A patchwork quilt of plantation sticks out across the blanket bog. Where funds and sales allowed, the RSPB bought up the plantations, taking out the trees and starting the long, slow process of re-wetting the bog so it could start to heal itself. Now the RSPB works with landowners to restore the bog. It is a slow process, and the restoration work can look rather brutal to the untrained eye, but it is making a difference.

There are, however, blocks of trees that are privately owned. Those plantations, and others, that are still to be restored release thousands upon thousands of seeds. They germinate often in the damaged bogs, but also at drier margins, near roads and streams where they, too, release seed. So, the consequences of these plantations linger. Those trees are known as 'regen', as in regenerated forest, and when they grow too large to be hand-pulled, contractors have to scrub them out.

When they are small in diameter volunteers can either hand-pull, saw or lop them out. Our task was to pull and chop down every baby pine and spruce we found. We did this on plantations that had been felled where the land was being restored to bog, as well as on bog that sat next to intact plantations. We also worked on land that appeared not to be near plantations because the conifers' seed is dispersed by wind and there's plenty of that up there.

Removing regen is surprisingly satisfying, mildly competitive (we were put into teams), fulfilling work. Until you look to the horizon and spot all the outliers. It is not a task that will be finished any time soon. But neither is blocking old drains or bund restoration work. Decades of work lie ahead. Pulling up trees, walking slowly over a bog and over felled plantations, with trip hazards and deep, wet ditches to fall into, you have plenty of thinking time.

When I wasn't marvelling at how beautiful it is, for even the wrecked bits have glimmers of hope – the first sphagnum mosses, the brilliant gleams of sundews that love to colonise bare peat, the good bits of the ancient club mosses. Lilliputian mountains of hummock-forming mosses in their scarlets, rusty browns and vibrant greens, the heavy drone of bumble bees, the wild call of startled birds, the sometimes gentle caress of wind, the warmth of the sun so soon after rain – I came to a chorus of beings and happenings and found communion in it all: the aliveness of this land, not just the animated above but what lies deep below.

Over and over again I find myself thinking and voicing aloud the idea of the bog as a beast, not assigning some mythical being to the place but the actual being that is each bog. Of course, the bog is alive. It is an ecosystem. It is by its very nature participating in a community of beings.

The bog-as-a-being is shaping not just the lives that inhabit it but the landscape it sits on and even the landscape beyond it. The science community call this the 'role of the reciprocal organism-landform interactions' with 'biogeomorphic feedbacks'. That means the mosses and the rocks commune with the waters and together they move and mould the world around them. These are the biological imperatives of the bogs and the wider system. Scientists argue that landscapes with such biogeomorphic feedback have a profound effect on the earth: they may cover just 1 per cent of the earth's entire surface (and peatland even less because this number includes all biogeomorphic wetlands, including mangroves, seagrass beds and salt marshes), but they store 20 per cent of the global organic ecosystem carbon.[*]

In other words, if you leave the bog in charge, it will look after far more than its mosses. All ecosystems act responsibly to all of us, if they are allowed to function in their natural state. Bogs are just like any other: if allowed to exist as they please, with sovereignty of their waters, they will nurture us as well as the many other beings that seek refuge in them, including our ancestors buried there.

*   *   *

[*] Ralph J.M. Temmink *et al.*, 'Recovering wetland biogeomorphic feedbacks to restore the world's biotic carbon hotspots', *Science* 376, eabn1479 (2022).

When I first went to the Flow Country I thought of it as one continuous blanket, but by my second visit, the following spring, I knew just enough of its shape, to start to see it like any other landscape that is made up of parts, in name at least. In the field centre at Forsinard there was a huge detailed Ordnance Survey map of the area the RSPB reserve covered. Four or five chunks of land marked out in green, broken up by forestry plantations, each bit with its own name, and then there were the bens and the smaller mountains and hills, the lochs, lochans and rivers, some ancient monuments, farmsteads, fields, drovers' routes, some notable rocks and boulders . . .

On my first visit, I went out with Milly and Quinten, one of the residential volunteers, a quietly deadpan Belgian who had fallen in love with bogs as a student at university and had cycled to Forsinard to spend a month learning more about the Flow Country. We traipsed across some very beautiful bog to survey one of the quadrats used to understand deer population numbers. There are many different landowners in the Flow Country and they all have different opinions on how many deer you might want onto your land. But too many deer have damaged the bog in overgrazing and compaction. Deer, of course, do not know or care about estate boundaries or numbers and travel miles across the landscape often in herds of at least thirty members.

There are several ways in which you can count deer. Several times a year you can send your fittest volunteers to a number of high points with a good pair of binoculars and, at the same time, everyone will count as many deer as they can see. It's a great snapshot of the deer populations at any one time; repeat it often enough and you will start to see patterns. The other way is to have quadrats in known locations and to peer at and measure the plants in the quadrats.

Deer show preference in what they eat: they like the young shoots of heather, particularly common heather, less so cross-leaved heather, which they find unpalatable. You can return to a quadrat and note what has been nibbled and what has new growth; if there's nibbled cross-leaved heather, there's an over-grazing issue, because deer only eat that as a last resort.

So, there we were with our GPS to locate the quadrats, with the sun blazing and the clouds racing across the lochans and many small pools. Every footstep offered a new way of combining mosses, lichen, club mosses, bear- and cowberries, the uniquely bog trick of a landscape that is miniature and mammoth, of the microtopography of tiny mountains of hummock mosses and a wider view of actual giants.

Although it was varied and wonderful, it also looked, if you spun yourself round several times, exactly the same. I had no sense of north and, with the sun high in the middle of the sky, little of east or west. If Milly wasn't there, I am pretty sure Quinten and I would have walked round and round in circles, even with a GPS. I quizzed her, 'How do you it? How do you make sense of this huge landscape?'

She admitted that when she'd started the job, she hadn't believed she'd ever make sense of the space, but little by little the slight slope of the landscape, the distant mountains and the lochs started to take on their particular shapes and she could match name to form. We could be at a particular quadrat in a sea of bog and she'd confidently walk east, knowing she'd meet a lochan, and over that rise our truck would come into view.

That makes it sound as though you can see these features in advance but mostly you can't. Maybe it's part of the magic-carpet ride, but because the walking is difficult, with no firm surfaces, and you spend so much time looking at your feet you can't always tell you're going uphill until suddenly you have a slightly different view. With the shifting nature of the near and far distance, it's as if the middle distance doesn't exist. It reminded me of sea swimming, where you understand what's far, far away and what is upon you, but beyond that wave, there's always a bit of unknown. I am not alone feeling at sea in this landscape.

Tacitus wrote, in *Agricola*, about the Flow Country:

The Flow Country

But when you go farther North you find a huge and shapeless tract of country, jutting out towards the land's end and finally tapering into a kind of wedge . . . Nowhere does the sea hold wider way; it carries to and fro in its motion a mass of currents, and, in its ebb and flow, is not held by the coast, but passes deep inland and winds about, pushing in among the highlands and mountains, as if in its own domain.[*]

We know that the sea does not shape the bog, different waters do, but the sense of a body of water running over and under the landscape certainly evokes something visceral about its shifting nature.

After lunch, we walked back around a lochan that had a quaking mat of sphagnum moss doing its best to reclaim the waters. It was thick enough to walk over and we saw the landscape in front of us wave forward with each step and ripple till it hit a slight incline. We were walking on water, kept (just) afloat by that magic carpet of mosses. It's certainly trippy out there.

It was a good day. I liked Quinten's humour and Milly's effervescence. I loved peering very closely at plants under a big blue sky. I've added it to a handful of days that I can call on when I meet darker moments, days of sheer luck to be alive and to be in a place where happiness can attend so readily. It also gave me a little more terrain to fold into my map of the Flow Country.

I'd taken *Setting Foot on the Shores of Connemara* by Tim Robinson to read on this trip. It's a book of essays on mapmaking. I'm very interested in how we map things: landscape, but also emotions, and the Flow Country had piqued this obsession again. If you go to any Ordnance Survey map and look for bog you see the tell-tale etching of five or so vertical lines in blue, denoting rushes, and nothing else. Robinson's work aims to address what happens when the paucity of general maps fails to rise to the

---

[*] Tacitus, Publius Cornelius; Mattingly, H.; Handford, S.A. *The Agricola and the Germania (Book X)*, (Penguin, 1970).

diversity of a place, and I wanted to linger, in his thoughts, in a place that matched that idea.

I was doing this rather unsuccessfully, though, because all that good clean air had me dropping off to sleep the minute I got into the bottom bunk and picked up the book. But the snippets I stayed awake for made me consider how you make sense of landscape through being in it. In 'Listening to the Landscape', an essay on how a place gets a name and keeps it, or not, he writes,

> Thus we personally, cumulatively, communally, create and recreate landscapes – a landscape being not just the terrain but also the human perspective on it, the land plus its overburden of meanings . . . There is a difference between a mere location and a real place, between a placename and a map reference; there may even be conflict between them.[*]

That made me think of the conifer plantations, how they divide up the undulating landscape with neat edges, geometric in shape in a place of soft curves: they carve up not just its waters but its identity too. Because one thing is very apparent about the Flow Country when you stand anywhere at some elevation: it does what its name suggests. It flows endlessly. The name Flow comes not from its continuous blanket of growth, but the Old Norse *floi*, meaning 'soft or marshy ground'.

The conifer plantations are what Robinson calls a 'conflict' between a map and the ground, if you were to look for them on an online map for direction you wouldn't find them, they'd have magically disappeared. And yet, if you put 'Flow Country' into the satellite function and zoom in far enough, the plantations reappear as dark green blobs and eventually you can detect even the straight access lines between them. If you physically wander

* Robinson, Tim, *Setting Foot on the Shores of Connemara and Other Writing,* (The Lilliput Press, 1996).

up these access lines into the plantations the bog is often rather deliciously claiming back as much as it can. The access lines exist so that the machines can get in to harvest trees, and in those open spaces the mosses colonise, a verdant green carpet, while the gloom of tightly spaced conifers looms at either side. We'd often sit in those spaces to have lunch after hours of pulling out conifer seedlings: they offered shelter from wind and rain and were soft, if wet, to sit on.

Veronica, a fellow working-holiday volunteer, called this 'bog weeding' when asked what she did on a bog for a week. She's so enamoured with bog weeding that she might be Forsinard's most loyal working-holiday volunteer. I think she'd done about five different trips. She's so enthusiastic and cajoles any number of friends to come with her. She persuaded me to come for a second week too. I jumped at the chance to be back in that landscape and spend another week in her good-humoured company.

You shouldn't, of course, have to weed a bog, but the conflict of the plantation is that it's not just a spot on a map: it's a Sisyphean seed bank endlessly replenishing everything we pull out. On a single day we'd removed more than two thousand saplings. Trees from a few centimetres high to several metres, a team of ten of us walking in a line, bending, pulling, lopping, sawing, counting, clicking as the ticker records the number (each seedling has to be logged so that the numbers can be compared). As far as the eye can see the miniature forests of seedlings continue, a conflict of conifers.

This struggle causes a different identity crisis. It is not just how we perceive the bog, but how others, the more-than-human, do too. If you are a bird, one of the many that think of the bog as a familiar place, you, too, want the bog to endlessly roll over the landscape because when your ancestors first sought a safe place to breed and raise young, they chose this because it was open. That was what made it safe, its lack of tall cover.

The dunlins, the European golden plovers and the common greenshanks raise their families on the bog. The Flow Country is home to 66 per cent of the common greenshank population, 35 per cent of the dunlins and 17 per cent of the golden plovers. That's at least seven thousand golden plovers, six thousand dunlins and fifteen thousand common greenshanks, so not just a handful of birds.

Golden plover chicks are camouflaged to look like balls of golden and green moss. A dunlin chick has the colours of hare's tail cotton grass in winter, and a common greenshank does a good study in the greys of heather stems. Both the chicks and the adults of these birds can disappear into the landscape by hunkering down in its openness. A forest is quite the opposite: it hides predators, pine martens, hooded crows, red foxes, and, once upon a time, wild cats (currently being reintroduced elsewhere in the Highlands) and wolves. The birds know this. They need a place where they can have clear views of approaching predators.

A study looked at the wider effect of plantations on these waders; it found that golden plovers and dunlin won't and don't go anywhere near wooded areas, and this is known as the edge effect. The plantation steals more land than just what it sits on. As the Flow Country became fragmented by the conifer plantation, the birds started to change where they would nest. The study found the effect was strongest within 700 metres, that's almost half a mile, of the forest edge. All three species wish to occupy flatter, more exposed ground close to bog pools that offer plenty of insects to feed the chicks. The edge has another effect: it changes the hydrology and habitat of adjacent bogs up to 40 metres from plantation boundaries, affecting prey availability for breeding birds.*

Not all birds are affected equally. The common greenshank hurls violence at the problem: they mob any predators that

* Wilson, J.D., Anderson, R., *et al.*, 'Modelling edge effects of mature forest plantations on peatland waders informs landscape-scale conservation', *J Appl Ecol* (2014), 51: 204–213.

approach their chicks. The corncrake quite likes the forest edge, while the black grouse and common cuckoo may benefit from the ecotone habitat of forest edge and open land. So, the conifers either fragment the landscape or create a mosaic of novel habitats.

Sitting beside a salmon stream as we ate lunch one day, Milly told me that there is a very steady population of common cross-bill now on the bog, a brilliant red, stocky finch with a huge overbite for a bill, hence the name, that likes to eat pine seeds. As great as it is that the crossbills are thriving, they aren't supposed to be there because the trees aren't either. This is the identity-shifting element that the conifers bring. The plantations are novel recombinant habitats, meaning that they are mixing genomes. From such novelty new ways appear. You may say, 'It's sad that something is lost, but nature has filled the gap with something else.' Nature is ever-evolving in its need to move forwards. Something will always move into a new space.

It's not just on the near-pristine Flow Country. Cors Fochno has a population of whinchat and Cors Caron a population of willow tit because fragments of woodland are growing from drained margins of their bogs. The willow warblers are in decline from habitat loss, so the woods stay but they further damage the bogs, which are in decline because of habitat loss from drainage for agricultural land. Round and round we go.

21

Thinking

Being in the Flow Country gave me so much to think about, partly because many of the tasks kept my hands busy but left my mind free to wander. And when you look up from the task, however damaged by plantation and wind farms, there is just so much of it.

The Flow Country has many near-pristine elements, a gold, red, green and yellow standard of moss diversity and a water table that sits always at or just below the surface. Compared to the many bare peat sites I'd visited in Bannau Brycheiniog (the Brecon Beacons), the Pennines, across Ireland, Dartmoor, the Dales and just round the corner from my home, in the uplands around me, this is a landscape that is doing very well. And that is due to the work of many scientists, conservationists, and the charities that make up the Flow Country Partnership. They have worked tirelessly for it to be recognised as one of the world's greatest expanses of blanket bog. It was recently awarded UNESCO World Heritage status, a welcome and much-needed accolade recognising its importance.

As I left Forsinard a second time, I lingered in the field centre until I had to run to catch the train home (the joy of having a station in the middle of a bog). I overheard Marjoleine, one of the peatland restoration officers, telling Elaine, a member of our volunteer crew, what she'd been up to that day. She'd visited a recently restored forest-to-bog site and there were already surface pools appearing – not infillings of ditches, but the bog starting its process of hydrological magic, happening in just months of a wet winter. Her happiness and awe that this could happen was almost palpable. Give it back its water and this landscape's readiness to repair itself is clear. It has an extraordinary resilience.

Earlier in the summer, I had managed to pin down the incredibly busy Dr Roxane Andersen, professor of peatland science at the University of the Highlands and Islands. A poet of the bog landscape as well as one of our leading experts, she had just finished a Leverhulme-funded study of how resilience works in the Flow Country. She had found that every element of the bog mattered, even the dry margins that had largely been overlooked as an important part of the hydrology. I could concur with that: in literature, in conversations, the dry edges with their encroaching scrub were always talked about as less-than bog.

It turned out that when drought approached and took hold over the summer, the drier edges were doing something amazing. They collapse on purpose, their soils slumping and flattening around the edge of the bog. Then when the waters in the wetter middle parts dry out, as they do in drought years, and the pools are drained to their mud bottoms, the waters that remain aren't drawn out to the edges to be lost to the surroundings because those slumped edges have sealed off the bog. The water doesn't move horizontally in drought years but recedes down: the bog sucks in its belly and waits.

When the rain comes back, the waters rise, the pools fill, the wet middle is saturated, the edges straighten, the bog survives and the mosses thrive again. Given a chance as a whole landscape, it can and will replenish itself. It's that notion of autonomy. I asked Roxane if she thought it was odd that I thought of bogs as beasts. She smiled, and sent me a poem she's working on turning into a children's book about how the Flow Country is actually a dragon hiding beneath the moss. It's a story about how we make sense of our world, a story with roots as old as the bogs, for there certainly was a time when you wouldn't ask a scientist whether it was mad to think of a place as a being. But what of the bogs where the beast has vanished? Can you restore resilience to a place that has seemingly lost its soul?

What if restoration has to start as far back as bare deep peat, the catotelm or even the mineral soils, with no living layer in decades or even a century? What does it mean to restore this landscape? What if some mosses return but others are always lost? Is this the healing of the old beast or the making of a new one?

Restoration is a complex idea because it has to factor in time, how long it might take to get the ecosystem to function on its own. But at what point do we restore a system that is ever naturally fluctuating? Restoration often makes an ecosystem's time linear. It gives a timeline to an idea in terms of how long it will take to do the work, when the work is considered satisfactorily finished, when the ecosystem is recovered or recovering (essentially when the ecosystem takes over from the intervention), but also importantly the reference point for the work. It sticks a pin into the history of the space, or nearby spaces, and says, 'This is what we are aiming for.'

But no ecosystem thinks like that. Their time is different from ours because it can jump back and move forward at once. On a bog there's a complex depth–time relationship that is as physical as it is philosophical. A sphagnum moss can clone itself potentially perpetually, if conditions don't change. Sphagnum can be centuries, perhaps millennia old, the same individual ever reaching upwards. The central growing rosette, the capitulum, is 'eternally young', as the older respiring tissue is buried in the peat. This means the sphagnum you see growing on the surface of a bog that has been little disturbed may be the same genetic individual as the first sphagnum that took hold as the peat was forming. The peat's timeline, metaphorically and physically, is both now and then. It is not building on time, but a continuum of it. But, as necessary as it is, restoration is on some level an attempt to claw back time, to make up for past mistakes. Restoration is also driven by our fleeting, hurried desires and our impetuous notions of change. The cynic would say that peatland restoration is getting the level of funding right: it's an easy win for a government to pay lip service to any meaningful environmental change. If you stop the bogs releasing carbon, you need not chase the transportation industry to change more rapidly.

There a pattern you see with restored habitats that some species jump back in quickly, other take decades or longer and some never return. This happens on bogs: once lost, certain species of mosses never make it back. We don't know why – perhaps it's the conditions, the time frame, the genetic pool – but something is missing in many restored spaces. The quick-to-establish hollow and pool plant species, like *Sphagnum cuspidatum,* often make their home again without even being introduced: their spores or fragments of their kin fly in on the winds of the upper atmosphere. We rightly celebrate their return, but they are not the bog-building species.

It's the shifting base-line syndrome of habitat loss, the generational degradation that says I hold my childhood habitat as a standard, but my great-grandparents would be horrified at the losses and my great-great-grandparents might not even recognise the landscape.

How do we recognise and give ethics to the depth–time relationship that the bog is having with its past, present and future self? Sphagnum moss is very old, not just as an ancestral lineage, but potentially as an individual. We love to venerate the ancient: perhaps we should give some moral consideration to something that's been around that long. This is why preservation of 'good' bogs is as important as restoration of 'damaged' ones.

We should look at this biocentrically, rather than, say, anthropocentrically: we should consider not what the bog and its being are worth to us and our needs, but what it means to itself, as a living being within the system, and what it means to those outside, the value of its interconnectedness and interdependence. Then the moss, as an ecosystem engineer, creating and driving the ecosystem's development, surely has some ethical status, particularly in terms of environmental protection.

We rightly celebrate restoration work that is closing the gap, when a forest-to-bog restoration project has sphagnum colonising in the first year or so, when we've moved from felled Sitka to the ghostly white limbs of root stumps to surface pools and soft, green sphagnum. 'Look at that, look how quickly Nature moves to restore the bog.' But is it a bog yet?

It's a finicky question, but as the bog didn't choose to be cut for fuel, or drained of its water when we thought it was useless land, or the animals that we brought to shear its living layer, or the trees we planted on it, or the machines we brought onto it to make up for the mistakes, or the mosses we decided, unwittingly or not, to reclothe it in. And all of this is restoring the bog to an idea we have of it in the past, when we have no sense of what the future will bring. What if we are trying to restore our bogs to a point that can never be reached? Particularly in light of a climate that continues to change, with more potential for fires and drought, rising seas, increased atmospheric pollution and on and on . . .

None of this is to say that those who are doing the practical work on the ground, the theoretical work in the lab, the building of pile dams and contour bunds, the recording of gases and water tables, water quality and microbial activity, of vegetation assemblages and invertebrate numbers, the flowering and breeding of the living as a bog, should not be doing exactly what they are doing. Theirs is hard work that needs to be done and the best examples jumpstart ailing ecosystems back into control on a timescale that suits the bog.

I worried about the ethics, how the work was to be financed:

what if buying up bogs became the new land-grab for carbon credits? What if the moral agency of these spaces wasn't recognised beyond their fragmented state? Is a bog whole if its lagg is not intact? If that field was once part of the bog, doesn't it, too, deserve to be in control of its waters? The frantic, sometimes frenetic timescale of current restoration is often at the mercy of grants and funding bids, and is dictated by bureaucracy, not healing. The modern way of the contract job means that the people who started the knitting together are often not the same people who finish it. What of continuity of people and place? Sometimes I voiced this aloud, but often I didn't: who needs *that* outsider when the task ahead is so big? And I certainly didn't have the answers.

At some point on this journey, I stumbled upon a newsletter by the UK branch of the IUCN Peatland Programme. It was full of what you might expect – training programmes, funding opportunities, discussion of financial schemes, jobs, a selection of recently published papers and call-outs – but if you dipped in past the titles you found a lot of joy, of community bog projects and returned life caught not in the published papers but in phone-snapped shots: a wisp of snipes in full flight at Hafod Elwy in north-west Wales, increasing in numbers because the birds were drawn to the bog pools that had reappeared after bunding restoration, or a text message: *Water voles everywhere. I found them within two minutes of searching. It took ages to get to 100m upstream, there were so many signs. I also saw one swimming in a new pool. It really is wonderful news*, wrote an ecologist to a manager about the animals' return to a restored peatland in Tywi Forest. Or of the return of the aquatic monsters of Wester Ross, of dragonflies, damsel flies and whirligig beetles increasing in species richness year after year on restored peatland sites. Nature wasn't returning because the place of return was now gone: it was seizing the newness of all this wetness. I heard in these stories and saw in re-wetted areas, colonised anew with mosses, that Nature was saying something else: let's start again.

I realised that perhaps part of my issues with restoration was its notion of returning to some point in the past, an idea of a landscape, a time when we felt things weren't broken. It's a place that can't exist because present regressions aren't erased by going backwards. I realised then that sometimes the notion, less so, perhaps, the practice, of restoration is missing something essential. It misses the apology. I want us to say sorry to the bogs and actually mean it. Then I think we can join in with the rest of Nature and, too, start afresh.

22

Returning

On my second visit to the Flow Country, I spent a lot of time pulling out conifers and the same amount planting native deciduous trees, albeit in very different spaces. As part of their management plans for the reserve, the RSPB carries out compensatory planting: if they fell trees as part of their restoration work, they replant native trees along the straths and banks of rivers that wind through the Flow Country. The trees are a mixture of natives, mostly birch, rowan, some willow, holly, oak, which create the much-needed fragments of riverine woodland. There are many benefits to this: for the soils, and the waters downstream, to provide shade for the salmon that spawn in the river, food and housing for the birds that flit about, but also food and habitat for foraging insects. All of this would benefit the bog. No ecosystem is an island: the health of other ecosystems and ecotones around them matters. It is part of the overall resilience of a wider landscape.

I love planting trees. I've spent a good part of my life doing it and I find the rhythm of spade, turf and tree is a muscle memory I am always pleased to exercise. Plus a day with no emails, no computer, just sky, the promise of biscuits, tea and, hopefully, sun while eating sandwiches on the riverbank is a good day, an honourable one. And the sun came out and stayed for lunch, and we craned our necks to watch two golden eagles circle high above. Tracy, another working-holiday volunteer and serious birder, lent me her binoculars and I saw in detail the fine wingtip feathers spread like fingers as the birds glided about.

I'd been talking to Milly and Tamara about the tricky ways of money and investments, the complicity that is intertwined into all we do. I casually glanced at my emails on my phone. I hadn't been looking at them all week. Twenty minutes ago, finishing off one sapling and moving on to the next spot, I realised I was in a small dip and no one could see me if I lay back. Stripped down to my shirt sleeves in the first good rays of spring I listened to the birds and water running and leaping beyond, to the wind coming down off the bog and running up to a conifer plantation, the way it whipped and circled through the trees. I heard the wings of a crow, the distant chatter of my fellow volunteers, and for a few blissful moments I heard nothing man-made, no engine noise, no car, no machine, nothing, and looked up to nothing but pure blue sky. That's some kind of peace. Ridiculous, then, to punctuate it with emails.

Amid the drudge of administration, I saw an email from Justin. I'd asked him a few weeks ago if I could come and see some restoration work happening on Cors Fochno. Perhaps I had a growing excavator fetish, but I wanted to make sure I understood how the bunds that held back the waters were built. I wanted to see the stitches that embroidered the bog back to wetness. And he'd said they were behind but he'd let me know when they were on the bog.

The beginning of the email was just a date, but beyond that he had written there was something else I might be interested in. I read on, hoping for something rare and unusual to see. What

I got were some pictures of algal gunk. Something awful was happening to our beloved bog.

Justin is always measured, never hasty, unless he believes he's late. I once watched him run towards me on the boardwalk on the bog. I was a mile or so out in the middle, and as I watched him, I feared something awful must have happened. I discovered that he didn't want me to think he was sauntering to meet me. Justin looks at everything carefully before he makes a statement. This email was uncharacteristic. I felt its urgency, even a slight panic.

I read the briefing Justin attached and saw pictures of those wonderful *Sphagnum pulchrum* lawns and fine *Sphagnum beothuk* hummocks, rare and beautiful, covered with a greyish-green slime. The algal gunk was seemingly rotting the sphagnum. Justin, ever the dutiful observer, had placed red flags by any affected spots and photographed the worst examples. He noted some hummocks were fine, with no observable effects, while others were covered with gunk. It seemed to be affecting non-sphagnum moss species too, such as *Leucobryum*, which can form satisfying, tightly knitted, extensive hummocks on bogs, and really does look like plump velvet cushions, and the heath plait-moss, *Hypnum jutlandicum*, which has fractal fern-like leaves. Both were either covered with slime or bleached out.

I scanned a forwarded email from a man called Sam, a bryophyte specialist who has written extensively about atmospheric nitrogen pollution.

I looked up from my phone to the peace of the Flow Country. Home felt very far away. I asked Milly if she had heard of anything similar up here in the Flow Country. She said, no, she wasn't even aware of such a thing as algal gunk (a term coined by Sam for unknown green slime). She didn't think much about bogs and pollution, she said, waving her sandwich at the wider landscape.

There are farms all over the Flow Country, but they are small, mostly sheep and Highland cattle. There may be plenty of industrial conifers, but the landscape is unaffected by industrial farming.

223

Not so the rest of the country. As I whiled away hours on the train home, I caught up on the outrage at the industrial chicken farming and chicken-feed units of mid-Wales that were linked with the decline of the River Wye, and of similar tales from industrial-level dairy farming, of excessive slurry pits and regulations. The BBC World Service fed me daily bulletins from farmers in Holland and Germany who felt strangled by the red-tape legislation of slurry injecting, the more environmentally friendly but costly and slower process of injecting slurry into the soil rather than spreading it. They couldn't compete with other EU producers so they were going to vote out all this red tape.

Back home, river lovers and wild swimmers, even the *Daily Mail*, were planning to fight to save our waters. It painted a very angry picture, which seared itself into my mind over that of the beautiful mosses rotting away.

You cannot endlessly pump certain elements into our system. There is a cycle and flow of certain resources that need to stay within their boundaries for our and the planet's health. Carbon is obvious, but there are others, such as phosphorus and nitrogen. The latter is particularly problematic when it gets stuck in the atmosphere.

As soon as I got back from the Flow Country, I arranged a date with Justin to look at the excavator restoration work, but also to see the algal gunk, the nickname we were using for mucilaginous algae. Justin couldn't tell me exactly what it was, but he worried it was linked to atmospheric nitrogen.

Atmospheric nitrogen pollution is a complex subject, Justin explained, then rattled through the basic science as we stood looking at one of the beautiful *Sphagnum pulchrum* lawns receding beneath the white beak-sedge. Dairy is the primary contributor according the Centre of Ecology and Hydrology. These deposits can come locally, nationally and much further afield. On Whim Bog in southern Scotland, nitrogen deposits were found from local sources, but also from England and as far away as EU agriculture.

The local stuff was dry ammonia and nitrous oxide. It doesn't travel far, maybe a kilometre or so, if the bog is near a cluster of farms or an intensive agribusiness. But because chemistry is not interested in ownership and boundaries, the dry ammonia and nitrous oxide can convert atmospherically into ammonium ions, nitric acid and nitrates. Once up in the clouds it becomes wet deposits, which can travel great distances.

Justin had sent samples to find out what the algae might be and was rapidly developing a crisis plan. I sensed he wouldn't wait for some high powers to intervene. But first he sent me off on the boardwalk alone as he went to check on progress with restoration.

I walked out, alert for slime. It had been a while since I last visited the bog. I'd brought my friend Ingrid, who lived just down the road in Machynlleth and had recently fallen hard for lichen and bryophytes. If that sounds like an unusual predilection, then you need to get to our bit of the world – the woods, the rocks, the walls of our houses, our roofs, our path edges are dripping with lichen and moss. It's wet out here. If you peer curiously at even the most ordinary of cushion mosses on top of a wall coping, you fall into a marvellous miniature world that is surprisingly easy to capture on a smart phone, and that is exactly what Ingrid likes doing. It's the *kawaii* (the cute) of the plant world, snapping mosses and lichen.

Anyway, this was back in January 2024. As I walked out, I was thinking, Where are the mosses? The winter was famously the 'wettest' yet and, of course, if you peered you found mosses, but they seemed to be hidden by the sedges. That was not something I remembered of bog at this time of year. At the time, as Ingrid and I knelt down to look at the different mosses, I read out their descriptions from the great tome that is the British Bryological Society's *Field Guide to Mosses and Liverworts*. I thought perhaps it looked a little flat because I'd forgotten about winter. I'm pretty fair-weather about my bog visits. I don't really know the January bog and I concluded that it must be that. We were layered up, with thermals and waterproofs, hats and gloves. Perhaps the mosses hunkered down when the cold heart of winter beat loudest. Or that was what I tried to tell myself. But it felt too brown, as if the mosses were hiding.

When Justin came out to meet me on the boardwalk he immediately said as much. He thought the white beak-sedge was suddenly doing a little too well. He was ever cautious with this observation, but he is, almost exclusively, one of the only people who could make such a statement. I've never asked his age, but I'm going to take a punt that he's spent almost thirty years or so with the bog. He's one of the few people who visit the space regularly and he looks at all of it with a great deal of care. That's his job. He sped through atmospheric nitrogen cycles and various depositions, looking up at the hills beyond as we talked about how farming was changing in the area and waving across the Irish Sea to explain how wide the problem was. He was not pointing the blame at farmers – if anything, it seemed the weight was on his shoulders alone. I realised I was one of many to whom he'd fired off an email and for the first time I heard a note of desperation in his voice.

All bogs are very low-nitrogen environments and the little that comes into the system falls from the sky in the rain, but also from the mosses' relationship with cyanobacteria (nitrogen-fixing bacteria) that live on or in their cells. The mosses' role as ecosystem engineers is to filter the little nitrogen there is, utilise it quickly to grow and then to reallocate it from the older leaves that are about to turn to leaf litter to the younger leaves. This way the nitrogen is not lost to sphagnum and critically not given away to other plants, keeping the moss in chief position on the bog. If there is too much nitrogen it starts to accumulate in the mosses' tissues.

Among the many things the moss does to maintain the bog is to act as a nitrogen filter. If there's too much, the mosses stop filtering and the excess is released to other bog plants, the vascular ones that can thrive on higher nitrogen levels. In particular, the graminoids: the purple moor grass, the sedges and rushes, but also species like birch and willow. This has a knock-on effect. Initially, the more the grasses and trees grow, the more they shade out the mosses, which start to die back, releasing the nitrogen they normally hold on to, further increasing the nitrogen-enriched litters. At the same time, the grass and tree litter rots easily, sphagnum litter doesn't (that is why it builds peat so successfully). Suddenly there is more easily decomposable litter, which further stimulates rotting and mineralisation. This cycle does one thing very well: it slows peat accumulation. In short, increased nitrogen not only means the mosses are outcompeted, but hugely affects the capacity of the system to act as a carbon sink.*

Like many pollutants, you can't see nitrogen depositions; you can't taste it in the air; you can't feel it in the rain. It's all but invisible until the mosses start shrinking back behind the grasses. It is thought that the algal gunk is related to the nitrogen deposition, but the details of how it all works and interplays are still being worked out.

And you see the problem, right? We're racing to conserve and restore our bogs on the one hand, and on the other we're raining down nitrogen. Once we talked about air quality, in terms of acid rain and sulphur dioxide, but now we must talk about nitrogen. We stemmed the sulphur pollution and we can stem this too: it's not just the bogs in danger, it's the temperate rainforests, the precious few wildflower meadows, the sand dunes, the salt marshes, the heathlands. More of our natural systems are low-nitrogen than not.

As we walked back from the centre of the bog to look at the restoration work happening to the south, Justin talked more than perhaps he'd ever done of how he felt about Cors Fochno.

I've said it before but trudging along a single-file boardwalk is a funny way to listen to a story: you're always either behind

* Rowe E.C., Mitchell Z. *et al.*, 'Trends Report 2020: Trends in critical load and critical level exceedances in the UK', Report to Defra under Contract AQ0843, CEH Project NEC05708 (2020).

or ahead and there's no place for eye contact or, for that matter, writing anything. I end up paying a strange kind of attention to listening, always straining around the wind, but held in that vastness. When I think of the bog conversations I've had, they have a clarity I don't find elsewhere.

Justin talked about meeting various folk from the peatland restoration community at conferences, of hearing tales of bare peat restoration, of starting from the very bottom, and he said he'd always thought of that as someone else's problem, not something he'd ever have to think about for Cors Fochno, rich in diverse sphagnums, rare orchids, hunting ground for hen harriers, adders and its untold masses of strange invertebrates. 'I was like a proud dad, showing off my bog.' I couldn't see his face when he said this, but I felt his grief. He said quietly that he worried this might be an ecosystem collapse. Words not said lightly by someone who can name all those that make up the world around them. It's a crushing thing to hear, even harder to say.

There's a Welsh term *y filltir sgwar* that translates as 'the square mile of ground that is your home', an area you know intimately, but it has another meaning, which is that you can love a place so deeply that it becomes part of you, influencing your core identity: an idea that the land is as much kith and kin as neighbours, friends and relatives.

We walked over to meet Peter Watkins, one of Justin's trusted mini-digger operators who was building bunds to help re-wet a bit of bog on the edge of the public boardwalk. It had tell-tale signs of having been drained in the past. There were swathes of purple moor grass, beloved of moving water, a little too much common heather and a small coppice of young birch. We climbed on top of one of the bunds just made and watched Peter work with the excavator, scraping up the top layer, carefully laying it aside, digging down into the peat, using it to create a contour mound that would hold back the water, then covering with the living layer, knitting the bog back together. The mini-diggers have extra wide treads to lessen the impact, but they have to move either on specialist tracks so they don't sink or, in this case, on a series of wide wooden beams, laid in a row. Periodically, to move forward, the mini-digger would swing behind to pick up a beam as if it was a toothpick, then place it on the other side to inch forward.

It was nearing lunchtime and Peter was ready to stop, so we went over to say hi and I quizzed him about a lifetime of this work. He's been doing some version of restoration at local bogs for the last forty or so years. He and Justin discussed a lineage of bog restorers, Justin's former boss and *his* former boss, the reserve manager and the one before that, so-and-so over the hill, and this farm and that. It was a very Welsh chat, another element of the *y filltir sgwar*, my folk, your folk and our folk. It dawned on me as I listened to decades of work, of hours and days and weeks spent in this wild and beautiful place, that Justin and Peter were part of a long line of people who'd dedicated their lives to looking after it. As we stood on top of the bund, watching the digger move methodically about, Justin told me he has a document full of the names of all the people who had worked tirelessly for decades to have Cors Fochno recognised as a nature reserve, the layers upon layers of negotiation to find out who owned which bit of the land, who'd sell and who wouldn't, patching back the bog so it could come under protection as one parcel of land. Ecologists, naturalists and conservationists, whose journey towards getting the bog to heal started by following a paper trail before any practical on-the-ground work could even start. And I understood, as these two talked of all the folk they could remember, how many people it takes to care, that this conversation was keeping alive a different kind of history of place. Many people think the bog is the empty, unpeopled middle of Borth, but it is quite the opposite. There's a ghostly Greek chorus of actors, whose care gives a collective voice to the action needed to keep Cors Fochno safe.

I'd often wondered if I'd made a mistake in falling for gardening over ecology, who or what I might be part of if I'd taken a different path. Would I be looking after a bog now? I saw how fulfilling it is to be out on the land, walking it, looking at it, caring about it, truly paying attention to who the land is. And sometimes this was accompanied by a feeling of deep regret: my twenties had been full of chasing life in cities. I thought of those who I'd met on this journey, Claire and Milly at Forsinard, Ben tending to mosses up at the upland research centre at Pwllpeiran, Chris the philosophical peat-prober in South Wales, Sam up on Bannau Brycheiniog, Bryn mapping all the afforested sites in Wales: they'd never fallen for all the bright lights. But when I walked away from this conversation with Justin and Peter, I realised I had a chance, if not exactly to join the chorus, at least to amplify their voices.

I caught up with Dr Janna Barel over email. Janna is the brilliant young Dutch specialist in plant-soil dynamics in the context of carbon storage – I'd met her the summer before on Cors Fochno, she of the pot worm, who'd introduced me to the complexities of the peatland soil food web and exposed me to the idea that acidic soils had just as valuable and detailed a microbial community as others, just a far less studied one. I told her I had a whole suite of questions, some related, some random, about peatlands: could we catch up on a video call? Some people are born communicators of complex ideas, able swiftly to take the knotted intricacies of the biological world, pull apart each thread until their audience is ready to look at the whole picture. Janna is one of them. She is also funny and easy-going.

The day arrived for our video call. I pummelled her with questions to which she raised an eyebrow when she thought they were amusingly off the wall. But, first, I wanted to know how her research was going, her findings from a summer spent on bogs. She told me she was wrapping things up because she had a tenured teaching position at Utrecht University. I'd spent long enough with academics on this project to know that tenure was the holy grail, a position secure enough that would allow her to pursue long-term research. I was thrilled to think of future students being taught by such a quick, clever mind. The short, insecure contract is killing many industries, and the business of learning is no different from the restoration business. The likes of Justin and Janna, who get to stay put, are sadly rare.

There is one question that all biological systems scientists hate. You can see them ready themselves for it in every conversation about climate and futures: have we enough time? And then: will it work? The older ones talk of the fleeting nature of life; the younger ones seem to steady themselves on some imaginary mountain of more research, more evidence, more will.

I was stuck on the thorny question of restoration in the light of many factors over which there is no control: emissions from industries, land-grabbing, road-building, anthropogenic fires, habitat loss. In short, the effects of capitalism, We tell ourselves a story about capitalism that translates to an idea about a commodity chain: gather resources, transform them into goods, distribute to consumers; a series of links connecting the many places of production and distribution. But this isn't a chain. Capitalism is a web that is as complex and as nuanced as a biological ecosystem; governed by a few, but held together by many actors, unwittingly or not. So much of our policy work and restoration efforts are held only by a single link back out to the world we have created. Restore the bog, replant the forest, restock the mussels and oysters, but it goes no further into the web. Does the man who is funding the enhanced breeding for feed-efficient dairy cows know anything of the woman who is recording the gas exchange of the ailing bog?

And on top of all of this is the unknown of our future climates. Climates that might be too radically different to support bogs at least in the places where they currently sit. There's evidence that peatlands are moving further north as the climate warms. What lies currently beneath ice could quite possibly become a bog.

Janna was measured and calm. Nature is always changing, relentlessly so. 'But is a bog really a bog if it doesn't have its mosses?' I worried.

She reframed it. If it can be considered a mire, if it is still growing, which are the species we should promote to create a resilient system? What are our expectations? 'It has always been unrealistic,' she said, 'to think we can restore to a near-natural state.'

There it was. At the heart of my worry there was the grief for what is already lost. Things neither of us had ever seen, resilience last noted by our great-grandparents.

We talked on about nitrogen depositions, about moss filtering, the issues and complications with long-term monitoring of sites, the needs for very long-term experiments at a network of sites, so you know that in ten years you can go back to build up the data-base of findings and start to make predictions based on studies that are rooted in place and time. That there will never be a one-size-fits-all solution: each bog, each peatland is specific to its place, its time.

I thought a lot about this conversation over the next month. I took solace in knowing that Janna is part of the solution: teaching, studying, questioning, adding to an ever-growing body of knowledge.

I also thought a lot about time and place. Like all of my good thinking, these days, it happened on the bog. The spring had been late and cool, and by May there was, like elsewhere, a funny mixture of on-time species and those running late all out at once. The new leaves of the bog myrtle were still just taking on the serious business of scent, soft and light in their spring colours, yet to harden in the bright sun of summer. The dragonflies, the darters and chasers, the damsels and demoiselles were dancing together and then apart, coming to peer curiously at my intrusion, then rushing off.

The skylarks lived up to their name and cavorted across the bog that was waving in hare's tail cotton grass, white tufts of seed heads ready to take to the wind when the time came. The bog cottons were just starting to flower when I visited the Flow Country – they are often one of the first things to get going and now, on Cors Fochno, they were getting on with the next stage of life. It was a resplendent sight that distracted me from the moss problem. When I peered closely, though, the mosses looked fragile, not plump and prepared for the summer ahead, like a Persian carpet fraying from wear. Yet when you looked up and the wind calmed enough so you could hear the bog's many inhabitants go about their days, my world let up on its insistence for futures and, for a second, I was held suspended in this vision of another world in the full lilt of desire, relentless in the face of change.

When I was up in the Flow Country, I got to know Tracy, who like me was back for a second visit. Claire said we'd found our people: it was becoming a self-help group for peat heads. 'Hi, I'm Alys and I'm a little obsessed with bogs.' One of the many interesting and charming things about Tracy was that she'd taken the idea a step further than the rest of us and bought one. A bog on the edge of her village, just behind a sea loch on the west coast of Scotland. Like many bogs in Scotland, it had been cut over for fuel and was, she said, very damaged, but she had a plan: she would restore it into a tiny nature reserve for locals and visitors alike. She is a true naturalist, lover of all things wild, from tiny lichens to the broad-winged sea eagles that soared over her bog. She came in part on these holidays to learn how to restore bog, but also, I think, because it so nice to be with people to whom you don't need to explain why you love bogs so much. We joked that when I'd finished writing this, I'd ghost-write her book, *I Bought a Bog*.

There were many reasons why she'd bought that bog. Life had aimed great blows at her and she had found, like so many others, solace in the natural world. Now she found herself able to give a little of that back. She said that most people thought she was mad to sink her money into a slightly wrecked bit of land that you couldn't build on or profit from, but she had her reasons and a steely will. I held a secret wish to do the same, to take a little bit of misunderstood land and give it back its sovereignty. I understood that desire.

It is great testament to my wife that when she told me she'd booked three weeks off for us to travel that summer I pointed out that that was exactly the same time as my deadline for this book. I would go away for a tiny slice of her time off, but only if we went to see some bogs. She agreed *and* drove most of the five hundred or so miles to see Tracy's bog in Poolewe. That, and she gamely stopped off at every bog I excitedly pointed out on the way up, so I also got to tick off the Flanders Moss intact original lagg (and probably some of the best interpretation boards of the trip), several very good stands of late northern marsh orchids and saw some really good machair-to-bog transitions dotted with heath spotted orchids. I peered at some very good bog pools with flowering waterlilies and bog beans, among acres of blanket bog, some poor, some terrible, and some in a very good state.

Finally we were at Tracy and Roger's little croft cottage, which is surrounded by blanket bog. I don't think I'd put two and two together but the west coast of Scotland is as much blanket bog as it is white beaches and granite crags. Between the crofts and the villages, bog sprang. It ran over the hills and down to the beach edge until the sands drained it away. It seemed curious to buy bog in the land of it, I said. Tracy agreed. Most people kept asking her, she said, if she was rewilding the bog, and if so, did that mean she'd be planting trees? Along the steep hillside, she was hoping to fence off the area so that the trees could naturally regenerate. There were a lot of deer up there, but the bog, she told everyone, would remain resolutely a bog.

The following day we went to see it, Roger resplendent with his long walking stick and plus-fours, Tracy in neat outdoor wear and us in a mismatch of rather ill-suited clothing for bog-hopping. I'd forgotten to pack wellingtons and we had only one pair of good waterproof trousers. It was truly a dreich day, and full of midges, too.

The bog is nestled behind the village, a long flat plain of blanket bog, with a burn running through it, then a steep hillside mostly covered with bracken. It once had a much heavier cover of trees. I could clearly see where it had been cut over and where that intervention had also led to erosion, so there were haggs and exposed peat. Tracy had shown me pictures at Forsinard, so I was aware that it was 'damaged' bog, but I wasn't prepared for how alive it still was. The bad bits weren't good, but between the deer compaction and the erosion, there was such life.

I spotted *Sphagnum fallax*, *Sphagnum cuspidatum* and the classic pompom-shaped *Sphagnum capillifolium*, the deep wine-red of *Sphagnum magellanicum*, white beak-sedge, bog myrtle, cross-leaved and common heather – on the latter Roger found a small emperor moth caterpillar in neon pink and green. There were impressive strands of common hair-cap moss, the bleached reindeer lichen, *Cladonia portentosa*, there was bog pondweed, *Potamogeton polygonifolius*, in pools that were near the burn, where we also found a young newt. Roger was desperate to turn it upside down to identify it, Tracy firmly making the case to leave it be.

It was a lot of fun being with Tracy and Roger, so curious about every small element of the world around them. We pointed at and pondered over what things could be, Roger dutifully taking snaps of everything so we could work out what they were at home. Tracy expanded on plans and dreams, an accessible board-walk and better access for walkers, a little field centre perhaps, a community food-growing area on a non-bog corner, but all this would cost money and buying the bog had cleaned her out. It would take time, she said, but it was what she wanted to do with this next chapter of her life. It was a project that would take her into old age and would be her and Roger's legacy to a bit of the world they had fallen in love with twenty years ago on holiday and promptly moved to.

I couldn't really explain why I was so drawn to drive all this way to see that bog, until I stood next to Tracy and gazed out on it. It is a crazy, optimistic leap of faith to buy a bit of bog. It was just what I needed. After two years of being well mired in all the politics and complications of bog restoration, of the vast piles of scientific papers, the acres of bare peat and miles of purple moor grass, here was a woman embracing all of those future challenges with such hope. She knew it would be hard work but she was rolling up her sleeves and getting on with it.

I caught Ele's eye as we made our way to the western corner. She was not so wrapped up in the great promise of re-wetted peat. She was swatting a cloud of midges and had very wet feet. When I looked down, I, too, was soaked, my trousers stiff with water, but I was so thrilled with exploring that I'd hardly noticed. Plus the midges are attracted to effort, so the more you sweat, the more they bite. The best option is to distract yourself, but I am bog preoccupied and bitter to taste while Ele is sweet: she was coming up in welts left, right and centre. 'I understand how important they are. I just don't want to stand in them any more,' she implored. It was time to leave.

I promised we'd spend the rest of the holiday exploring beaches, and in the car, travelling further north, I said, 'It'll be over soon, my bog obsession, and we can go to other places.'

'Do you really think it's going to end?' she asked. 'It isn't like you're going to suddenly fall out of love with bogs. Maybe we'll just take different holidays. You can come up and hang out with the midges and I'll take a beach holiday.'

I fiddled with the satnav to take us to a beach quick. We meandered along the coast to the end of the peninsula and I gazed out at all the blanket bog rolling by. 'Why are there so many midges?' Ele asked.

'Because of the bogs. They create the damp environment necessary for them. But they also mean this landscape is empty of people and full of birds that feast off them,' I offered, in vain hope, while swatting away a cloud.

I'm not good when people don't fall for being on a bog. I fear it means I haven't done my job properly. I want – I need – you to love these spaces. But in the quiet afternoon, between achingly beautiful white sands and tracing-paper mountains across bays, the bogs continued to roll on by. And with each mile I quietened, as if the bog was telling me something, as if it was saying, 'Ssh now,' with its winds, 'let me roll on by, let me keep the air damp, let me fill the skies with midges, let me stay mutable and difficult to pass, let me fold over the landscape unnoticed.'

Bogs, fens, peat: they are unbelievably successful at what they do, despite us throwing failure at them, in unsuccessful interventions and attitudes. We may have done our best, unwittingly, to ruin them but, given sovereignty of their waters, they jump back into the game. I finally heard part of their song clearly that afternoon: be willing to fail, particularly if that means adopting conventional notions of being lovable; be difficult; be different; be willing to get lost; find counterintuitive forms of resistance; be water; be land; be both; be cooperative; be beyond. Hold secrets. Outlive it all.

I let the peat speak silently for itself in big skies and distant views, and sat back in gratitude for thousands of years of softness soaking our breath and more, for the love of a woman who'll travel to the end of the earth with me.

Acknowledgements

With gratitude to:

Justin Lyons for not only teaching me so much, but for taking care of such a beautiful bit of our world. Richard Lindsay for unwavering support and graciousness in answering so many bog questions. Dr Fred Slater, Dr Rob Law and Professor Andy Baird for patiently guiding me through wetland hydrology. Professor Susan Page for talking to me about tropical peatlands, Professor Emeritus Jan Zalasiewicz for guiding me through deep time and ways of looking at layers, and Dr Emma Hinchliffe at IUCN Peatland Programme for helping me make sense of funding all this work. Dr Ben Roberts at Aberystwyth University for taking time to answer so many questions on top of a cold mountain. Sam Ridge for taking me up to see the restoration at Waun Fach and Pen Trumau in Bannau Brycheiniog and the good folks at the Lost Peatlands of South Wales Project.

My Irish bog lovers, Ella McSweeney, Faith Wilson, Fionnuala and Anthony Brabazon, Doug McMillan, Robert Miller and Kerri ní Dochartaigh.

My bog family up at Forsinard, Claire, Milly, Veronica, Alf, Lou, Alison, Tracy, Quinten, both Elaines and all the other volunteers. Thanks to the RSPB Scotland for letting us be part of your work.

Naomi, Ruth, Amy, Kate, Row, Bridget, Mai, Jaun, Clare, Sarah, Pip, Cath, the Hawley-Reids, Gil, Stephen, mum and dad and everyone else who's put up with this obsession.

I would not have been able to write this book if it wasn't for the support of Society of Authors whose grant allowed me to travel, and the Royal Literary Fund fellowship which gave me a warm office, a writing community and space financially to do this.

My publisher, Rupert Lancaster, for being game and only making a handful of bog puns with every email. Hazel Orme for giving life to this text with her careful eye. I couldn't have asked for a better editor. To Cath and Annabel White at Curtis Brown and Lucy Buxton at Hodder & Stoughton.

Finally, Ele and the small dog, despite all the wet paws and socks, the gnat bites, you still choose to come to bogs with me.

Select Bibliography

Aldhouse-Green, Miranda, *Bog Bodies Uncovered: Solving Europe's Ancient Mystery* (Thames & Hudson, 2015).

Bain, Clifton, *The Peatlands of Britain and Ireland: A Travellers Guide* (Sandstone Press, 2021). This book informed many of my travels and a true treat for any bog lover.

Burnet, Elizabeth-Jane, *Twelve Words for Moss* (Allen Lane, 2023). Exquisite poems about moss.

Charman, D.J., *Peatlands and Environmental Change*, (John Wiley & Sons, 2002).

Chronister, Kay, *Bog Wife*, (Titan Books, 2024). A gripping, supernatural tale of one family's legacy of living with a bog.

Coles, Byrony and John, *People of the Wetlands: Bogs, Bodies and Lake Dwellers* (Thames & Hudson, 1989).

Fenton, J.H.C., *An Illustrated Book of Peat: The Life and Deaths of Bogs: A New Synthesis*, (Pemberley Books, 2021). I owe a lot to these two spiral-bound books. Fantastic diagrams, illustrations and photographs of all the bog's processes; niche, but very satisfying read.

Giles, Melanie, *Bog Bodies: Face to Face with the Past*, (Manchester University Press, 2020).

Joosten, Hans, *Mires and Peatlands in Europe: Status, Distribution and Conservation*, (Schweizerbart Science Publishers, 2017).

Magan, Manchán, *Listen to the Land Speak: A Journey into the Wisdom of What Lies Beneath Us*, (Gill Books, 2022).

Moore, P.D. and Bellamy, D.J., *Peatlands*, (Elek Science, 1974).

Moss, Sarah, *Ghost Wall*, (Granta Books, 2018). A haunting, spell-binding tale set on a bog.

Robinson, Tim, *Setting Foot on the Shores Of Connemara and Other Writing*, (The Lilliput Press, 1996). An excellent set of essays about map-making.

Rydin, Hakan and Jeglum, John K., *The Biology of Peatlands*, Second Edition, (Oxford University Press, 2013).

Shrubsole, Guy, *Who Owns England: How we lost our land and how to get it back*, (William Collins, 2020).

Wall Kimmerer, Robin, *Gathering Moss: A Natural and Cultural History of Mosses*, (Oregon State University Press, 2003). A brilliant, accessible read about the importance of moss.

Williams, Mark and Zalasiewicz, Jan, *The Cosmic Oasis: The remarkable story of the earth's biosphere* (Oxford University Press, 2022).